The Evolving Science of Reading

Building a Continuum from Foundations to Fluent Thinking

Anthony J. Fitzpatrick, Ed.D

Copyright © 2026 by Anthony Fitzpatrick, Ed.D.

All rights reserved. No part of this publication may be reproduced, distributed, or transmitted in any form or by any means, including photocopying, recording, or other electronic or mechanical methods, without the prior written permission of the publisher, except in the case of brief quotations embodied in critical reviews and certain other noncommercial uses permitted by copyright law.

Published by: Inedvation

The Evolving Science of Reading: Building a Continuum from Foundations to Fluent Thinking

Print ISBN: 978-0-986-43777-7-9

Digital ISBN: 978-0-9864377-8-6

Dedication

For Liz, whose high expectations, patience, and unwavering support provided the foundation upon which this work was built.

And for the educators, leaders, and students who grapple with the beautiful complexity of literacy every day. May this book serve as a useful map for your vital work.

Acknowledgements

This book represents a synthesis of years of learning, practice, and conversation. It would not have been possible without the intellectual and personal generosity of many colleagues, mentors, and friends.

My deepest gratitude goes to the researchers and thinkers whose work forms the intellectual spine of this book. While I cannot name all who have influenced my thinking, I am particularly indebted to the foundational work of scholars like John Hattie, Louisa Moats, and Michael Fullan. Their insights into learning science, reading science, and coherence provided the clarity and inspiration to build this continuum. Any new light this book sheds stands on the shoulders of their brilliant contributions.

Ideas are only as good as their application in the real world. I owe an immeasurable debt to the school communities I have been privileged to serve. To the students, teachers, and leaders at Kingsway Regional, Haddon Township, and Delsea Regional/Elk Township, thank you. You were the living laboratories for my career and where these ideas were tested, challenged, and refined. Your willingness to engage in hard questions, embrace coherence, and keep students at the center of every decision is the true heartbeat of this work.

Finally, to my family and friends, thank you for your endless encouragement and for graciously accepting the long hours this work required. To Michael, your support is the anchor that makes everything possible.

Any errors or omissions in this work are, of course, my own.

Advance Praise for The Evolving Science of Reading

Building Literacy Ecosystems That Work: Research, Coherence, and K–12 Alignment

The Evolving Science of Reading is a groundbreaking and much-needed contribution to the literacy field—one that genuinely moves the conversation, the practices, and the profession forward. Anthony Fitzpatrick, Ed.D., masterfully dismantles the false binary between "learning to read" and "reading to learn," replacing it with a clear, developmental continuum that extends from preschool through high school. His central message is both urgent and refreshing: literacy is not a series of isolated stages or siloed initiatives, but a coherent progression of language, cognition, and instruction.

What makes this book remarkable is its integration of neuroscience, linguistics, cognitive psychology, and **system design**. Fitzpatrick explains how decoding, linguistic comprehension, fluency, morphology, syntax, background knowledge, and reasoning work together to support deep reading. His framework bridges foundational skills with higher-level thinking in a way that is accessible to teachers and transformative for leaders.

Particularly powerful is the book's exploration of **system coherence**—how curriculum, intervention, professional learning, MTSS, assessment, and leadership must function as a unified ecosystem. Fitzpatrick offers practical tools, reflection guides, and developmental progressions that districts can immediately use to redesign both instruction and professional learning around a shared continuum.

But the book's greatest contribution may be its vision of literacy as a social, moral, and intellectual act. Fitzpatrick argues persuasively that reading must ultimately lead to independent thought, empathy, identity formation, and civic reasoning.

The Evolving Science of Reading is essential reading for educators, administrators, and policymakers seeking a research-grounded, coherent, and human-centered approach to literacy. It is a landmark text—both visionary and deeply practical.

Amelia Larson, CAO - Summit K12
Licensed School Psychologist

For most of my career, I taught students well past the point of basic reading instruction. Year after year, I could see the long shadow cast by early reading instruction, sometimes coherent, sometimes fractured, but always consequential. This book explains why. Rather than reopening old battles over phonics versus comprehension, it reframes the Science of Reading as what it has always been: a developmental continuum. From sound to symbol, from language to meaning, and ultimately to reasoning, reading is not mastered in a single grade, it grows alongside the learner. What makes this book essential is its insistence on coherence. It honors the science without reducing it, respects teachers without blaming them, and offers a practical vision for literacy that connects early foundations to the more sophisticated thinking that we expect of adolescents. I saw firsthand what happens when those connections are missing, and how powerful it can be when they are made.

Jessica Hawk, Ed.D
Retired English Teacher
@myteacherface

The Evolving Science of Reading offers a timely and much-needed reframing of literacy across the PreK–12 continuum. Rather than treating reading as a set of disconnected skills or initiatives, Dr. Fitzpatrick presents literacy as an interconnected system shaped by language, cognition, instruction, and time.

Grounded in the Science of Reading and informed by implementation theory and systems thinking, this book offers a clear path for aligning literacy within a coherent MTSS framework. One that supports teachers, honors development, and can be sustained over time. The focus remains on building shared understanding and coherence across classrooms, schools, and grade levels.

At its core, this work centers teachers as the true architects of the brain. It positions teaching reading, writing, and thinking as deeply intellectual work that shapes how children learn over time. When educators understand the full arc of literacy development and their role within it, student learning deepens, collective efficacy grows, and coherence becomes visible in classrooms, conversations, and communities.

Our children are not initiatives. When they experience a truly aligned literacy system, they recognize it. They talk about it. And the evidence appears far beyond the classroom walls. This book invites leaders to design systems that reflect how children actually learn and to build literacy cultures that endure.

Nicole Moriarty, Ed.D.
Former Assistant Superintendent for Curriculum and Instruction | Educational Consultant

-

Contents

Dedication iii
Acknowledgements iii

Preface: Beyond the Binary xi
The Illusion of a False Divide xi
The Continuum We Forgot xii
The Pervasive Problem of Silos xiii
A Developmental Science xiii
The Vision Forward xiv

Part I: Rethinking the Science of Reading 1

Chapter 1: The Myth of Mastery 2
Introduction 2
Section 1: The Pendulum Problem — Decoding vs. Meaning 2
Section 2: The Third Grade Cliff — What Happens When Systems Stop at Phonics 6
Section 3: From Code to Cognition — The Neuroscience of Reading Development 8
Section 4: Why Literacy Plateaus and How to Extend Growth Through Linguistic and Cognitive Complexity 10
Section 5: Extending Growth Through System Design 11

Chapter 2: From Code to Cognition 14
Introduction 14
Section 1: What the Brain Does When It Reads — Decoding to Meaning-Making 14
Section 2: The Continuum of Automaticity → Comprehension → Reasoning 16
Section 3: The Role of Morphology, Syntax, and Fluency in Bridging Word Recognition and Comprehension 17
Instructional Bridge Table: Morphology – Syntax – Fluency 19
Section 4: How Linguistic Awareness Supports Inferential Reasoning 20
Closing Reflection: From Neural Pathways to Systems of Learning 21

Chapter 3: When Science Meets System Design 24
Introduction 24
Section 1: The Danger of Siloed Reading Reforms 24
Section 2: How Curriculum, Intervention, and Professional Learning Must Function as One Literacy Ecosystem 27
Section 3: The Architecture of Coherence — Connecting Classroom Practice to District Vision 29
Section 4: The Leader's Role in Sustaining Alignment Beyond Initiatives 30

Section 5: Closing Reflection: The Shape of Coherence 31

Part II: The Developmental Architecture of Literacy 34

Chapter 4: The Foundations — Phonemic Awareness to Automaticity. 35
Introduction 35
Section 1: Why Explicit, Systematic Instruction Builds Equity. 36
Section 2: The Mechanics of Orthographic Mapping and the Role of Working Memory 37
Section 3: Fluency as a Bridge to Comprehension, Not Just Speed 38
Section 4: Embedding Foundational Routines within Knowledge-Rich Content 39
Closing Reflection: The Living Architecture of the Foundations. 40

Chapter 5: The Bridge to Meaning — Vocabulary, Syntax, and Morphology 43
Introduction 43
Section 1: The Cognitive Leap from Decoding to Linguistic Comprehension 45
Section 2: Morphology as the Meaning-Maker: Prefixes, Roots, and Suffixes. 46
Section 3: Syntax and the Architecture of Meaning 48
Section 4: Contextual Vocabulary Instruction through Morphology and Syntax. 49
Section 5: Oral Language and Prosody as Comprehension Accelerators 50
Closing Reflection: The Bridge That Language Builds 51

Chapter 6: The Deep Reading Phase — Comprehension and Reasoning 54
Introduction 54
Section 1: What Comprehension Really Is (Snow's Simple View of Reading Expanded) 55
Section 2: The Role of Inference, Background Knowledge, and Schema. 56
Section 3: Teaching Comprehension through Discussion, Questioning, and Analysis. 58
Section 4: The Rise of Metacognition: Readers Monitoring Their Own Understanding 59
Section 5: Strategies That Cultivate Reasoning and Critical Literacy 60
Closing Reflection: Reading as the Practice of Thought 62

Chapter 7: The Transfer Phase — Reading as Reasoning 65
Introduction 65
Section 1: The Nature of Transfer: From Visible Learning to Visible Thinking 66
Section 2: How Disciplinary Literacy Extends Comprehension into Analysis. 67
Section 3: Rhetorical Reading — Connecting Literacy to Writing, Argument, and Civic Reasoning 68
Section 4: Designing Transfer Tasks That Build Synthesis and Independence. 70
Section 5: Reading as Identity — Students as Meaning-Makers and Contributors 71
Closing Reflection: The Architecture That Thinks 72

Part III: Designing Systemwide Coherence..........75

Chapter 8: Building the K–12 Continuum..........76
Introduction..........76
Section 1: Mapping the Developmental Literacy Progression..........77
Section 2: Integrating MTSS and SoR for Seamless Tier 1–3 Design..........78
Section 3: Aligning Teacher Learning and Student Learning Around the Same Continuum....80
Section 4: Balancing Explicit Skill Instruction with Knowledge Building..........81
Closing Reflection: The Spine That Holds the System..........83

Chapter 9: From Curriculum to Culture..........86
Introduction..........86
Section 1: Building Professional Clarity and Collective Efficacy..........87
Section 2: Coaching Conversations Anchored in the Learning Phases..........88
Section 3: Literacy Walkthroughs: Observing for Transfer, Not Just Task..........91
Section 4: The Feedback Loop: How Data Informs Practice Without Narrowing It..........92
Closing Reflection: The Heartbeat of Coherence..........94

Chapter 10: Measuring What Matters..........97
Introduction..........97
Section 1: Designing Balanced Literacy Metrics (Accuracy, Fluency, Reasoning)..........97
Section 2: Using Formative Assessment for Learning, Not of Learning..........102
Section 3: Rubrics for Reading Transfer — Independence, Metacognition, Synthesis..........103
Section 4: Leading Data Dialogues That Inspire Inquiry, Not Fear..........105
Closing Reflection: When Systems Learn to See..........106

Part IV: Teaching for Transfer and Agency..........109

Chapter 11: From Reading to Thinking..........110
Introduction..........110
Section 1: Why Cognitive Transfer Defines True Literacy..........111
Section 2: The Neuroscience of Independent Thought..........112
Section 3: How Reading Builds Empathy, Civic Reasoning, and Identity..........114
Section 4: Reimagining Secondary Literacy as Intellectual Apprenticeship..........115
Section 5: A Vision for Reading as a Social, Moral, and Cognitive Act..........116
Closing Reflection: The Thinking Heart of Literacy..........118

Chapter 12: Leading the Literacy Evolution 121
Introduction 121
Section 1: Moving from Fragmented Initiatives to Coherent Design 122
Section 2: Leadership Mindframes for Literacy: Clarity, Curiosity, Collaboration 123
Section 3: Building System Momentum Through Visible Results 125
Section 4: The Next Frontier: Integrating AI, Analytics, and Human Expertise............. 127
Closing Reflection: Leadership as the Literacy of Systems.................................... 129

Epilogue: From Science to Humanity 133
The Literacy of Understanding... 133

Appendices: How to Use These Tools.. 135

Appendix A: The K–12 Pillar Continuum 136
The Developmental Spine of Literacy Learning... 136

Appendix B: Visible Learning Phases in Literacy Instruction 143
Turning Cognitive Science into Classroom Clarity.. 143

Appendix C: The Literacy System Audit Tool 147
A Framework for Coherence, Alignment, and Sustainability 147
Usage Guidance 152

Appendix D: PLC Reflection 153
Collaborative Inquiry for Continuous Literacy Growth 153
PLC Evidence Menu – Appendix D: Evolving Science of Reading 156

References 158
Additional Conceptual and Leadership References 159

Glossary of Key Terms 161

About the Author 165

Preface: Beyond the Binary

The kindergarten teacher leans over a carpet of eager five-year-olds, holding a small card with the letter 'm'. Her voice is patient and deliberate as she guides them: "Listen: /m/ ... /a/ ... /p/. Now blend it — *map*." In this foundational moment, she is igniting the very first spark of literacy.

Across the hallways of time and grade levels, a high school teacher stands before a group of juniors, the classroom air thick with the gravitas of Martin Luther King Jr.'s *Letter from Birmingham Jail*. "How does King's syntax create rhythm and urgency?" she asks, challenging them to discern the craft of his message. "Where do you see evidence of moral reasoning shaped through language?"

These are two distinct moments in two very different classrooms, yet they are united by a single, powerful truth: **one science.** Both teachers, whether meticulously blending phonemes or incisively analyzing rhetoric, are applying the enduring principles of the Science of Reading. Their methods may differ, but their work unfolds along the same continuous trajectory of linguistic and cognitive development. Each is teaching students to connect sound to symbol, language to meaning, and meaning to profound thought. And critically, both are grounded in the same scientific understanding: the human brain is not innately wired to read, but it possesses an exquisite capacity to be taught.

The Illusion of a False Divide

For far too long, essential conversations about how to teach reading have been framed as intractable battles—phonics versus whole language, discrete skills versus holistic comprehension, scientific rigor versus humanistic interpretation. In reality, these imposed binaries have done more harm than good. By framing reading instruction as a perpetual pendulum swing between opposing camps, we have inadvertently fractured a unified body of research into a patchwork of disconnected initiatives and isolated grade-level silos.

Consider the common fragmentation: kindergarten teachers often speak a language rich with decoding and phonemic awareness. Middle school teachers shift focus to text complexity and abstract comprehension strategies. High school educators, in turn, emphasize the nuances of argumentation and disciplinary literacy. Each group, while correct in its immediate focus, operates in an unfortunate isolation, remaining incomplete without the context of the whole. This fragmentation leaves schools with systems that may be strong in parts but ultimately incoherent as a unified whole. Much of the 'reading war' is not about the science itself, but about its failed implementation—a failure that has left teachers feeling attacked rather than supported. This book is designed to heal that divide. It provides a humane, coherent, and practical framework for leadership and system design that honors the expertise of educators and builds collective efficacy from the ground up.

Clearly, the consequences are severe: children often receive explicit phonics instruction in early grades, only to encounter implicit comprehension expectations later on, without the vital linguistic and cognitive bridge that should connect one to the other. Districts celebrate promising early literacy gains that, alarmingly, plateau by Grade 4, mistaking temporary fluency for an enduring, integrated understanding. The problem, then, isn't that the Science of Reading doesn't work; it's that, too often, we have applied it incompletely. We've treated its essential foundations as the finish line, rather than the crucial floor upon which all further literacy development must be built.

The Continuum We Forgot

The Science of Reading was never intended to conclude with decoding. The robust research base—from Jeanne Chall's foundational stages of reading development to Hollis Scarborough's iconic "reading rope" and a wealth of subsequent cognitive studies—has consistently described a continuous and evolving process: from phonological processing to automatic word recognition, then advancing to language comprehension, leading to inference and reasoning, and culminating in transfer and synthesis.

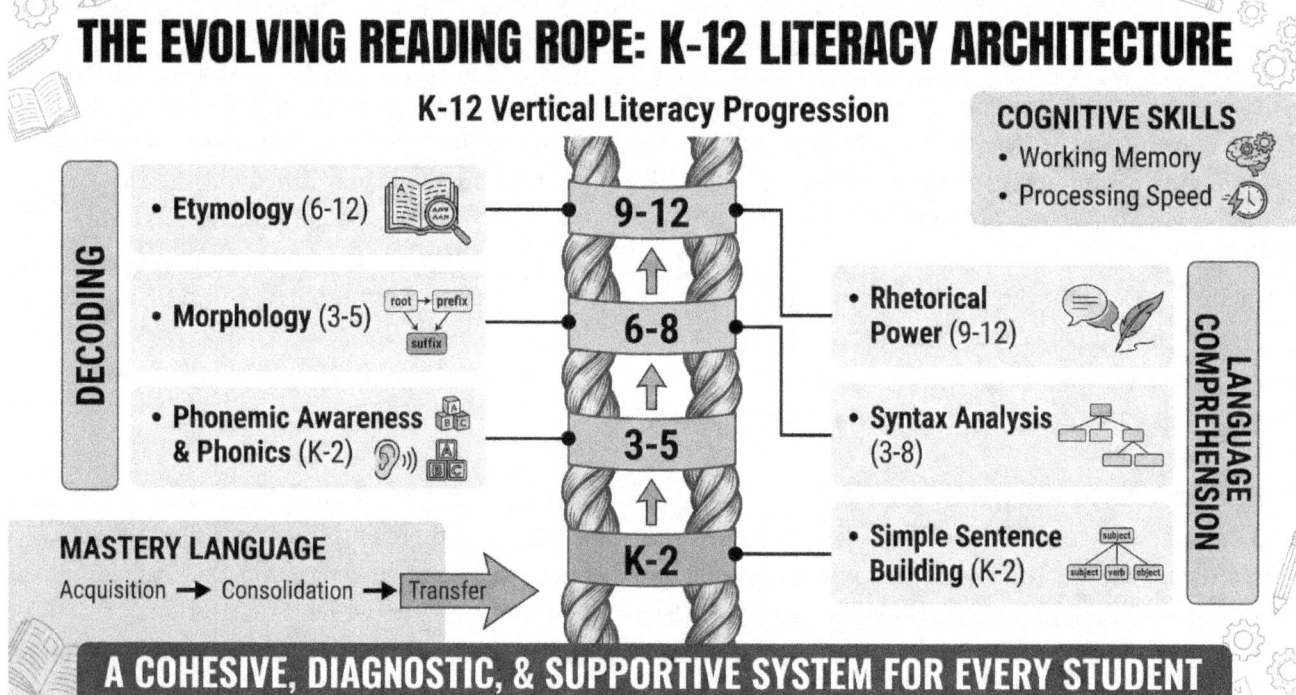

As Louisa Moats (2020) powerfully reminds us, "Teaching reading is rocket science." That science unequivocally includes phonology and orthography, yes—but it extends far beyond, encompassing morphology, syntax, semantics, and discourse. It reaches from the initial acquisition of foundational skills all the way to complex reasoning about texts and sophisticated engagement with ideas. It is, as Catherine Snow (2002) eloquently articulated, both a linguistic and a cognitive endeavor.

The perennial issue has never been whether phonics or comprehension "wins." Rather, it is our collective failure to connect these interdependent elements within truly coherent systems of instruction. What John Hattie (2018) champions as Visible Learning depends precisely on this kind of developmental progression: students must move from surface learning (accuracy and knowledge) to deep learning (integration and reasoning) and, ultimately, to transfer (application and independent learning). The Science of Reading, fully understood, follows precisely the same trajectory—from foundational accuracy to profound cognitive agility.

This misunderstanding of the continuum is at the heart of the most potent, good-faith critiques of the movement. Critics who claim the Science of Reading "erases context" or is a conservative force that ignores diversity are, in reality, mistaking its *foundations* for its *entire architecture*.

A system that stops at phonics may be vulnerable to this critique.

But as this book argues, a *fully-realized* Science of Reading continuum does not end at decoding; it *culminates* in the very civic reasoning, empathy, and critical analysis of perspective that these critics rightly champion. The foundation exists to *enable*, not replace, this deeper, more diverse humanistic inquiry.

The Science of Reading has been ill-served by a public narrative that reduces its vast body of research to a simple phonics mandate. This reductionism is the very source of the 'Third Grade Cliff' this book seeks to repair. This book aims to restore the full science—which extends from phonology to reasoning—to its rightful place in our professional discourse and to promote a holistic, developmental model of literacy that unites the early, middle, and later phases of reading growth into one continuous, rigorously research-grounded journey.

The Pervasive Problem of Silos

In the vast majority of school districts, early literacy initiatives and secondary literacy efforts often operate as entirely separate ecosystems. Foundational reading programs diligently address phonemic awareness, phonics, and fluency, while upper-grade curricula pivot almost exclusively to comprehension and writing. Interventions are then introduced, often as discrete programs, attempting to bridge the ever-widening gaps that emerge. Each operates from its own distinct set of professional texts, favored assessments, and specialized instructional vocabulary.

As Shanahan and Shanahan (2012) astutely observed, "The problem of adolescent literacy is not that students cannot read, but that they cannot read well enough for the demands of new disciplines." This statement illuminates the precise missing link in the Science of Reading's evolution: the critical process by which the foundational architecture of reading—its sounds, symbols, and structures—seamlessly transforms into linguistic, cognitive, and rhetorical sophistication. Without this vital link, we risk producing readers who can skillfully decode words but struggle profoundly to decode complex ideas.

A Developmental Science

The Science of Reading is not merely a method, a specific program, or a political movement. It is, fundamentally, a **developmental science**—one that inherently evolves in complexity alongside the learner. Every grade band, every new stage of schooling, represents not a new subject to be taught, but rather a new, increasingly sophisticated stage of cognitive demand placed upon the reader.

The very same brain that first learned to map phonemes onto graphemes must, in later stages, learn to map complex concepts onto arguments, robust evidence onto compelling claims, and nuanced language onto specific perspectives. This profound understanding means that teaching basic reading in kindergarten and teaching sophisticated rhetoric in high school are not disparate acts; they are, in fact, continuous extensions of the same neurological and linguistic continuum.

Consider this progression:

- Phonological awareness seamlessly grows into morphological reasoning.
- Initial word recognition matures into precise lexical understanding.
- Basic fluency develops into sophisticated rhetorical delivery.
- Foundational comprehension transforms into critical literacy and, ultimately, into active civic agency.

When viewed through this comprehensive lens, the Science of Reading is not merely the *beginning* of literacy instruction—it *is* all of it, encompassing the entire journey from initial foundations to fluent, critical thinking.

The Vision Forward

Imagine, then, what could happen if every district chose to treat literacy not as a series of disjointed programs, but as a single, beautifully coherent continuum? What if every single teacher—from the preschool classroom to grade twelve—deeply understood precisely where their crucial work sits along that entire developmental arc? What if the Science of Reading were embraced not merely as another reform initiative, but as the essential backbone of a unified system that robustly connects decoding, rich language development, and advanced reasoning?

That, precisely, is the profound purpose of this book: to reconnect what has been fragmented, to translate powerful research into actionable coherence, and to reframe reading not only as an exact science but also as an intrinsically human act of meaning-making. For the Science of Reading, when fully understood and comprehensively applied, is not a pendulum swing between phonics and comprehension—it is the dynamic, continuous movement of the learner: from sound to symbol, from language to meaning, and from foundational comprehension to the very act of thinking itself.

PART I
Rethinking the Science of Reading

Every generation of educators inherits a version of the reading debate. The vocabulary changes, the research deepens, the policies shift—but the rhythm is always the same: a swing between competing truths. One year, the pendulum arcs toward phonics and precision; the next, toward meaning and comprehension. Each time, the profession braces for reform, promises renewal, and begins the cycle again.

And yet beneath this familiar motion lies a quieter story—the story of progress disguised as disagreement. Every argument about how to teach reading has, at its heart, a shared conviction: that every child deserves the chance to make sense of words and the worlds they open. What we call the "Science of Reading" is not a side in this debate but the thread that runs through it—the accumulated knowledge of how the human mind learns language, connects symbols, and turns recognition into thought.

But somewhere along the way, that thread became tangled in translation. The Science of Reading, born from decades of cognitive and linguistic research, was reduced to a checklist, an early literacy initiative, a political shorthand for phonics. The science itself never changed; our interpretation of it did. We forgot that the science describes not a program, but a process—a living continuum that begins with sound and ends with reasoning, that starts in the ear and ends in the mind.

To rethink the Science of Reading is not to abandon what we've learned, but to expand it. It means recognizing that decoding and comprehension are not opposing forces, but sequential expressions of the same neurological journey. It means seeing that a third grader sounding out words and a high school student analyzing argument are engaged in the same science at different stages of maturity. And it means accepting that literacy reform, no matter how well intended, will never reach its promise until systems are built to honor this developmental truth.

Part I explores that rethinking. It begins by dismantling the myth of mastery—the belief that reading ends once words are decoded. It then follows the brain's pathway from code to cognition, revealing the elegance of the system that makes reading possible. Finally, it turns outward to the organizational world of schools, where the science often fractures in translation, and coherence must be rebuilt from within.

To rethink the Science of Reading is to see it not as a pendulum, but as a spiral—ever refining, ever ascending, pulling us closer to the heart of how minds learn and how systems can rise to meet them.

CHAPTER 1
The Myth of Mastery

Introduction

The story of early reading is often told as a triumph of progress. We picture small voices blending sounds, eyes widening with recognition, teachers smiling as words begin to take shape. It is one of education's purest joys—the moment when print becomes sound and sound becomes meaning. For a child, it feels like discovery; for a teacher, it feels like proof.

But beneath that moment of celebration lies a quiet misconception that shapes entire systems: the belief that once students can read, the journey is complete. We call it mastery. We measure it in fluency scores, reading levels, and color-coded progress charts. And yet mastery, as we define it, has become a ceiling rather than a floor. We stop teaching just as the mind is ready to think most deeply.

The Science of Reading was never meant to end at phonics. The brain's learning network—its intricate circuit of sound, sight, and meaning—continues to develop long after words can be recognized automatically. The same cognitive structures that once struggled to map a letter to a sound later learn to connect ideas, arguments, and evidence. The code is only the beginning; comprehension and reasoning are its natural inheritance.

This chapter begins where most systems stop. It examines the illusion of mastery—the way our definitions of proficiency have narrowed the science into an early literacy reform rather than a lifelong developmental journey. It asks why we have come to mistake accuracy for understanding, and what happens when systems are built around the first half of the reading brain's work while neglecting the second.

To rethink reading, we must first dismantle the myth that it can be mastered. Reading is not a skill we finish; it is a way of thinking that matures. This chapter invites us to step beyond the comfort of early success and look again at what the science has always shown: that the true end of reading is not fluency, but thought.

Section 1: The Pendulum Problem — Decoding vs. Meaning

If you listen closely to the literacy conversations happening across the country right now, you can almost hear the rhythm of a pendulum swinging. One year, the focus is on phonics and foundational skills. The next, on comprehension and critical thinking. Back and forth it goes—each side defending what research has already proven to be true, but only partially.

For decades, reading instruction has oscillated between two poles: the science of decoding and the art of meaning-making. Each movement has advanced our understanding of how children learn to read. Each has also created blind spots. When we privilege the code, we risk losing sight of purpose and meaning. When we emphasize comprehension without the code, we risk leaving students without the cognitive foundation they need to access text in the first place. The truth, of course, is not at either extreme—it lives in the continuum that connects them.

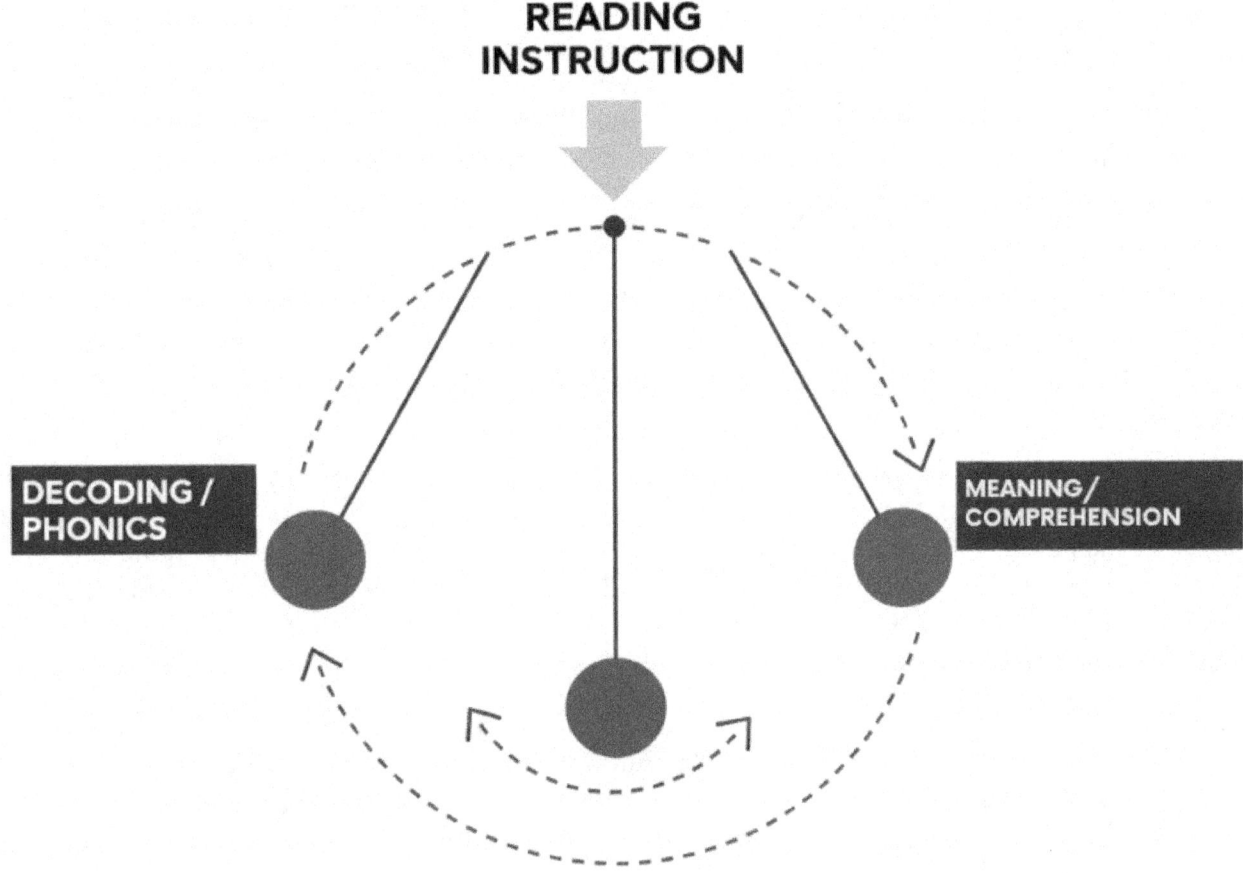

This pendulum isn't new. In the late twentieth century, reading wars defined generations of teachers. Advocates for explicit phonics argued that reading begins with mastering the alphabetic principle—the ability to connect letters to sounds and sounds to words. They were right. Others, influenced by whole-language philosophy, reminded us that reading is an act of constructing meaning through authentic experiences with text. They were right, too. The problem wasn't that either side was wrong—it was that we kept pretending they couldn't both be right at the same time.

Emerging as an attempt to end that debate, the Science of Reading grounded instruction in cognitive and linguistic evidence. But instead of integration, we often found implementation reduced to the earliest grades—a reform focused on decoding rather than development. The result was a new kind of imbalance. We built strong foundations but often failed to extend the structure upward. Many systems began to treat the Science of Reading as an early literacy intervention rather than a lifelong framework for how the brain learns language.

This misunderstanding created the illusion of mastery. When a first grader accurately sounds out map or sunset, it feels like victory—and in that moment, it is. Yet those victories can be deceptive. Fluency data rise, benchmark targets are met, and schools celebrate "proficiency" as though reading development were a staircase with only three steps. But mastery of decoding is not the finish line; it is merely the threshold to comprehension, reasoning, and independent thought.

The cognitive work of reading continues long after a child can pronounce words on a page. The same brain regions that once connected sounds to letters must later connect language to logic, structure to syntax, and syntax to reasoning. What begins as orthographic mapping in the early years evolves into morphological analysis, complex sentence processing, and abstract comprehension in adolescence. Yet when instruction stops at phonics, students are left with strong foundations and unfinished architecture.

This is the pendulum's hidden cost. Every swing toward one end neglects the continuum that makes reading development durable. Districts that devote resources to foundational programs sometimes assume the upper grades will take care of comprehension "naturally." Middle and high school teachers, in turn, inherit students fluent in word reading but unprepared to analyze or synthesize ideas. When scores plateau around fourth grade—a moment sometimes called the "reading cliff"—we interpret it as student failure rather than system design failure.

The truth is, the Science of Reading was never meant to be confined to kindergarten through second grade. Louisa Moats (2020) reminds us that teaching reading is "rocket science"—an ongoing interplay of decoding, language, and meaning that evolves with the learner. Catherine Snow (2002) extends this argument, describing comprehension as a dynamic cognitive act dependent on the same neural systems that first enabled decoding. When we stop teaching the structure of language just as texts become more complex, we abandon students precisely when they need that science most.

John Hattie's work (2018) on Visible Learning offers a helpful parallel. He describes learning as a movement from surface to deep to transfer phases—each dependent on the other. Foundational skills represent the surface phase of reading development: essential knowledge that allows learners to access print. But true literacy emerges when those surface understandings become deep learning—when readers begin to make inferences, analyze structure, and evaluate meaning. And finally, in the transfer phase, they apply those skills independently across disciplines and contexts.

The Science of Reading, in its truest form, follows the same progression. It begins with sound and symbol but matures into thought and reasoning. What we call "phonics" in kindergarten is not separate from what we call "rhetorical analysis" in high school; they are different expressions of the same neurological process—the brain's capacity to construct meaning from language.

To visualize this unified science, we must replace the reductive metaphor of the pendulum with a more dynamic one. Neuroscientist Maryanne Wolf offers a powerful alternative in her **"Elbow Room" model**. She illustrates the reading journey with two arms: one representing **"Expanded Foundational Skills"** and the other representing **"Comprehension Processes."**

In the early years, the Foundational Skills arm is held *high* (heavy instructional emphasis), while the Comprehension arm is *lower* (present, but with less emphasis). As reading develops, the arms **dynamically shift**. The Comprehension arm rises to become the primary focus, while the Foundational Skills arm moves *lower* to serve "in support"—it never disappears.

This model perfectly illustrates the fallacy of the "Myth of Mastery." The goal is not to "finish" foundational skills and then "start" comprehension. The goal is a fluid, developmental *hand-off* where skills like advanced morphology and syntax continue to support deeper and more complex reasoning for a lifetime.

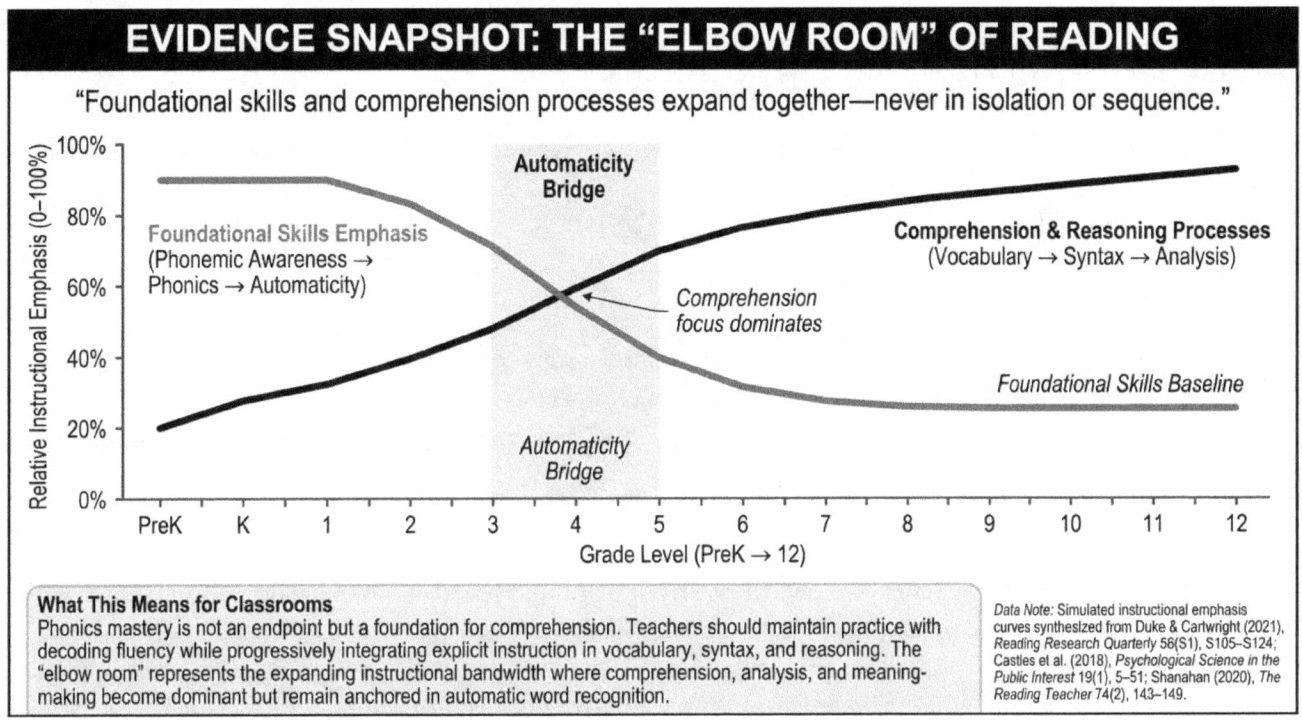

The challenge before us is not to stop the pendulum but to transform it into a continuum—a coherent, developmental trajectory that connects early decoding to advanced comprehension, and foundational literacy to critical literacy. That coherence begins when educators see their place not as endpoints on opposite sides of a debate, but as collaborators along the same developmental arc.

Imagine a system where a kindergarten teacher's explicit phonemic instruction and a high school teacher's Socratic seminar are viewed as two expressions of the same science—each contributing to the construction of a literate, reasoning mind. That is not idealism; it is what cognitive science has always shown. Reading is cumulative. Each layer builds upon the last.

The pendulum problem is not, at its heart, a question of method. It's a question of momentum. Every time we fixate on a single phase of reading development, we lose the forward motion that propels learning across years. Early decoding becomes isolated success. Fluency scores rise, teachers are praised, and systems exhale with relief—as though the destination has been reached.

But reading is not a static skill to be mastered and filed away; it is a living system of cognition that must be nurtured and extended. The moment we treat the early mastery of code as completion, we invite what researchers have long called the plateau effect—a gradual slowing of progress once the visible benchmarks have been met.

In too many schools, that plateau arrives around the end of third grade. Students who once soared through early literacy assessments suddenly begin to stall. Their rate, accuracy, and even confidence remain high, but their comprehension falters as texts grow more complex. The vocabulary becomes denser, the syntax more intricate, and the inferential load heavier. The foundation holds—but the structure above it was never built.

That is the quiet crisis of modern literacy systems: the "third grade cliff." It is not a failure of phonics. It is a failure of continuity.

And it is where the myth of mastery does its greatest harm.

Section 2: The Third Grade Cliff — What Happens When Systems Stop at Phonics

It often begins with a quiet celebration.

In the early grades, classrooms hum with the rhythm of success—children blending sounds, decoding new words, and reading short books aloud with pride. Teachers cheer as once-hesitant readers find their voices. Assessment graphs rise, benchmark reports glow green, and for a moment, it feels like the work of literacy is complete.

Then, something changes.

By fourth grade, the same students who once flew through phonics practice now slow down when faced with a page dense with academic vocabulary. They can read every word, but their eyes start to glaze somewhere in the middle of the paragraph. The story is still there, but the meaning slips through the cracks between sentences. They've learned to say the words—but not yet to live inside them.

This is the moment educators call the third grade cliff.

It's a quiet collapse, not a dramatic one. No single lesson or test marks its arrival. Instead, it's seen in the gradual flattening of reading scores, the subtle disengagement of students, the way comprehension questions begin to stump even those who once read "above level." It's as if the momentum that carried them so far in the early years suddenly fades.

And the truth is—it does.

The third grade cliff is not a mystery of ability; it is a consequence of design. We built a system that treats early reading instruction as a finite task instead of a foundation that must be expanded and reinforced. When we celebrate fluency as the final milestone of literacy, we mistake the opening of the door for the journey itself.

For years, the prevailing narrative has been that children first "learn to read" and then "read to learn." The phrase is tidy and reassuring, but it's also dangerously misleading. It suggests a linear process—a crossing of a threshold after which reading becomes automatic and self-sustaining. In reality, reading development is recursive and cumulative. The same neural networks that once connected sounds to letters must later connect ideas to one another, building layers of inference, logic, and conceptual understanding.

By the end of third grade, the very nature of reading changes. The texts that children encounter become more abstract and less predictable. Stories shift from concrete experiences to metaphor and theme. Informational passages introduce unfamiliar content and academic language. Sentences grow longer, syntax more complex.

To comprehend at this level, readers need more than decoding skill—they need language knowledge, mental flexibility, and background understanding that allow them to build meaning beyond the words themselves.

When instruction stops at phonics, this next stage of growth is left to chance. Some students continue to thrive because their language environments outside of school are rich—filled with conversation, reading, and exposure to complex ideas. But for many others, the scaffolding simply disappears. They can pronounce the words, yet their comprehension stalls. Their reading fluency, once a source of pride, becomes a mask for misunderstanding.

Educators see it every year. Students who once topped the charts for reading accuracy suddenly fall behind as the curriculum demands deeper analysis and inference. Their confidence erodes, and by middle school, many begin to internalize a quiet belief that reading is "not their thing." The joy of decoding turns into the fatigue of decoding endlessly without purpose.

This is the hidden cost of a literacy system built on short-term mastery rather than sustained development. We designed early success criteria around what could be measured easily—accuracy, rate, and basic fluency—without building equal structures to cultivate reasoning, vocabulary, and linguistic comprehension. The Science of Reading gave us the tools to build the foundation, but too often, we stopped building before the structure was complete.

Catherine Snow once wrote that comprehension is "the ultimate purpose of reading, but also the most complex." That complexity is why the science must stretch beyond the primary years. Reading does not plateau because children stop learning; it plateaus because our systems stop teaching what the next phase requires. Morphology, syntax, and discourse are rarely given the same instructional intensity as phonics, yet they are the very engines of understanding in later grades.

The third grade cliff, then, is not a failure of phonics—it is a failure of continuity. It is what happens when the early gains of structured literacy are not extended through explicit instruction in how language and thought evolve together.

Louisa Moats has described this as the unfinished business of reading instruction—the point at which we mistakenly believe the science has done its work. But reading is not a skill that stabilizes; it's a system that grows. As texts become more layered and ideas more abstract, the science of reading must become the science of thinking through reading.

There is, however, good news in this realization. The cliff is not inevitable. It is not neurological destiny. It is architectural. And what has been built can be rebuilt.

When districts design literacy as a continuum instead of a checklist, the landscape changes. Foundational programs merge seamlessly into language and comprehension frameworks. Vocabulary study connects to morphology and syntax. Teachers in every grade see themselves as part of the same system—each reinforcing the linguistic and cognitive infrastructure that reading demands.

In such systems, the third grade cliff becomes something entirely different: a moment of acceleration. Students reach a point where decoding is automatic enough to free cognitive space for reasoning, discussion, and interpretation. They climb, not fall.

The lesson of the third grade cliff is simple but profound: reading mastery is not a moment to be celebrated—it's a momentum to be sustained. Our challenge as educators is not to push children faster up the early slope, but to make sure the hill keeps rising.

The Science of Reading is not only about how the child learns to read; it is about how the reader continues to learn.

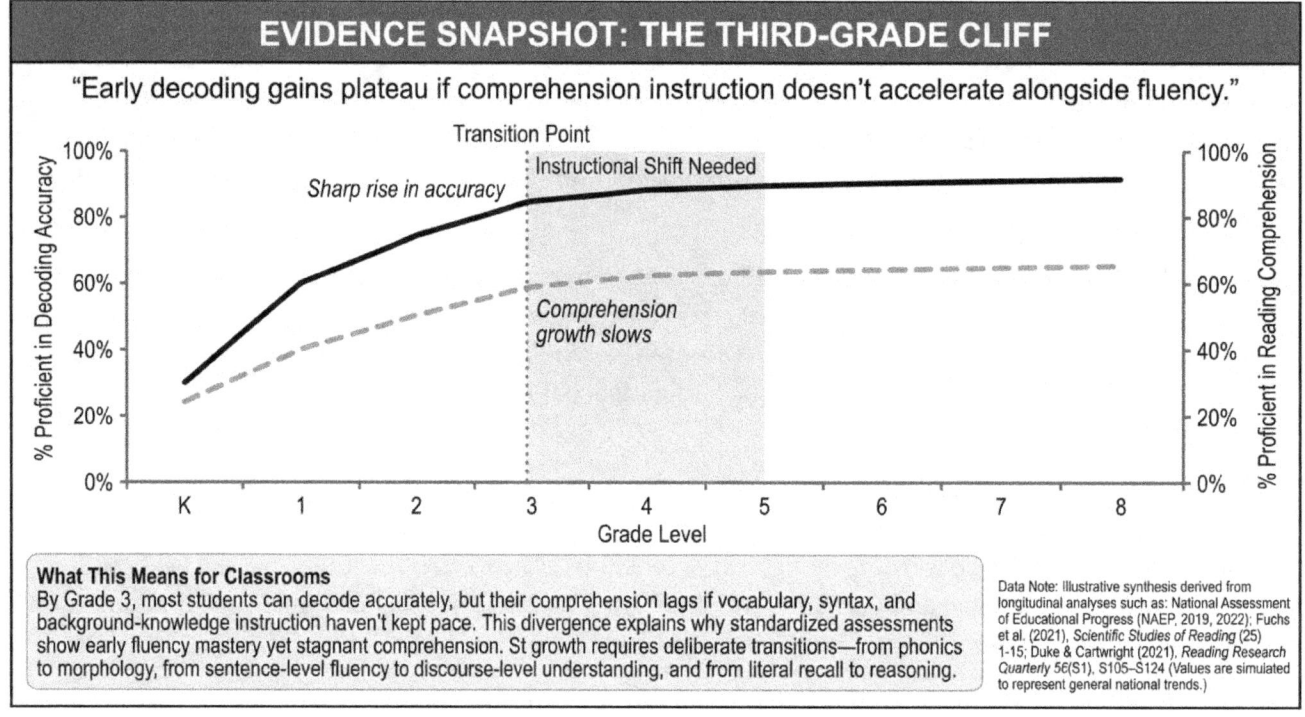

Section 3: From Code to Cognition — The Neuroscience of Reading Development

If we could look inside a child's brain as they learn to read, we wouldn't see a light switch turning on; we would see a landscape gradually coming to life. At first, small regions of the brain glow in isolation—the parts that recognize shapes, the areas that attend to sound. Then, like pathways cut through snow, faint lines begin to connect those glowing points. Over time, those lines strengthen into highways of thought: letters link to sounds, sounds join into words, words begin to carry meaning. The brain, once a place of scattered lights, becomes a network—what neuroscientists call a reading circuit.

Reading is not something the human brain evolved to do. It is a remarkable act of invention. To read, the brain repurposes systems that once handled vision and spoken language and teaches them to work together in a new way. The process begins as mechanical but quickly becomes cognitive, then linguistic, and eventually philosophical. Each phase depends on the one before it, just as a tree's highest branches depend on the strength of its roots.

When a five-year-old sounds out map for the first time, the brain is engaged in a fierce kind of labor. Every letter demands attention; every sound is a decision. The child's neural energy is spent almost entirely on accuracy. But with practice—thousands of repetitions across days and years—the mapping of sound to symbol becomes automatic. That moment of fluency is more than a milestone; it is a release of cognitive space. Once the brain no longer has to think about how to read, it is free to think about what it reads.

From that freedom, comprehension begins to bloom. The visual and auditory regions that once fired separately now pulse in synchrony with areas responsible for reasoning, planning, and emotion. The brain's focus shifts from decoding letters to constructing meaning. Words begin to summon images, connections, and judgments. Language becomes thought.

This transformation continues quietly throughout childhood. As texts grow more complex, the reading circuit recruits new partners—regions that handle syntax, morphology, and background knowledge. The same system that once labored over cat now processes irony, symbolism, and argument. Reading becomes an act of interpretation rather than recognition. In adolescence, that system expands again, linking language with reflection and moral reasoning. The brain that once asked, What does this word say? now asks, What does this idea mean, and why does it matter?

Neuroscience confirms what experienced teachers intuitively know: every level of literacy instruction builds upon the previous one. Decoding, fluency, vocabulary, syntax, comprehension, and reasoning are not separate skills—they are sequential expressions of the same biological capacity. When we continue to nurture that capacity, the reading brain becomes increasingly efficient and flexible, capable of transferring understanding from one discipline to another. When we stop too early, the circuitry plateaus. The brain retains its accuracy but loses momentum; it can read words without grasping worlds.

Yet the story does not end there, because the human brain is never fixed. Even in adolescence, even in adulthood, those neural pathways remain open to growth. Every encounter with challenging text, every moment spent analyzing language or grappling with ambiguity, strengthens the connections that make comprehension deeper and reasoning sharper. The reading brain is plastic by design—it was built to evolve.

Understanding this changes how we think about teaching. The Science of Reading is not just about helping children unlock print; it is about constructing the architecture for lifelong thought. Phonics lessons and rhetorical analysis are not opposites; they are points along the same continuum of neural development. The child decoding a sentence and the senior interpreting a sonnet are drawing on the same system, tuned to different frequencies.

When educators see this clearly, the old arguments lose their power. There is no need for the pendulum, no need to choose between the mechanics of code and the wonder of meaning. The reading brain has already chosen: it does both, and it keeps doing both, again and again, refining itself with every act of understanding.

The challenge before us is simple and profound—to teach as the brain learns, extending the science of reading until it becomes the science of thinking. When we do, mastery ceases to be an endpoint. It becomes movement: the brain, always reaching, always connecting, always learning how to turn symbols into sense and sense into knowledge.

Section 4: Why Literacy Plateaus and How to Extend Growth Through Linguistic and Cognitive Complexity

What looks like a plateau in skill is often a pause in opportunity. Everywhere in education, there is a season when growth seems to stall—data flattens, energy dips, and the thrill of early decoding fades into a quiet routine. Yet, this stagnation is rarely a failure of the student; it is a signal that the brain has outgrown its scaffolding. The learner hasn't stopped growing, but the instruction has stopped changing. Newly fluent in the code, the brain is ready for a more demanding task: understanding not just how words work, but how words *mean*.

For too long, systems have mistaken efficiency for completion. We define mastery by speed and accuracy—metrics that matter immensely when wrestling with the alphabetic code but offer diminishing returns once fluency is achieved. Fluency was never the destination; it was merely the clearing of the path. Without a subsequent invitation to explore language as a living, complex system, the reading brain becomes restless, like a pianist forced to play scales long after they are ready for a concerto.

Lifting students beyond this moment requires depth, not just acceleration. A child who once decoded letters must now learn to decode ideas. This shift demands that we trade the comfort of correctness for the wonder of discovery. Rather than teaching vocabulary as a static list to be memorized, we must reveal it as a web of relationships. Rather than presenting grammar as a set of rules for correction, we must teach it as a tool for design.

Consider the cognitive leap required here. Students need to see that the same prefix shifting *kind* to *unkind* also transforms *justice* to *injustice*—that language carries moral weight. As texts grow denser and syntax more intricate, the work of reading evolves into the work of reasoning. The reader's task shifts from reaching the end of the sentence to making sense of what that sentence reveals about the world.

Instruction designed to honor this growth turns the plateau into a launchpad. When we explicitly teach the architecture of language, students begin to notice how an author's word choice shapes emotion or how a sentence's rhythm dictates its power. Reading may slow down, but thinking speeds up. In this phase, the teacher's role transforms as well—from an instructor of mechanics to an interpreter of meaning, guiding students to discover how thought is constructed.

Ultimately, the plateau is not an ending. It is a structural demand. It is the Science of Reading reminding us that the brain has mastered the foundations and is waiting for the walls and windows to be built. When we meet that moment with richer language, deeper questions, and the courage to move beyond the safe territory of accuracy, reading evolves into what it was always meant to be: a bridge between thought and understanding.

Section 5: Extending Growth Through System Design

The problem with most literacy reforms is not that they are wrong, but that they are incomplete. Each new movement captures one essential truth and then builds an entire system around it, as though the truth existed in isolation. Phonics, comprehension, vocabulary, fluency—each becomes a banner, a faction, a new vocabulary of urgency. Yet learning has never worked in single lanes. It happens as a network, each idea linking to another, each skill dependent on the next. Reading is not a sequence of isolated achievements; it is a living system that grows by connection.

Schools rarely fail because they lack programs or evidence-based strategies. They falter because they lack coherence—because the pieces don't talk to each other. A kindergarten teacher may work tirelessly to build phonemic awareness, but by middle school, that work is treated as something long completed, a chapter closed. A fifth-grade teacher builds background knowledge, but without knowing how that connects to the morphological patterns that make meaning possible. A high school teacher asks students to analyze rhetoric, unaware that many are still decoding slowly, their fluency just strong enough to mask fragility. In these disconnections, the science itself is lost. The pendulum doesn't just swing between philosophies; it swings between grades.

When systems stop at mastery, they stop at the easiest part to measure. We can count words read per minute, but not ideas built per conversation. We can quantify accuracy but not insight. Data become the story, and the story becomes small. But literacy—real literacy—is expansive. It cannot be reduced to a single graph or proficiency line. It lives in how students use language to reason, to imagine, to enter into dialogue with the world. That growth is slower, subtler, harder to quantify, and therefore often invisible in the places where decisions are made.

The irony is that teachers sense this long before the data do. They notice the moment when fluency no longer guarantees comprehension, when a student can recite but not relate, summarize but not synthesize. They feel the dissonance of a system that praises what can be charted while neglecting what matters most. And they keep teaching anyway—adding complexity, introducing richer texts, modeling how to question, infer, and connect—often without realizing that they are keeping the science alive.

The next evolution of literacy work requires systems designed to sustain what teachers do intuitively. It means aligning every grade, every program, every layer of support around a shared understanding: that reading is both a linguistic and a cognitive progression. It means treating foundational skill instruction as the base of a pyramid, not the peak, and ensuring that language, knowledge, and reasoning continue to be taught explicitly long after students can decode. It means giving teachers permission to slow down when the work demands depth and courage to move past the comfort of speed.

In districts where this coherence exists, something extraordinary happens. The pendulum still swings in the broader world—new research emerges, new debates rise—but the system itself remains steady. The early years feed the later ones, the later years reinforce the early, and literacy becomes a continuous conversation rather than a series of reforms. Students move through their schooling with a sense that reading is not a stage they once completed, but a habit of mind they are still mastering. By graduation, they can decode complexity itself—not only in text, but in the world around them.

When I think about the future of reading instruction, I no longer imagine one fixed destination. I see a current that moves through the system, connecting classrooms like tributaries of the same river. The work of early literacy builds the banks, the work of upper grades gives it direction, and together they carry students forward—each year deepening, widening, becoming more capable of holding meaning. That is what the Science of Reading was always meant to be: not a moment, but a motion. A structure designed to endure, and within it, the steady hum of teachers and students discovering—over and over again—how language makes thinking possible.

Reflection Questions:

1. This chapter argues that "mastery, as we define it, has become a ceiling rather than a floor." In what ways have you observed this phenomenon in your own professional context (e.g., in student data, curriculum design, or teacher discussions)?

2. Consider the "Pendulum Problem" described in Section 1. How has this oscillation between decoding and meaning-making impacted literacy instruction in your experience? Can you recall a time when one was privileged over the other, and what were the consequences?

3. Maryanne Wolf's "Elbow Room" model suggests a dynamic shift in instructional emphasis over time. How does this model challenge or confirm your existing understanding of reading development beyond early phonics instruction?

4. The chapter describes the "third grade cliff" as a "consequence of design." What aspects of your current system might inadvertently contribute to this cliff, and how might that design be reimagined to support continuous growth?

5. Section 3 highlights that "Reading is not something the human brain evolved to do. It is a remarkable act of invention." How does understanding the neuroscience of the reading circuit's continuous development inform your perspective on literacy instruction across all grade levels?

Application Steps:

1. **Map the Pendulum:** As a department or school team, identify a recent period (e.g., the last 5-10 years) and map out the dominant literacy instructional focus. Was it decoding-heavy, meaning-heavy, or a blend? Discuss the perceived strengths and weaknesses of each focus.

2. **Audit "Mastery" Definitions:** Examine your school or district's current literacy benchmarks and assessments, particularly those around or before third grade. Are they primarily measuring surface-level skills (accuracy, rate, basic fluency) or are they also explicitly assessing deeper comprehension and reasoning skills? Discuss what adjustments might be needed to reflect a broader definition of "mastery."

3. **Initiate a Cross-Grade Dialogue:** Convene a small group of teachers from different grade bands (e.g., K-2, 3-5, 6-8, 9-12). Discuss how foundational skills are taught and reinforced at each level, and how comprehension and reasoning are developed. Identify any perceived gaps or disconnections that might contribute to the "third grade cliff."

4. **Visualize the "Elbow Room" in Practice:** Using Maryanne Wolf's "Elbow Room" model as a guide, discuss how your school/district's instructional emphasis shifts (or *should* shift) from early reading to deep reading. What does "Expanded Foundational Skills" look like in middle or high school?

5. **Review Systemic Coherence:** Reflect on Section 5's call for "coherence." What is one area where your current literacy system feels fragmented (e.g., separate programs, lack of shared vocabulary, isolated grade-level initiatives)? Begin to brainstorm how a more unified "developmental architecture" could address this.

CHAPTER 2
From Code to Cognition

Introduction

If Chapter 1 exposed the limits of how we think about reading, this chapter explores its wonder—the astonishing precision with which the human brain learns to transform print into thought. Reading is often described as a skill, but it is closer to an orchestration: dozens of cognitive systems learning to play in harmony until language becomes music.

Every fluent reader carries within them an invisible miracle. The act seems simple—eyes moving across lines of text, sounds forming in the mind—but it represents one of the most sophisticated feats the brain can perform. What begins as visual recognition evolves into phonological processing, semantic integration, and reasoning. A pattern of ink becomes an idea. The journey from code to cognition happens in the blink of an eye, but it is the product of years of deliberate instruction and neurological design.

The Science of Reading, stripped to its essence, is the study of how this transformation occurs: how letters and sounds fuse into words, how words assemble into sentences, and how sentences give rise to meaning. Yet what makes the science truly powerful is not its complexity, but its continuity. The same processes that help a five-year-old sound out map also help a fifteen-year-old evaluate a metaphor or trace an argument. The code never disappears; it simply deepens, branching into morphology, syntax, and inference.

This chapter invites us inside the reading brain. It follows the path of neural connection from the earliest sparks of decoding to the fully illuminated network of comprehension and reasoning. Along the way, it reveals how fluency frees the mind to think, how linguistic awareness fuels understanding, and how inference—the highest act of reading—depends on the smallest acts of structure and sound.

To understand how reading develops is to understand how thinking develops. The more clearly we see what the brain does when it reads, the more clearly we can design systems that honor its natural progression—from accuracy to understanding, from recognition to reflection, from code to cognition.

Section 1: What the Brain Does When It Reads — Decoding to Meaning-Making

Reading begins as an act of translation. The eyes sweep across a line of text, gathering what appear to be meaningless shapes. The brain, an interpreter of patterns, begins to sort them into something recognizable. What is visual becomes linguistic; what is linguistic becomes conceptual. In less than half a second, black ink and white space give rise to understanding.

This process feels effortless to a skilled reader, but beneath that ease is a symphony of activity. Each word on the page sets off a cascade of neural events across the brain—visual regions in the occipital lobe identify the shapes of letters, auditory regions in the temporal lobe summon their corresponding sounds, and regions in the frontal cortex integrate those sounds into language and meaning. The brain is not a linear machine processing one step after another; it is a chorus, with each part anticipating the next.

Humans were never born to read. Speech evolved naturally over millennia; reading required invention. To make it possible, the brain had to repurpose existing systems—those built for recognizing objects, hearing sounds, and forming memories—and wire them together in a new way. Neuroscientists call this process neural recycling. When a child learns to read, their brain begins to build an entirely new circuit, connecting visual recognition to the spoken language network that already exists. The child does not simply learn letters; they learn how to fuse two previously separate worlds: sight and sound.

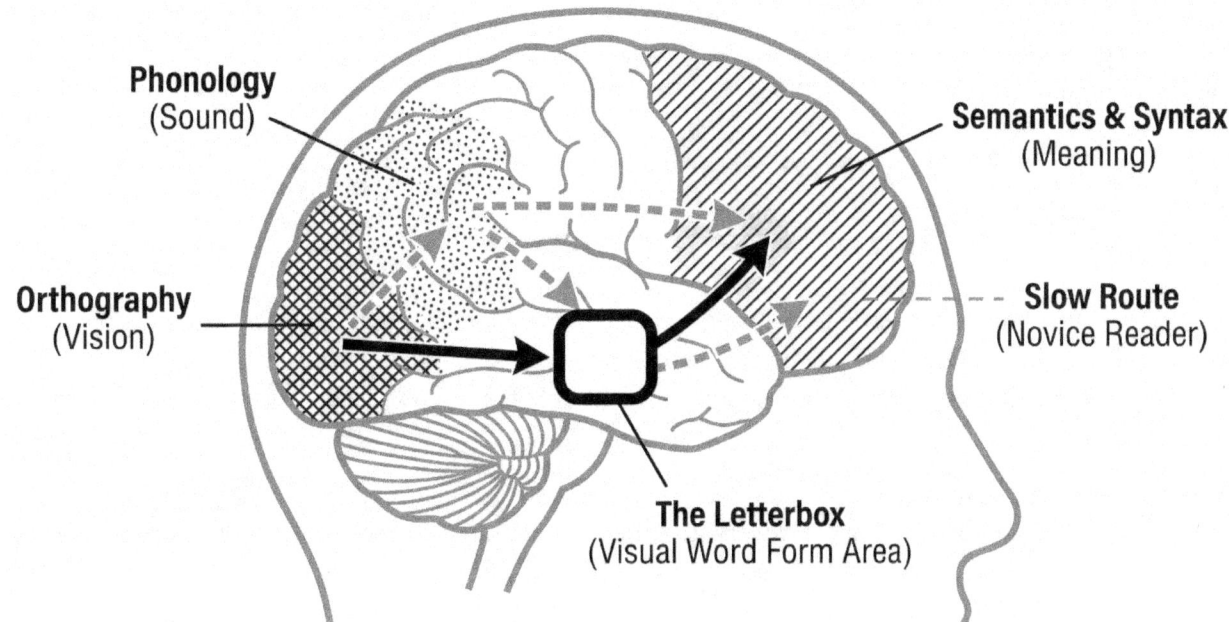

The Reading Circuit: Transforming visual symbols into language and thought.

At first, this is slow and deliberate work. Each letter demands conscious effort, each sound must be held in working memory long enough to be blended into a word. What looks like guessing or hesitation is, in truth, the brain constructing a new highway—one synapse at a time. Linnea Ehri called this process orthographic mapping, the moment when letters, sounds, and meanings link so securely that a word can be recognized instantly, almost without awareness.

Once this mapping takes hold, reading changes. The effort that once went into decoding can now be redirected toward comprehension. The brain shifts from labor to flow. The reader no longer has to think about how to read; their mind is free to think because they can read. Every fluent moment carries within it the invisible labor of thousands of past repetitions—sound paired with symbol, symbol paired with meaning, until the connections become automatic.

And yet, automaticity is only the beginning. As the reading circuit strengthens, it extends its reach. The brain begins to draw not only from stored sounds and symbols but from everything it knows—memories, emotions, background knowledge, experiences. Reading ceases to be an act of decoding and becomes an act of interpretation. The same neural pathways that once connected m to /m/ now connect freedom to the complex associations that word evokes.

It is easy to forget that this entire transformation—sight to sound, sound to sense, sense to thought—unfolds in milliseconds. But when it does, something extraordinary happens: the external world enters the mind, and language becomes the bridge between perception and understanding. Every time a student reads a sentence and pictures what it means, every time a phrase sparks an emotion or a question, the brain is performing its most sophisticated act—turning code into cognition.

The Science of Reading begins here, not in the mechanics alone, but in this miracle of connection. The teacher who helps a child sound out map is not just teaching letters and sounds; they are helping the brain invent a new way of thinking. The student who reads justice aloud is doing far more than pronouncing a word; they are activating a network of meaning that unites language, knowledge, and empathy. Reading, at its core, is the mind learning to see thought.

Section 2: The Continuum of Automaticity → Comprehension → Reasoning

Once the decoding circuit has settled into place—once letters no longer need to be sounded out and words appear whole in the mind's eye—the real work of reading begins. Automaticity is not an end point; it is a release of attention. The brain, no longer consumed by the act of recognition, can now devote its energy to the act of understanding.

In this new space, language unfolds differently. The reader is free to anticipate, to predict, to connect. Sentences become more than strings of words—they become containers of meaning, patterns that the mind learns to recognize and manipulate. Each sentence builds upon the last, forming a network of inference, implication, and idea. What was once effortful becomes elegant; what was once a task becomes thought.

This movement from automaticity to comprehension is the reader's first great cognitive leap. At the neural level, the change is profound. The visual word-form area continues to do its rapid recognition work, but now it interacts more dynamically with the brain's semantic and associative regions. Perfetti called this the lexical quality hypothesis: skilled readers possess richer, more interconnected word representations. A word is not merely known—it is understood, contextualized, and alive with nuance. Each word carries a shadow of experience, ready to illuminate meaning in new contexts.

Comprehension, however, is not simply the accumulation of word meanings. It is the art of construction. As readers, we build mental models of what we read—maps of meaning that blend linguistic cues with background knowledge. Duke and Pearson described this as the reader's active construction of understanding—a process that is neither linear nor passive. Every sentence prompts a small act of reasoning: what does this connect to, what does it imply, what must come next? The reader is not a recipient of information but an architect of coherence.

When comprehension matures, it becomes reasoning. The difference is subtle but transformative. Reasoning adds the capacity to evaluate, to question, to synthesize. The text is no longer just a story to be followed or information to be remembered; it is an argument to be examined, a lens through which to view the world.

The brain draws on executive functions—those regions responsible for judgment, planning, and reflection—and merges them with the language systems that once handled only decoding. Reading becomes an act of discernment.

This continuum—from automaticity to comprehension to reasoning—is the path of all literate thought. It mirrors Hattie's progression from surface to deep to transfer learning, but it is also the natural rhythm of the reading brain itself. The first stage is mechanical, the second relational, the third philosophical. Each depends on the one before it, each expands what came before. The reader who moves through these phases is not mastering separate skills; they are refining a single cognitive art—the ability to turn symbols into sense and sense into insight.

In classrooms where this progression is honored, reading instruction feels both grounded and ascending. Teachers still teach phonics, fluency, and vocabulary, but they treat them as gateways to something larger. They know that fluency without comprehension is hollow, and comprehension without reasoning is incomplete. They understand that the goal is not just to help students decode the author's words but to engage with the author's mind—to follow, question, and ultimately think alongside it.

When a reader reaches this level, the act of reading becomes indistinguishable from the act of thinking. The words on the page are no longer separate from the thoughts in the reader's head; they merge, blur, and expand each other. The page becomes a mirror of the mind's own reasoning process. And in that moment, reading is no longer something a person does—it is something they are.

Section 3: The Role of Morphology, Syntax, and Fluency in Bridging Word Recognition and Comprehension

As readers gain fluency, the brain hungers for something more intricate to grasp. The surface task of recognizing words has been mastered; what remains is to understand how words relate to one another—how meaning is built not only within a word but between them. In this transition, three forces begin to shape comprehension: morphology, syntax, and fluency. Together, they form the invisible architecture that holds language upright.

Morphology is the bridge between sound and meaning. It teaches the reader that words are not arbitrary symbols but small systems of logic. Each prefix, root, and suffix carries a fragment of sense—a clue to how the word functions in context. The word construction reveals its own purpose: con- meaning "together," struct meaning "build." To understand that relationship is to glimpse how language mirrors thought. The mind begins to see patterns, to predict meaning from form. Morphological awareness is therefore not a minor linguistic skill but a cognitive tool—it trains readers to notice structure, to expect coherence, to interpret nuance.

Syntax extends that structure from the word to the sentence. It governs how ideas are linked, ordered, and emphasized. A reader fluent in syntax doesn't merely decode; they navigate. They understand that where a word appears in a sentence shapes its meaning, that clauses and phrases carry relationships as precise as equations. Through syntax, the brain learns to trace cause and effect, to distinguish what is given from what is new. This is where comprehension becomes a kind of mental choreography: the reader moving in rhythm with the writer's intentions, anticipating turns, adjusting pace.

Fluency is the sound of all this coming together. It is not speed but alignment—the outward evidence of inner coordination. When a reader's phrasing matches the contours of syntax and the weight of meaning, fluency becomes expressive, almost musical. The rise and fall of the voice reflect comprehension itself. In that cadence, the mind and language move in concert, each reinforcing the other.

These three elements—morphology, syntax, and fluency—are the tendons that connect decoding to understanding. Without them, comprehension remains skeletal; with them, it gains movement and life. They allow the reader to interpret not just what a text says, but how it thinks. A student who understands morphological structure can decode a new term in science; one who grasps syntax can follow the logic of a historical argument; one who reads fluently can carry the weight of meaning across sentences without losing balance.

In many ways, these skills represent the hidden curriculum of literacy—the part often assumed rather than taught. Yet when instruction makes them visible, students' understanding deepens exponentially. They begin to read with precision and empathy, sensing how language reveals not only information but intention. The text is no longer a series of words to conquer, but a system of choices to explore.

When we teach these dimensions deliberately, we honor the true complexity of the reading brain. We teach students not merely to recognize language, but to work within it—to see how thought itself is constructed through morphology, syntax, and rhythm. This is the point at which reading transcends decoding and becomes design.

Instructional Bridge Table: Morphology – Syntax – Fluency

Grade Band	Morphology (Structure & Meaning)	Syntax (Sentence Construction & Cohesion)	Fluency (Automaticity with Expression)
K–2	**Mini-Lesson:** Introduce base words and simple prefixes (e.g., **un–**, **re–**) through word sorts and oral word play. **Why it matters:** Builds early awareness that word parts carry meaning, setting the stage for decoding and comprehension.	**Mini-Lesson:** Use sentence stems to combine ideas ("I can ___ and ___"). Color-code subjects and predicates. **Why it matters:** Establishes concept of sentence boundaries and agreement, critical for early writing and oral language.	**Mini-Lesson:** Echo read short patterned sentences, modeling phrasing and expression. **Why it matters:** Links decoding to meaning-making—students hear that fluent reading "sounds like thinking."
3–5	**Mini-Lesson:** Teach Greek/Latin roots (**bio, graph, spect**). Students create "root families." **Why it matters:** Expands vocabulary exponentially and deepens comprehension of academic text.	**Mini-Lesson:** Deconstruct complex sentences from content texts; rearrange clauses to see meaning shifts. **Why it matters:** Strengthens syntactic flexibility, enabling inference across clauses.	**Mini-Lesson:** Partner fluency practice with expression goals (pause at commas, emphasize contrast words). **Why it matters:** Reinforces syntax awareness—phrasing follows grammar, not speed.
6–8	**Mini-Lesson:** Compare derivational patterns (**nation → national → nationalism**). Analyze how morphemes change function. **Why it matters:** Builds cross-disciplinary vocabulary knowledge and connects word formation to argument precision.	**Mini-Lesson:** Examine mentor sentences to identify subordinate and relative clauses. Rewrite to shift emphasis. **Why it matters:** Deepens sentence-level reasoning, vital for analytical writing.	**Mini-Lesson:** Read excerpts aloud for rhetorical pacing; practice chunking by syntactic unit. **Why it matters:** Fluency now mirrors comprehension—students internalize rhythm of reasoning.
9–12	**Mini-Lesson:** Conduct morphological dissection of technical terms in science or civics (e.g., **photosynthesis, democracy**). **Why it matters:** Reinforces transfer of linguistic analysis to content learning and abstract reasoning.	**Mini-Lesson:** Analyze syntactic manipulation in persuasive texts (parallelism, inversion). Apply in argument writing. **Why it matters:** Syntax becomes a reasoning tool—students control logic flow through structure.	**Mini-Lesson:** Perform cold readings of complex passages, focusing on phrasing to reflect rhetorical relationships. **Why it matters:** Fluency becomes prosodic evidence of comprehension and author intent.

Section 4: How Linguistic Awareness Supports Inferential Reasoning

At a certain point in every reader's development, comprehension begins to reach beyond what is written on the page. The reader no longer asks, What does this say? but rather, What does this suggest? What lies beneath it? This quiet expansion marks the entrance into inferential reasoning—the ability to fill the spaces that text leaves open, to hear the writer's unspoken conversation with the reader.

All reasoning begins in language. To infer is to build bridges of meaning between fragments of information, and those bridges are made from words, syntax, and the reader's own conceptual scaffolding. Linguistic awareness is what makes this possible. It allows the reader to sense how a sentence implies more than it declares, how the order of words changes the weight of ideas, how tone and structure shape truth.

In a literal sense, the brain is constantly predicting what will come next as it reads. Each word triggers an intricate process of expectation: which grammatical structures could follow, which semantic categories are most probable, which ideas might emerge. Skilled readers navigate this invisible web of possibilities without effort. They don't consciously analyze the morphology of a term or the syntax of a clause; they feel them working together, silently updating their understanding with every phrase.

Kendeou and her colleagues describe this process as the construction and revision of a mental model—a dynamic map of meaning that shifts as new information arrives. Every sentence reshapes that model, either confirming what the reader expected or forcing the mind to reconcile something new. Inference lives in these moments of adjustment. The brain doesn't passively receive meaning; it negotiates it, combining linguistic signals with background knowledge, experience, and empathy.

This negotiation depends on awareness. Morphology signals subtle shades of meaning; syntax reveals hierarchy and emphasis; vocabulary evokes networks of association. Together, they guide the reader's reasoning about what must be true, what might be true, and what remains unsaid. Linguistic awareness thus becomes a form of metacognition—a reader's capacity to think about how language is working as they read.

When students develop this awareness, comprehension becomes less about recall and more about insight. They begin to notice patterns that hint at intention: a shift in tense suggesting a change in perspective, a repetition that underscores urgency, a metaphor that quietly reframes a concept. They read not only with their eyes, but with their intellect and intuition intertwined. The text becomes a living dialogue, and understanding becomes a form of participation.

Inferential reasoning, then, is not an add-on to literacy—it is its culmination. It is what happens when the systems built for decoding and comprehension mature into systems for judgment, interpretation, and empathy. The same neural pathways that once connected letters to sounds now connect ideas to one another. The reading brain has become a thinking brain.

When instruction nurtures this awareness—when teachers invite students to ask, How is this text working? What choices is the author making? What is left unsaid?—the distance between language and logic disappears. Students move from consuming ideas to producing them. They begin to see themselves as authors of meaning, not just readers of it.

This is the final transformation that the Science of Reading points toward but rarely names: reading as reasoning, language as the architecture of thought. To teach students to read deeply is to teach them to think deeply. And when linguistic awareness matures into inference and reflection, the written word becomes not just a tool for learning, but a space for thinking, questioning, and becoming.

Closing Reflection: From Neural Pathways to Systems of Learning

The story of reading is, at its core, the story of connection.

Neurons linking to neurons. Letters linking to sounds. Words linking to meaning. And finally, meaning linking to the endless complexity of human thought. The Science of Reading, when we see it fully, is not the study of letters and sounds in isolation—it is the study of how the brain builds bridges between them, how the simplest acts of recognition give rise to the highest acts of reasoning.

Every fluent reader is living evidence of this transformation. Each has rewired their brain to do something evolution never intended—to see thought. The circuits that first labored over sounds now carry entire constellations of meaning. Reading, in this sense, is not just a cognitive achievement; it is an act of humanity. It allows us to enter another mind, to experience the world through another consciousness, to think thoughts that are not our own.

Yet this transformation is fragile. It depends on systems of instruction that understand the sequence of growth and continue to nurture it long after decoding has become automatic. Too often, our schools stop teaching just as the mind is ready to think most deeply. We have built systems that reward mastery but rarely sustain it, systems that measure what can be counted while neglecting what continues to grow quietly within.

If the first task of literacy is to teach the brain to read, the second is to design schools that teach the reader to think. The movement from code to cognition cannot belong to a single grade band or program; it must become the shared spine of a coherent system—one that recognizes that the early lessons of phonology, morphology, syntax, and semantics are not separate parts of reading, but the very architecture of comprehension, analysis, and understanding.

In the chapters ahead, the focus shifts from the interior to the collective—from the neural networks within the mind to the instructional networks within schools. The question is no longer how reading happens, but how we create the conditions that allow it to keep happening—how we design systems where the science of learning is visible not only in the brain, but in the classroom, the curriculum, and the culture itself.

The journey from code to cognition is both biological and educational. It begins in the brain, but it reaches its full potential only when a system is built to honor it.

Reflection Questions:

6. **This chapter emphasizes that reading is an "orchestration" and a "remarkable act of invention." How does this perspective shift your view of reading instruction, moving beyond a simple skill to a complex cognitive process?**

7. Section 1 discusses "neural recycling" and orthographic mapping as the brain repurposes existing systems for reading. How does understanding this foundational neurological work inform your appreciation for the initial, often slow, stages of decoding instruction?

8. The continuum of "Automaticity → Comprehension → Reasoning" is presented as the path of all literate thought. Where do you observe your students (or school system) currently placing the most emphasis along this continuum? Where might there be opportunities to extend the focus?

9. Section 3 highlights the crucial roles of morphology, syntax, and fluency in "bridging word recognition and comprehension." Which of these three elements do you feel is most often "assumed rather than taught" in your current instructional context, and what might be the impact of that oversight?

10. "Linguistic awareness is what makes this possible." How does the concept of linguistic awareness, as described in Section 4, deepen your understanding of inferential reasoning? What instructional shifts might foster this awareness more explicitly?

Application Steps:

1. **Trace the Neural Pathways (Self-Reflection):** Reflect on your own reading habits. Think about a time you read something effortlessly (automaticity), then something you truly understood (comprehension), and finally something you critically analyzed (reasoning). Consider how these different levels of engagement feel and what cognitive resources they demand.

2. **Analyze a Text for "Hidden Architecture":** Select a challenging text that your students encounter. Go through it specifically looking for examples of:
   - Key **morphemes** (prefixes, suffixes, roots) that unlock vocabulary.
   - Complex **syntax** (long sentences, subordinate clauses, inversions) that might challenge comprehension.
   - How these elements contribute to the text's overall **meaning and inferential load**.
   - Use this analysis to identify potential instructional points.

3. **Evaluate Fluency Beyond Speed:** In a small group, watch a video of students reading aloud. Beyond measuring words per minute, discuss the nuances of their **prosody** (expression, phrasing, intonation). How do these elements reveal their comprehension (or lack thereof) of morphology and syntax? How could fluency instruction be refined to explicitly integrate these linguistic elements?

4. **Design an "Linguistic Awareness" Prompt:** For an upcoming lesson, craft a specific prompt or question that encourages students to think about *how* language is working in a text to create meaning, rather than just *what* the text says. For example: "What is the author trying to *imply* with this word choice, and what grammatical structure helps you see that?"

5. **Connect to Your Continuum (Early Planning):** Consider your K-12 Pillar Continuum (the focus of later chapters). How do the concepts of "Automaticity → Comprehension → Reasoning" and the roles of morphology, syntax, and fluency lay the groundwork for the specific instructional shifts you'll propose in subsequent chapters? Begin to mentally map these connections.

CHAPTER 3
When Science Meets System Design

Introduction

The story of reading does not end in the brain. It continues in the places where teaching happens — in classrooms, hallways, faculty rooms, and the quiet architecture of schools. What the mind does with language, a system must learn to do with people: connect, align, and grow through shared purpose.

The Science of Reading gave us clarity about how learning unfolds inside the individual. But in the absence of coherent design, that clarity often dissolves in translation. One school adopts a new phonics program; another invests in comprehension workshops. Intervention teams operate separately from classroom instruction. Professional learning becomes a calendar rather than a culture. Each initiative begins with conviction and ends in fatigue. The science survives, but its spirit fragments.

To move from evidence to impact, systems must become as integrated as the reading brain itself. Just as phonology, orthography, and semantics work in concert to produce understanding, curriculum, intervention, and professional learning must operate as a single literacy ecosystem. Coherence replaces compliance. The question shifts from Are we doing the right program? to Are we designing the right conditions for learning to thrive?

This chapter examines that shift. It explores what happens when the Science of Reading meets the reality of schools — when research must coexist with leadership, resources, and time. It asks how we can build systems that learn as the brain learns: through alignment, feedback, and adaptation. And it challenges us to see that the greatest failure of reform is not ignorance of science, but neglect of structure.

When science meets system design, literacy stops being a series of reforms and becomes a living framework — one that moves with the learner, the teacher, and the organization itself.

Section 1: The Danger of Siloed Reading Reforms

The classroom looks exactly as it should: shelves lined with decodable readers, students whispering phonemes under their breath, teachers kneeling beside small groups with precision and care. On the surface, the Science of Reading has arrived. There is fidelity, structure, and purpose. The charts on the wall are clear, the routines are practiced, the assessments are timely.

Yet just beyond the classroom door, the system begins to fray. The intervention teacher uses a different set of materials, the reading specialist a different diagnostic lens, the upper-grade teachers a different vocabulary of practice altogether. Each is working hard, each with good intentions, and each in isolation. The coherence that the science demands is lost in the shuffle of reform.

This is the quiet paradox of literacy improvement: we know more than ever about how the brain learns to read, and yet schools often remain fragmented by design. The Science of Reading, meant to unify instruction through evidence, sometimes splinters practice through implementation. Districts adopt programs that promise alignment but deliver silos—one for early literacy, one for comprehension, another for intervention. Professional learning cycles revolve around discrete goals rather than shared understanding. The system works in parts but not in concert.

An Example from the Field: The K-2 / 3-5 Silo

In one district, this silo was stark. The K-2 team had spent two years implementing a new, explicit phonics program. Their early decoding and fluency scores were rising for the first time in years, and they were rightfully proud. But just down the hall, the 3rd-grade team was launching its first nonfiction "Reading Workshop" unit, focusing on "Main Idea" using leveled readers and comprehension strategies that made no mention of the linguistic structures the K-2 teachers had worked so hard to build.

The 3rd-grade team, driven by state testing pressures, saw phonics as "a K-2 job that's finished." The K-2 team felt their work was "being dropped the moment it mattered." Students were hitting the 3rd-grade cliff not because they couldn't decode, but because no one was explicitly teaching them the morphological and syntactic bridge to comprehension.

The first step to breaking this down wasn't a new program; it was a new conversation. We brought the K-2 and 3-5 teams into one room with a single, shared problem: 4th-grade writing samples. The writing revealed a clear pattern: students could spell simple words correctly but collapsed when trying to use or spell multisyllabic academic words like construction or unpredictable.

The "a-ha" moment was when a 3rd-grade teacher pointed to unpredictable and said, "They can read 'predict,' but this word stops them cold." A 1st-grade teacher replied, "We teach the prefix 'un-.' They just don't know it's the same 'un-.'" The silo wasn't broken by a memo; it was broken by this shared diagnosis. The first step, then, was to create a vertical "K-3 Continuum Team" tasked not with adopting a new curriculum, but with mapping the linguistic connections—and disconnections—in their existing ones.

The result is a pattern of partial progress. Early reading scores rise, then plateau. Middle school teachers inherit students who can decode but not analyze. Secondary ELA becomes the domain of comprehension strategies divorced from linguistic roots. At every level, teachers work diligently within their lane, unaware that the lane itself is the problem.

Bryk and his colleagues, in Learning to Improve (2015), wrote that "every system is perfectly designed to get the results it gets." In literacy, that truth cuts deep. Fragmented systems produce fragmented outcomes. When one part of the system advances while another stands still, growth cannot hold. Students who learned to read through explicit phonics instruction in primary grades need a parallel system of explicit instruction in language, morphology, and reasoning as they progress—but that bridge is rarely built.

The danger of siloed reform lies not in its intent but in its architecture. Initiatives often begin as solutions to urgent needs—closing foundational gaps, raising proficiency, accelerating struggling readers. But without vertical design, each new layer of reform becomes another layer of noise. Schools begin to chase compliance instead of coherence. Teachers learn to implement, not to integrate. They follow the program rather than the progression of learning.

In one district, I watched as a new phonics curriculum transformed the early grades. Teachers became confident in direct instruction, children read aloud with growing fluency, and for the first time in years, first-grade scores exceeded expectations. Yet by fourth grade, the same students began to stumble. Teachers, unsure how to extend the science of reading into content-area literacy, reverted to strategies rather than systems. "They can read," one teacher said softly, "but they can't think through reading."

That sentence captures the heart of the issue. Reading reforms that live only at the foundational level are like building a strong foundation and forgetting to add walls. Without vertical alignment—without a plan that extends decoding into language, comprehension, and reasoning—the science stops short of its own promise.

Michael Fullan (2020) reminds us that coherence is not the absence of conflict; it is the presence of shared meaning. Coherence is what happens when a teacher in kindergarten and a teacher in high school both understand that they are part of the same continuum of learning. It's what happens when a district stops asking whether its programs align to the Science of Reading and starts asking whether its people align to one another.

The Science of Reading was never meant to be a checklist or a compliance document. It is a description of how the mind grows, and minds do not grow in silos. They develop through integration—of sound and symbol, word and structure, language and thought. Schools must do the same.

When we treat reading as an ecosystem rather than a sequence of disconnected parts, the fragments begin to reconnect. The kindergarten phoneme lesson and the eighth-grade argument essay reveal themselves as different expressions of the same science: the development of a thinking reader. The work becomes collective. The pendulum stops swinging, and the system begins to hum.

Section 2: How Curriculum, Intervention, and Professional Learning Must Function as One Literacy Ecosystem

In a healthy ecosystem, everything is connected. The soil feeds the roots, the roots sustain the branches, and the branches gather light for the whole. No single part can thrive without the others. When one weakens, the system compensates until balance is restored. Schools, at their best, operate the same way—curriculum, intervention, and professional learning functioning not as separate initiatives, but as interdependent parts of a single, living design.

Yet in most districts, these elements exist in parallel rather than in partnership. Curriculum teams design units in one office, intervention specialists purchase programs in another, and professional development unfolds as a separate calendar of events altogether. Each layer is well-intentioned, but the alignment stops at logistics rather than learning. The system may appear organized on paper, but it behaves like three overlapping worlds sharing the same space without speaking the same language.

A true literacy ecosystem works differently. It begins with the shared belief that every child—regardless of grade, background, or reading level—is part of the same developmental continuum. From this belief grows coherence. Curriculum becomes the architecture of opportunity, defining the core experiences every student will encounter. Intervention becomes the adaptive support, designed not as a separate path but as an extension of that same architecture. Professional learning becomes the connective tissue that keeps both alive and evolving.

In this model, Tier 1 instruction is not simply "core curriculum"—it is the collective expression of the Science of Reading across grade levels. Teachers know not only what to teach, but why and how it aligns with what came before and what comes next. A first-grade teacher introduces morphology through prefixes and suffixes that a fourth-grade teacher will later connect to academic vocabulary. A middle school teacher builds comprehension strategies grounded in the same syntax awareness cultivated years earlier. The instruction changes in form, but not in essence. The continuum remains visible.

Intervention, then, is no longer remediation; it is acceleration through precision. In a coherent system, interventionists use the same language of learning as classroom teachers. They draw from the same phonological, morphological, and syntactic understandings, adjusting only the intensity and scaffolding. The student who moves between small-group intervention and classroom discussion experiences consistency rather than contrast. Support feels like reinforcement, not detour.

Professional learning, too, must live inside this system, not outside it. The most effective professional learning is not a series of workshops or mandates—it is the ongoing study of the system itself. Teachers learn together how reading develops, how instruction interlocks, and how their collective decisions shape student growth. Fisher and Frey (2021) describe this as "professional clarity"—the point at which teachers see not only their own impact but how it connects to others'. When that clarity emerges, collaboration becomes the culture rather than the exception.

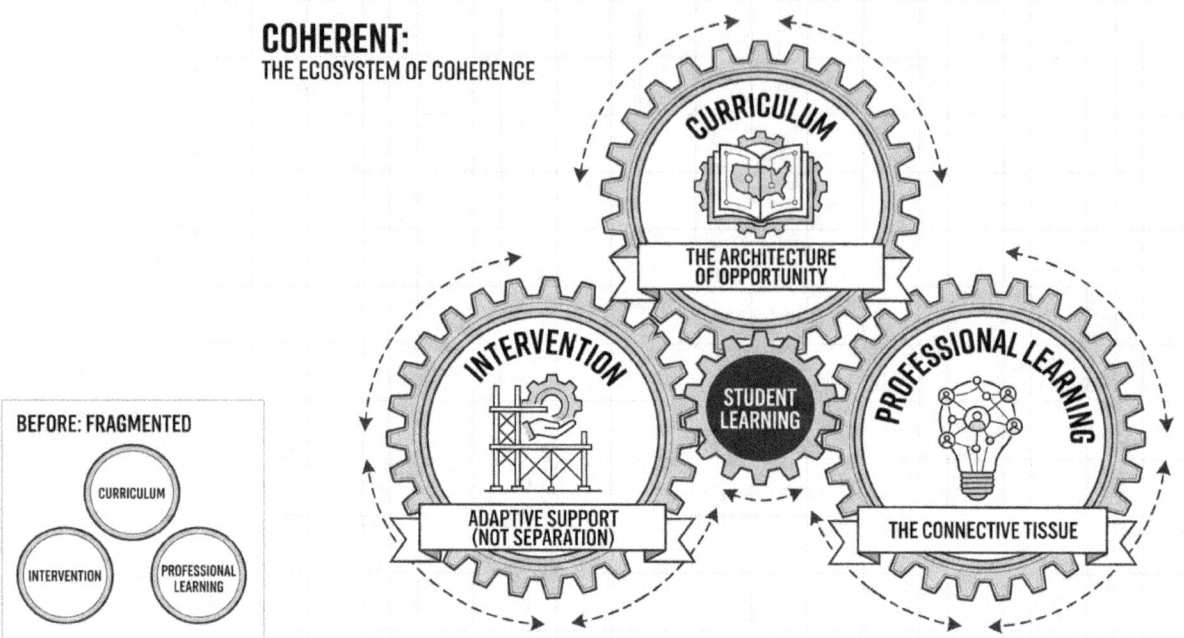

The Ecosystem of Coherence: Curriculum, Intervention, and Professional Learning functioning as one.

In districts that operate as ecosystems, conversations shift from compliance to curiosity. Teachers ask not, "Am I doing this program right?" but "How does this practice advance the continuum?" Leaders stop measuring success in isolated metrics—fluency rates here, comprehension scores there—and start looking at the throughline of growth. They begin to see that literacy improvement is not the sum of isolated gains but the outcome of aligned motion.

This kind of system coherence is not accidental; it is cultivated. It requires leadership that treats every reform not as a new layer to stack on top of the old, but as an opportunity to integrate. It means pausing before adopting a new program to ask how it fits the developmental architecture of the system. It means designing professional learning that deepens, rather than distracts from, instructional alignment. It means teaching teachers not just what the Science of Reading says, but how to see themselves as part of its living structure.

When curriculum, intervention, and professional learning begin to move together, literacy stops feeling like a set of separate tasks and starts to feel like an ecosystem of purpose. The soil enriches the roots, the roots strengthen the branches, and the branches gather light for the next generation of growth. Every part of the system feeds the others. Every action becomes cause and consequence.

This is the difference between doing the Science of Reading and becoming it.

Section 3: The Architecture of Coherence — Connecting Classroom Practice to District Vision

Every successful literacy system begins as a conversation that refuses to stay small. It starts with one teacher asking why a student can decode but not comprehend, another wondering how early gains could flatten so quickly, a principal noticing that what happens in second grade has no echo in sixth. These questions gather momentum until they reach the district level, where the realization dawns that the problem is not people, or even programs—it is architecture.

Coherence is an architectural idea. It is the structure that allows every part of a system to bear the same weight, the same purpose. Without it, even good instruction bends under the strain of inconsistency. Each grade builds what it can, but the floors do not align, and by the time students reach the upper levels, the staircase no longer connects. Teachers work harder, not smarter, because the blueprint guiding their work has vanished.

The goal of system design is to rebuild that blueprint—to create visible connections between the classroom and the district office, between daily instruction and the long arc of student growth. When coherence is in place, the teacher's lesson plan and the district's literacy plan read like two versions of the same text, written at different scales but with the same intent.

This kind of alignment does not happen by decree; it grows through design. Leaders begin by identifying the non-negotiables—the principles of reading development that hold true across age, context, and content. These are the anchors: the understanding that phonological awareness, orthographic mapping, and fluency remain essential; that morphology and syntax extend their reach; that comprehension and reasoning emerge through deliberate practice. When these principles are named, the system can finally build around them.

Curriculum frameworks become the scaffolds of this architecture, translating the science of learning into tangible experiences. Each unit, text, and lesson contributes to a progression of knowledge and skill that spans years rather than weeks. The work of reading, writing, and thinking unfolds as a single continuum. Teachers no longer wonder whether what they teach connects—they can see it in the design itself.

At the same time, the architecture must remain flexible. Coherence does not mean uniformity; it means intentionality. It allows for variation, creativity, and responsiveness within a shared structure. A district grounded in coherence understands that innovation is sustainable only when it grows from common roots. Teachers can adapt materials and methods to meet their students' needs precisely because they are anchored to a system that will not tip under the weight of change.

Michael Fullan (2020) calls this "the coherence of meaning." It is not compliance or consistency for its own sake, but a shared story about why the work matters. When a district operates from that story, teachers stop viewing reform as something being done to them and begin to see themselves as co-authors of the system itself. The classroom becomes the smallest expression of a district-wide belief: that reading is a human right and a cognitive journey that no child should navigate alone.

In coherent systems, the language of leadership echoes the language of instruction. A superintendent can walk into a kindergarten classroom and hear phonological precision, then visit a high school seminar and hear rhetorical reasoning—and both sound like different dialects of the same conversation. The vision has become visible.

Coherence turns abstraction into alignment, alignment into culture. It transforms the Science of Reading from a set of practices into a shared identity. When architecture replaces improvisation, teachers are not isolated innovators—they are builders working from the same blueprint. Every lesson, every discussion, every act of reflection becomes a beam in the same structure, each one carrying a part of the weight of student understanding.

In the end, the architecture of coherence is not built in boardrooms or through mandates; it is built in the rhythm of classrooms and conversations that connect them. A teacher who understands their place in that structure does not ask, Am I aligned with the initiative? but Am I aligned with the learning? That is how the Science of Reading becomes something larger than instruction—it becomes design made visible.

Section 4: The Leader's Role in Sustaining Alignment Beyond Initiatives

The most fragile moment in any reform is not its beginning but its success. The moment a new initiative begins to show results—when data rise, when classrooms hum, when teachers start to believe—the system's attention shifts. The focus that once united people around a common purpose disperses into the next wave of priorities. What began as coherence dissolves into compliance once again. The science remains, but the story fades.

Sustaining alignment requires leaders who understand that coherence is not a project but a practice. It is built in daily decisions, in the quiet constancy of purpose that outlasts any single program or framework. Leadership, in this sense, is not about managing reform but about cultivating a culture of continuity—a place where the principles of learning are so embedded that even when initiatives come and go, the system still moves in the same direction.

True literacy leadership begins with a kind of listening. It is the superintendent sitting in a first-grade classroom, hearing the deliberate rhythm of phonics instruction, and recognizing it as the same learning process that will later appear in a middle school debate or a high school research paper. It is the principal who can trace a student's confusion with a text back to a missing thread in linguistic understanding years earlier, and who sees that connection not as blame but as design opportunity. It is the coach who walks into a room not to check for fidelity, but to look for flow—how instruction aligns with cognition, how teachers connect what students are learning today to what they will need tomorrow.

Bryk's research on improvement science reminds us that sustainable change depends on "learning in practice." Systems improve when they create the conditions for people to study their own work and see its impact in real time. Literacy leadership must do the same. It replaces inspection with inquiry. Instead of asking, Are teachers implementing the program correctly? it asks, Is the program serving the learning progression our students need? The question shifts from compliance to coherence—from doing things right to doing the right things together.

Fullan often writes that coherence is not imposed from above but discovered from within. A leader's task, then, is to create the structures where that discovery can happen. Professional learning communities become the laboratories of coherence—spaces where teachers analyze student work, trace learning trajectories, and refine practice in dialogue with one another. Leaders sustain alignment not by tightening control, but by deepening collective understanding. The goal is not fidelity to a script but fidelity to the science of how learning grows.

Fisher and Frey describe this as "visible systems for visible learning." It means that teachers can see the throughline of instruction as clearly as leaders can see its outcomes. When coherence reaches this level of visibility, accountability transforms. Data no longer feel punitive; they feel instructive. Teachers use results to adjust their own practices rather than defend them. The system becomes self-correcting, because its people are self-aware.

This kind of leadership demands patience and presence. It means saying no to initiatives that compete with the existing architecture and yes to conversations that strengthen it. It means measuring progress not by the novelty of a program but by the depth of a shared belief. It means understanding that alignment cannot be mandated; it must be modeled.

In districts where coherence endures, leadership feels less like direction and more like gravity. The vision holds everyone in orbit—not through pressure, but through pull. Teachers, coaches, and administrators move in rhythm, guided by a common sense of purpose rather than a checklist of tasks. The system no longer needs constant reminders to "stay aligned," because alignment has become the culture itself.

When that happens, the Science of Reading stops being a reform and becomes an identity—a way of seeing, teaching, and leading that transcends initiatives. The language of coherence replaces the language of compliance, and the entire system breathes a little easier. Reading instruction becomes what it was always meant to be: a human endeavor, sustained by human clarity.

In the end, sustaining alignment is not about protecting a program—it is about protecting the promise that brought the work to life in the first place. The science gives us the evidence; leadership gives it endurance. And when the two move together—research and resolve, knowledge and care—the system stops chasing improvement and starts embodying it.

Section 5: Closing Reflection: The Shape of Coherence

Every strong system begins with a pattern of trust.

Teachers trust that their work today will still matter tomorrow. Leaders trust that clarity will outlast compliance. Students trust that what they learn in one classroom will help them in the next. Coherence, in the end, is not built from programs or protocols—it is built from those acts of trust, repeated and protected over time.

When a district finds that rhythm, the work of improvement stops feeling like reform and starts to feel like culture. Conversations change. Meetings no longer revolve around initiatives to launch but around learning to sustain. Teachers begin to see how the smallest decision—a word choice in a read-aloud, a scaffold in a small group, a question in a conference—echoes through the system. The distance between the classroom and the district office shrinks until it disappears. Everyone is working inside the same design.

This is what it means for the Science of Reading to meet the science of systems. The brain and the organization follow the same law: they grow through connection. Just as neurons strengthen their pathways through repeated activation, coherence strengthens when people keep returning to shared ideas, shared language, shared purpose. Every conversation about instruction is another synapse in the district's collective mind. Every act of alignment deepens the circuit.

Sustaining that connection is the leader's greatest work. It asks for steadiness in the face of novelty, humility in the presence of expertise, and faith in the slow, deliberate beauty of systems that learn. It means recognizing that coherence is not a structure we build once and leave standing—it is a living architecture that must be walked, tended, and renewed.

When the system reaches this point, literacy becomes more than a subject; it becomes a shared identity. The sound of a phoneme in a kindergarten classroom carries the same purpose as the argument in a senior seminar: both are expressions of the same science and the same promise. Every teacher becomes a builder of understanding, every leader a steward of continuity, every student a traveler along the same continuum of thought.

And so the work turns back to where it began—not to reform what we do, but to remember why we do it. To return to the foundations, not as a step backward, but as a step inward, toward the core of how language and learning take root. Because coherence, at its truest, is not about keeping everything the same. It is about keeping everything connected.

Reflection Questions:

1. Chapter 3 opens by stating, "What the mind does with language, a system must learn to do with people: connect, align, and grow through shared purpose." How does this analogy between the reading brain and a school system resonate with your observations of literacy initiatives?

2. Section 1 highlights the "danger of siloed reform." Can you identify instances where well-intentioned literacy efforts in your own context became fragmented or created unintended silos? What were the consequences for students or staff?

3. The chapter argues that "Curriculum, intervention, and professional learning must function as one literacy ecosystem." How interdependent are these three elements in your current school or district? What benefits or challenges arise from their current level of integration?

4. Section 3 emphasizes that "Coherence is an architectural idea." How might your school's literacy practices currently resemble a structure with misaligned floors or missing staircases? What is one key "non-negotiable" principle you believe should anchor your system's literacy architecture?

5. Leaders are called to cultivate a "culture of continuity" that "outlasts any single program or framework." What practices or conversations could leaders initiate to shift from managing initiatives to sustaining a deep alignment to the science of reading?

Application Steps:

1. **Map Your Literacy Ecosystem:** Gather representatives from curriculum, intervention, and professional learning teams (or individual practitioners if the teams are small). On a large whiteboard or digital canvas, map out the current connections (or lack thereof) between these three areas in your school or district. Use lines, arrows, and notes to illustrate dependencies, overlaps, and gaps.

2. **Audit for "Silo Language":** Review your school or district's current literacy-related documents (e.g., curriculum guides, intervention handbooks, PD calendars, assessment reports). Look for any language that might reinforce silos or suggest disconnected efforts. Discuss how these documents could be revised to reflect a more coherent, ecosystem approach.

3. **Conduct a "Coherence Walk":** Arrange for a small team (e.g., a principal, literacy coach, and a teacher from a different grade level) to visit classrooms across grade bands (e.g., kindergarten, third grade, eighth grade). Observe and discuss:

   - How is the "language of learning" consistent (or inconsistent) across grades?
   - How do early foundational skills appear to be building (or not building) into later comprehension and reasoning instruction?
   - What evidence of your system's "developmental architecture" is visible in practice?

4. **Define Your "Non-Negotiables":** As a leadership team or literacy committee, identify and articulate 3-5 core, non-negotiable principles of reading development (drawing from the Science of Reading) that should anchor your K-12 literacy system. These should be principles that transcend any single program or initiative.

5. **Reframe Professional Learning:** Examine your upcoming professional learning schedule for literacy. How can existing or planned sessions be reframed or redesigned to foster "professional clarity" and strengthen the connections between curriculum and intervention, rather than treating them as isolated topics? Consider adding explicit opportunities for cross-grade dialogue around shared learning progressions.

PART II
The Developmental Architecture of Literacy

The science of reading begins in the smallest unit of sound, but it does not end there. What starts as a single vibration in the air—a child hearing a phoneme and matching it to a symbol—expands into a vast architecture of understanding. Each new skill adds another beam, another bridge, another room in which meaning can take shape. Reading grows not by replacement but by addition. The mind never leaves the earlier rooms; it carries them forward, using each to support the next.

If Part I traced the evolution of thought—the movement from code to cognition—Part II turns inward to the blueprint itself. This is where the science becomes visible, where the layers of literacy reveal their order and interdependence. The chapters that follow move through the structure of learning step by step: from the foundations that anchor equity, to the linguistic bridges that give language its texture, to the deep reasoning that transforms comprehension into thought, and finally to the transfer that turns reading into action.

Foundational instruction is the footing of this design, but not its ceiling. Phonemic awareness, phonics, and fluency remain essential precisely because they make later complexity possible. Vocabulary, syntax, and morphology give the structure dimension and color. Comprehension and reasoning supply its electricity—the current that moves ideas across rooms, illuminating connections that once lay dark. And transfer—the final stage—opens the doors and windows, allowing learning to circulate freely into every discipline and every life.

To build this architecture well is to understand reading as both an engineering feat and a human one. The science gives us the measurements; the craft lies in how we arrange them. Teachers become builders of thought, each lesson another layer of meaning carefully aligned to what came before and what will come next. When that alignment holds, the structure can bear any weight—new knowledge, new language, new ways of thinking.

Part II is an invitation to see literacy not as a series of tasks, but as a designed environment where understanding grows. Each chapter reveals another level of the design, another way the mind constructs its house of meaning. By the end, what began as sound becomes structure, and what began as instruction becomes insight.

CHAPTER 4
The Foundations — Phonemic Awareness to Automaticity

Introduction

Every act of reading begins in sound. Long before a child can recognize a printed word, their mind is already mapping the rhythm of language—the rise and fall of syllables, the subtle pause between words, the music of meaning embedded in speech. These early encounters with sound form the soil from which literacy grows. Phonemic awareness, phonics, fluency—each is a seed of cognition, a small act of precision that makes all later comprehension possible.

For years, these skills have been treated as the mechanics of reading—important, yes, but somehow separate from the deeper work of thinking. Yet the brain tells a different story. What we call "foundational skills" are not mechanical at all; they are the cognitive infrastructure of understanding. When a child learns to connect a sound to a symbol, they are learning to connect perception to idea. When they practice decoding, they are teaching their brain to recognize patterns, to anticipate meaning, to make predictions. Foundational instruction is therefore not a prelude to comprehension—it is comprehension's first draft.

Louisa Moats (2020) calls the explicit, systematic teaching of these skills "the equity work of our time." The children who benefit most are those who rely most on school to make the code visible. Systematic instruction ensures that opportunity does not depend on exposure or environment; it becomes a matter of design. Each carefully modeled phoneme, each deliberate connection between sound and print, is an act of inclusion.

This chapter explores those foundations not as ends to be mastered but as beginnings to be sustained. It follows the brain as it constructs its reading circuit, examines how orthographic mapping turns practice into permanence, and reveals why fluency, far from being a measure of speed, is the bridge that carries accuracy into understanding. It also argues that foundational instruction must live inside rich, meaningful content—not apart from it—so that every act of decoding is tethered to knowledge and curiosity.

The goal is not simply to teach children how to read words, but to help them build a mind prepared to read the world. The foundations are where that preparation begins: explicit, equitable, and enduring.

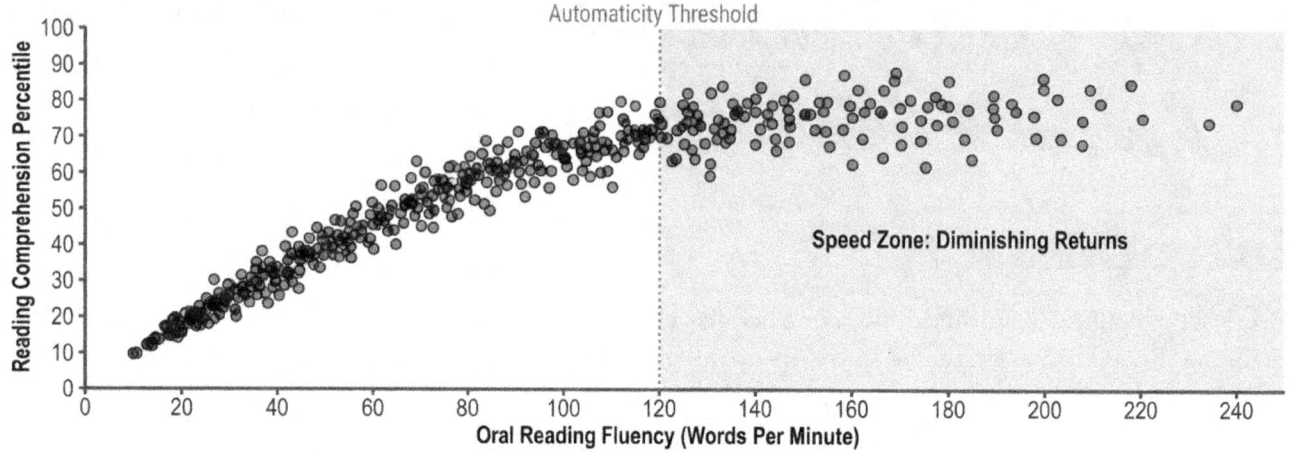

Section 1: Why Explicit, Systematic Instruction Builds Equity

Every child arrives at school carrying a language story. Some bring homes filled with conversation and books; others bring the rhythms of songs, stories told at the table, or the quiet patterns of thought formed in solitude. Each of those stories is linguistic capital—the brain's first curriculum. Yet the bridge from language to literacy is not evenly built. For many students, the connection between spoken sound and written symbol is fragile, and unless we teach it directly, it remains incomplete.

Explicit, systematic instruction is the act of building that bridge with intention. It is the decision to make visible what the brain cannot intuit on its own: that letters represent sounds, that patterns repeat, that print carries meaning. Teaching in this way is not mechanical; it is merciful. It recognizes that reading is an unnatural act, and that leaving it to chance privileges those whose environment already provides the code. Systematic teaching restores fairness by ensuring that knowledge is delivered, not inherited.

Louisa Moats (2020) calls this "the most democratic form of instruction we have." When a teacher models a phoneme, guides blending, or helps a child anchor a sound to a symbol, they are doing more than teaching literacy—they are offering access to language itself. Each direct, deliberate lesson gives the brain what it needs to connect sound to print, print to idea, and idea to understanding. What looks like precision is, in truth, compassion measured in seconds and syllables.

Equity in literacy does not mean identical experiences; it means universal opportunity to master the invisible architecture of language. Explicit instruction is the great equalizer because it removes luck from learning. It acknowledges that children differ in exposure, but not in potential—that clarity of teaching can replace the accidents of circumstance. When we teach systematically, we teach as though every child were capable of complexity, and that belief begins to shape reality.

This is why foundational work must never be dismissed as basic. The most advanced readers are those whose early instruction left no gaps for confusion to widen. The speed of comprehension in later years depends on the accuracy of instruction in the first. Each explicit lesson is a safeguard against future inequity, a line drawn in defense of understanding.

Equity, then, is not a slogan hung above a classroom door—it is embedded in every modeling of a sound, every moment of guided practice, every teacher who refuses to let a child guess at the code when they can be taught to master it. Systematic instruction is justice rendered in sequence and repetition, in the steady rhythm of teachers who believe that clarity is kindness.

Section 2: The Mechanics of Orthographic Mapping and the Role of Working Memory

Inside the mind of a beginning reader, every letter is alive. It holds a shape, a sound, and the possibility of meaning, but none of these elements yet know how to find one another. When a teacher guides a student through that act—when they stretch a word, isolate a sound, and connect it to a written symbol—they are, quite literally, teaching the brain to build a new network.

This process, known as orthographic mapping, is how words become known to the mind—not memorized as images, but stored as integrated units of sound, spelling, and meaning. Linnea Ehri's research revealed that readers do not remember whole words by sight; rather, they remember the precise relationships among letters and sounds. Each time a child encounters a word, the brain connects what it sees to what it hears and what it means. With enough successful repetitions, those connections strengthen until recognition becomes instantaneous.

For the brain, this is remarkable engineering. The visual word form area in the left occipitotemporal cortex specializes in recognizing letter patterns. The phonological loop in working memory temporarily holds sounds long enough for the reader to blend them. When these regions synchronize, the act of decoding becomes automatic. Working memory, once overloaded by the effort of keeping track of each sound, is suddenly freed to think about what those sounds signify. Accuracy gives way to fluency; fluency gives way to comprehension.

This is why explicit instruction matters so deeply in the early stages of reading. Orthographic mapping does not happen by exposure alone. The brain must be guided to notice patterns, to rehearse them, to strengthen their bonds. Each modeled sound, each blending routine, each cumulative review is not repetition for its own sake—it is the deliberate building of neural architecture. When teachers return to a familiar word family or pattern, they are solidifying the foundation that comprehension will later stand upon.

Working memory serves as both the bridge and the bottleneck in this process. It can hold only so much information at once, which means the clarity of instruction determines whether the bridge holds or collapses. When teachers sequence learning carefully—introducing only a few new patterns at a time, returning to

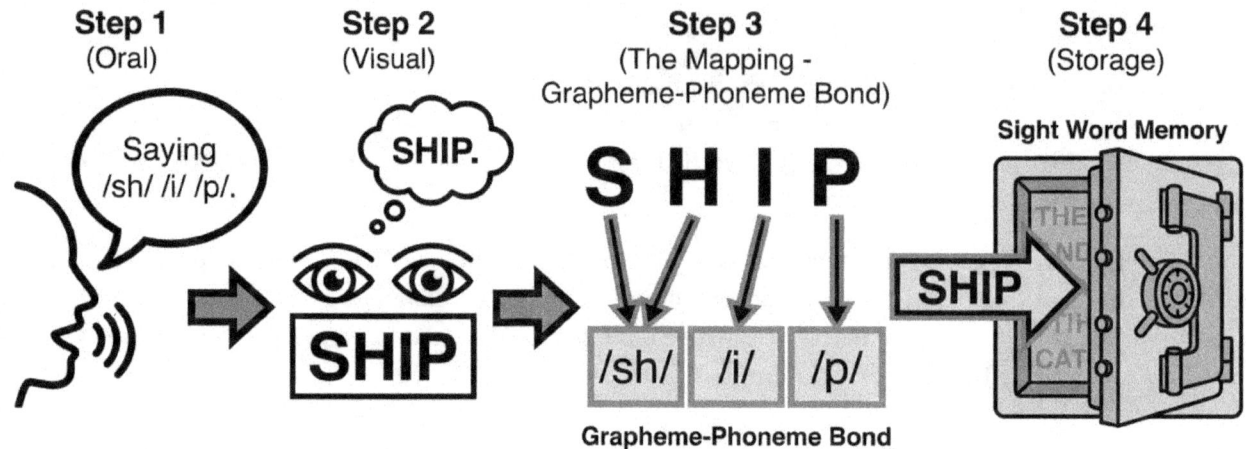

Orthographic Mapping: Bonding sound, symbol, and meaning

Over time, this system grows more efficient. A student who once labored to decode ship now recognizes shipment and relationship instantly. The orthographic map expands outward, creating a lexicon of known words and predictable patterns. Each new connection lightens the cognitive burden, allowing the brain to focus on comprehension rather than reconstruction.

This is the invisible transformation that marks the boundary between effort and understanding. When working memory is no longer consumed by the mechanics of print, it can begin to do what it was built for—thinking, reasoning, imagining. Orthographic mapping, then, is not just the science of word recognition; it is the threshold of literacy's higher work. It is the moment the brain stops learning to read and begins reading to learn.

Section 3: Fluency as a Bridge to Comprehension, Not Just Speed

At first, reading is halting—an audible labor. A child's voice rises and falls unevenly as they piece together sounds, each word a small victory earned through effort. Over time, that effort softens. Words begin to flow into phrases, phrases into sentences, sentences into stories. The rhythm changes. The reader no longer sounds out cat or ship; they speak through them. This change is called fluency, but it is often misunderstood.

Fluency is not a race. It is not the measure of how fast a child can move their eyes across a page, nor is it a contest of words per minute. Fluency is the sound of comprehension taking shape—the external evidence that the reader's brain has freed enough cognitive energy to think while reading. It is the harmony between decoding and meaning, between accuracy and interpretation. When a reader pauses appropriately, adjusts tone, or emphasizes a word to match its importance, they are not performing; they are understanding.

Maryanne Wolf (2008) described this transformation as the "reading brain's moment of liberation." Once the processes of decoding and word recognition become automatic, the brain's working memory can finally shift its attention to higher-level thinking. Fluency marks this release. It is the sign that the reading circuit has matured enough to operate with efficiency, leaving space for the subtleties of inference, emotion, and imagery. In fluent reading, the mechanics of literacy and the music of language become one.

Yet in many classrooms, fluency is still treated as a speed test rather than a bridge. Charts of rates and scores reduce the elegance of expression to a number. This misinterpretation misses the essence of what fluency truly represents—a mind learning to synchronize thought and sound. The goal is not faster readers but freer ones: readers whose cognitive resources are unbound from decoding and available for comprehension, analysis, and pleasure.

The most effective fluency instruction therefore begins not with timers, but with models. When teachers read aloud with expression, they demonstrate how print carries rhythm, tone, and meaning. When students echo that phrasing, they practice how comprehension sounds. Repeated readings, partner reading, and oral performance are not drills; they are opportunities for the brain to align pacing, prosody, and understanding.

Fluency also thrives when connected to content. When students read texts rich in knowledge and concept, their expression becomes more purposeful because the meaning matters. A child reading about migration, or planets, or justice will naturally infuse their voice with curiosity or conviction if comprehension drives the rhythm. In this way, fluency ceases to be a discrete skill and becomes the living evidence of learning.

The bridge from fluency to comprehension is built on this interplay between mastery and meaning. The reader who moves smoothly through a passage does so because each known pattern, each familiar word, each predictable syntax frees attention for the sentence as a whole. The melody of fluent reading is the sound of efficiency—every neural system working in time, every cognitive resource pointing toward understanding.

To teach fluency, then, is to teach balance. It is to remind students that the beauty of reading lies not in how quickly they reach the end, but in how fully they inhabit the words along the way. Fluency is what allows the reader to cross from recognition into reflection—to move beyond the code and into the current of comprehension itself.

Section 4: Embedding Foundational Routines within Knowledge-Rich Content

The earliest acts of reading instruction often unfold on the margins of meaning. We teach letters, sounds, and patterns in isolation, as if the brain can build understanding one syllable at a time. For a moment, that separation is necessary. The mind must first learn the mechanics before it can play the music. But if we linger there too long, the music never comes.

Foundational routines—phoneme blending, decoding practice, fluency drills—are essential scaffolds, but they are meant to hold something larger: knowledge. When students practice these routines within content that informs or delights, the brain does more than rehearse sound–symbol relationships; it begins to connect those relationships to ideas. Reading becomes not only accurate, but meaningful.

The power of embedding lies in the way it anchors cognition. A lesson on the long-a sound taught through a story about rain and grain is easier to remember because it binds phonics to imagery. A passage about pollination provides context for decoding multisyllabic words while simultaneously building background knowledge that will support comprehension in science later. The more connections a reader makes, the stronger the memory trace becomes. Meaning cements mastery.

Maryanne Wolf once wrote that reading "is a circuit built for meaning." The code itself is not the goal; it is the doorway. When foundational skills are taught through knowledge-rich experiences—stories, songs, poems, informational texts—the doorway opens into a room already filled with light. Students feel the relevance of what they are learning because each sound, each word, each sentence belongs to something larger than itself.

Embedding routines also nurtures curiosity. When children practice decoding within texts that teach them something new about the world, engagement replaces repetition fatigue. Motivation strengthens memory; interest sustains precision. The teacher's task, then, is not only to teach the code, but to curate the context—to select materials that align with both the phonological goals of the lesson and the intellectual goals of the curriculum.

This approach also honors time. Teachers in knowledge-rich classrooms do not need to choose between skill and substance, between phonics and content. Every moment of instruction becomes dual-purpose: building automaticity while expanding understanding. The same text that supports decoding supports background knowledge; the same sentence that strengthens fluency strengthens syntax awareness. Literacy ceases to feel divided.

When foundational routines live inside meaning, they acquire dignity. They stop being drills and become design—each repetition a rehearsal for comprehension, each sound a seed of knowledge. The youngest readers begin to understand that print is not a puzzle to solve but a tool to explore the world. And in that realization lies the true purpose of the foundations: not just to teach children how to read, but to give them something worth reading for.

Closing Reflection: The Living Architecture of the Foundations

Every structure we admire disappears beneath the surface once it does its work. No one walks into a cathedral to marvel at its footings, yet without them, the walls would never rise. Foundational reading instruction is much the same. When done well, it becomes invisible—its strength revealed not in the lessons themselves, but in the ease with which students move through them toward understanding.

The smallest routines—articulating sounds, tracing letters, rereading familiar lines—seem humble in the moment, but they are acts of immense significance. Each one builds access. Each one affirms a child's capacity to join the conversation of written language. When explicit, systematic teaching meets curiosity and meaning, the result is equity not as aspiration, but as architecture—strong enough to hold the weight of comprehension, reasoning, and identity.

The Science of Reading reminds us that mastery is not the point of arrival but the platform for ascent. Automaticity frees the brain to think; fluency frees the heart to feel. When foundational skills are anchored in knowledge-rich experiences, they cease to be preliminary—they become the living base of lifelong literacy.

As we move into the next chapter, the focus shifts from the mechanics of sound to the elegance of language itself—from the code that makes reading possible to the structures that make it profound. Vocabulary, syntax, and morphology are the beams and arches built upon these foundations, turning the solid footing of skill into the spaciousness of meaning.

The child who once worked to sound out words now begins to notice how words work—to see that language has texture, pattern, and power. The foundation holds, and from it, understanding begins to rise.

Reflection Questions:

1. This chapter argues that "Foundational instruction is therefore not a prelude to comprehension—it is comprehension's first draft." How does this perspective change how you view the purpose and importance of early literacy instruction?

2. Section 1 describes explicit, systematic instruction as "the equity work of our time." In what specific ways does this approach to foundational skills address historical inequities in literacy instruction? How can your system ensure this promise is met for all students?

3. "Orthographic mapping, then, is not just the science of word recognition; it is the threshold of literacy's higher work." Reflect on a time when a student's automaticity in word recognition seemed to "liberate" their cognitive space. What instructional practices contribute most effectively to this process in your classroom or school?

4. Section 3 challenges the common misconception of fluency as merely speed, redefining it as "the bridge that carries accuracy into understanding." How do your current fluency assessment and instruction practices align with this broader definition? What might need to shift?

5. The chapter emphasizes embedding foundational routines "within knowledge-rich content." What are the benefits of this approach, and what challenges might arise in ensuring that phonics and phonemic awareness instruction are consistently integrated with meaningful texts and concepts in your setting?

Application Steps:

1. **Audit Foundational Routines for Equity:** Select a common foundational skill routine (e.g., blending, segmenting, word sorts) used in your early grades. Discuss how explicit, systematic instruction ensures that *all* students, regardless of background, have equitable access to understanding the alphabetic code. Identify any areas where instruction might be inadvertently relying on implicit learning or prior exposure.

2. **Examine Working Memory Load:** Observe a foundational skills lesson (or reflect on your own teaching). Pay close attention to how much new information is presented at once and how opportunities for guided practice and cumulative review are provided. Discuss strategies to optimize instruction to support orthographic mapping without overloading students' working memory.

3. **Refine Fluency Instruction for Meaning:** Review your school's approach to fluency instruction. Beyond tracking words per minute, discuss how teachers could explicitly model and teach prosody (phrasing, expression, intonation) to reflect comprehension. Consider incorporating activities like repeated readings of conceptually rich texts, choral reading, or readers' theater with a focus on conveying meaning.

4. **Integrate Content with Code:** Select a specific phonics or phonemic awareness target for an upcoming unit. Brainstorm ways to embed instruction for that target within a knowledge-rich context (e.g., a science lesson, a historical narrative, a read-aloud related to a social studies theme). How can the chosen content make the foundational skills more meaningful and memorable?

5. **Professional Learning Dialogue:** Facilitate a discussion with early elementary teachers around the idea that foundational skills are "comprehension's first draft." How might this framing influence their planning and daily instruction? What support might they need to consistently connect early decoding to the larger purpose of understanding?

CHAPTER 5
The Bridge to Meaning — Vocabulary, Syntax, and Morphology

Introduction

Once decoding becomes effortless, the reading brain is ready for something more intricate. The scaffolds of phonemic awareness and automaticity have done their work; the mind now hungers for depth—for the meaning that lies within and between words. This is the moment when reading transforms from accuracy to artistry, from mechanical precision to linguistic grace.

If foundational instruction gives students the how of reading, this next stage gives them the why. Words are no longer puzzles to be solved; they are instruments of thought. The student who once celebrated reading cat now begins to wonder why cathedral and catalogue share its shape. The reader who once sounded out run begins to notice running, overrun, and outrun—how a single root can shift its identity through prefixes and suffixes. These are not trivial curiosities; they are the beginnings of cognition. The reader is learning to see language as system and design.

To build this bridge, we must adopt what Maryanne Wolf calls an "expanded conceptualization of foundational skills." For too long, the Science of Reading has been publicly (and incorrectly) reduced to just phonics . Wolf reminds us that the brain's reading circuit relies on a whole set of interconnected processes, which she captures in the **"POSSUM"** acronym:

- **P** (Phonology, Prosody)
- **O** (Orthographic patterns)
- **S** (Semantics / Vocabulary)
- **S** (Syntax / Language Structures)
- **U** (Understanding the alphabetic principle)
- **M** (Morphology / Meaningful parts)

This framework is revolutionary for our K-12 continuum. It makes clear that while systems are now rightly focused on the "P," "O," and "U," they have systemically neglected the "SSM"—**Semantics, Syntax, and Morphology**. These are what Wolf calls the "all too often missing links."

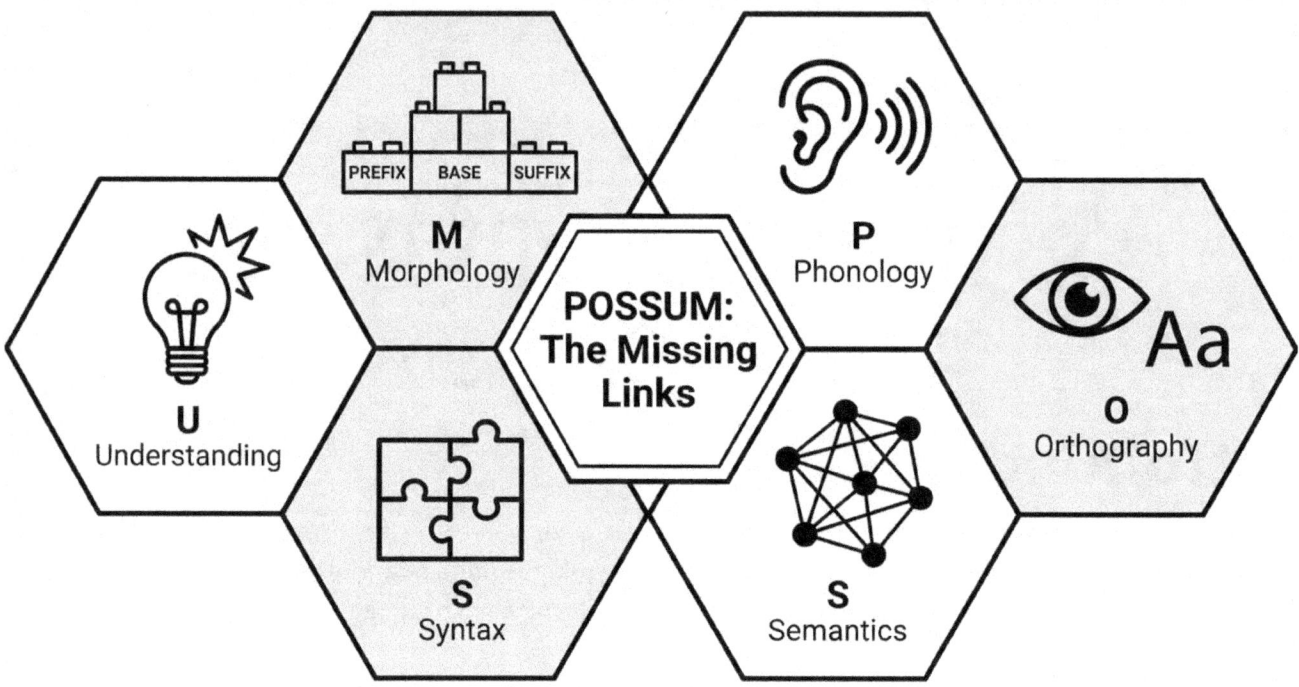

This chapter is dedicated to rebuilding those missing links. The "SSM" *are* the bridge to meaning.

This instructional framework is directly supported by leading-edge cognitive science. David Share's **Combinatorial Model** (2021) provides a powerful theory for *how* this developmental bridge is built in the brain. This 2025 model is a profound evolution of Share's (1995) own foundational "Self-Teaching Hypothesis" (STH). The STH established the critical *mechanism* by which phonological recoding—the act of "sounding out" a new word—allows a learner to acquire a vast orthographic lexicon. The "Combinatorial Model" is the evolution of this theory, explaining *how* that self-teaching mechanism functions at scale. Share's insight is that *combinatoriality* (at the phonemic, morphemic, and syntactic levels) is what *enables* the STH to function. As this chapter will detail, it is precisely the mastery of the 'morpho-lexical' phase that *powers* the STH beyond single-syllable words, allowing learners to build the robust, meaning-based lexicon required for deep reading.

Share describes reading acquisition as a "vertical growth" through additive phases.

6. First is the 'sub-morphemic' phase, where the novice reader builds foundational 'decipherability' (i.e., phonics).

7. Next, the reader must advance to the 'morpho-lexical' phase, where they learn to 'unitize' meaningful chunks—morphemes and words, not just letters.

8. This leads to the 'supra-lexical' phase, where sentence-level context and syntax are integrated for deep reasoning.

Share's model provides the theoretical blueprint for this book's continuum. It shows that systems that stop at the 'sub-morphemic' phase—treating phonics as the finish line—strand students before they can build the 'morpho-lexical' bridge. The 'SSM' (Semantics, Syntax, and Morphology) we just discussed are the very tools the brain needs to master this 'morpho-lexical' phase and achieve true fluency and comprehension.

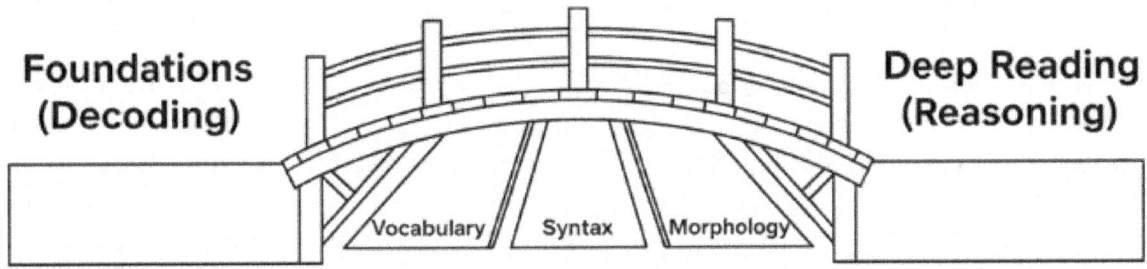

Vocabulary, syntax, and morphology form the bridge between word recognition and comprehension. Together, they provide the grammar of thought. Vocabulary gives words their color and precision; syntax arranges them into architecture; morphology reveals how meaning grows from within. The more a student understands how language works, the more flexibly they can use it—to infer, to reason, to learn.

This is also where equity deepens. Just as explicit instruction in decoding ensures that no child is excluded from the act of reading, explicit instruction in linguistic understanding ensures that no child is excluded from its interpretation. Knowledge of morphology, syntax, and vocabulary is not an enrichment—it is access to the deeper structures of knowledge itself.

This chapter traces how the reading brain evolves once the code has been mastered. It examines the cognitive leap from decoding to linguistic comprehension, explores how morphology and syntax give text its logic and texture, and demonstrates why vocabulary must be taught not as lists of words, but as patterns of meaning. It shows that language awareness is not a luxury—it is the engine of thought.

The bridge to meaning is the bridge to everything that follows. When we cross it, reading ceases to be an act of recognition and becomes an act of reasoning.

Section 1: The Cognitive Leap from Decoding to Linguistic Comprehension

When decoding becomes automatic, the mind does something extraordinary—it begins to think beyond the word itself. The eyes still move across the page, the voice still whispers the sounds, but beneath the surface, a new system is taking shape. The reader's attention, once consumed by letter–sound correspondence, shifts toward meaning. This transition, quiet and invisible, is one of the greatest leaps in human cognition.

In the earliest stages of reading, the brain's work is narrow but intense. It labors to connect what it sees with what it hears, converting print into sound. But once that circuitry stabilizes, new regions of the brain join the conversation—those responsible for semantics, syntax, and reasoning. The temporal lobe integrates sound with stored knowledge of words; the frontal lobe begins to analyze relationships between ideas. The act of reading, once mechanical, becomes conceptual.

This shift marks the beginning of linguistic comprehension—the reader's capacity to derive and construct meaning through language. It is the point where the Science of Reading expands beyond phonology into the full complexity of communication. Vocabulary, morphology, and syntax now become the tools through which comprehension is built, allowing the reader not only to understand a text, but to predict, infer, and reflect upon it.

Catherine Snow and her colleagues have long emphasized that comprehension is not a "stage" after decoding but a parallel system that matures in tandem. As decoding becomes automatic, linguistic comprehension accelerates, fueled by exposure, conversation, and intentional teaching. The relationship between the two is symbiotic: the stronger the code, the more cognitive space available for language; the richer the language, the more motivation and context for reading. Each strengthens the other until the distinction begins to dissolve.

At this point, reading instruction must evolve as well. A classroom built only around phonics will soon reach its ceiling. The human brain, having mastered recognition, now seeks complexity—new patterns, new connections, new ideas to organize. This is the moment to introduce the structure of language itself: how prefixes shift meaning, how syntax directs logic, how vocabulary encodes experience. The goal is not simply to read the words, but to read with the language—to understand how it builds, bends, and carries thought.

This leap also reshapes identity. A student who once saw reading as an act of decoding begins to see it as an act of discovery. They no longer ask, "What does this word say?" but "What does this sentence mean?" and, eventually, "What does the author want me to understand?" That change in question signals a change in cognition. The reader is no longer decoding text—they are decoding the world.

Instruction that honors this moment becomes a bridge rather than a divide. It connects the tangible mechanics of early literacy to the invisible reasoning of advanced comprehension. It treats vocabulary not as enrichment but as empowerment, syntax not as grammar drills but as logic training, and morphology not as memorization but as meaning-making. Each lesson becomes a small act of translation between code and consciousness.

The cognitive leap from decoding to linguistic comprehension is, in truth, the leap from reading as task to reading as thought. It is where the sound of language gives way to its sense—and in that transition, literacy becomes life itself.

Section 2: Morphology as the Meaning-Maker: Prefixes, Roots, and Suffixes

Every word carries a story. Beneath its surface lies a history of language—borrowed, adapted, and reshaped through centuries of human thought. To study morphology is to teach students how to read those stories, to see that words are not arbitrary symbols but structured systems of meaning. When we reveal this structure, we give readers the tools to unlock not just vocabulary, but understanding itself.

Morphology is the study of how words are built—how prefixes, roots, and suffixes combine to form meaning. A child who knows that tele means "distance" and graph means "write" can decipher telegraph, telephone, and television without having encountered them before. This is not rote memorization; it is reasoning through language. The reader begins to see that English, for all its quirks, is a code built on logic.

An Anecdote from the Field: The Fourth Grade "A-ha" Moment

I saw this cognitive leap happen in real-time during a 4th-grade PLC. The team was frustrated with vocabulary. Their students could decode fluently but struggled with academic words in their science texts. The teachers felt they were "pre-teaching" dozens of words, only to have students forget them a week later.

We decided to shift from pre-teaching lists to pre-teaching a single Latin root: spect (to see).

The team was skeptical. "This feels slow. We have so many words to cover." But they tried it. They built an anchor chart with the root and began "word hunting." A student found inspect. The teacher asked, "If spect means 'to see,' what does in-spect mean?" A student guessed, "To see in?" The room went quiet.

The "a-ha" moment came from a student in the back. "Wait. Does re-spect mean to 'see someone again?'"

The team leader paused, then said, "It's about 'looking' at someone in a way that values them. You 'look up' to them. You 'look' at them with honor."

Another student chimed in, "So a spect-ator is someone who 'sees' the game?"

In that 10-minute exchange, the teachers' entire perspective shifted. The "a-ha" was theirs as much as the students'. One teacher told me later, "I've been teaching for 15 years, and I never realized language had a logic like that. I thought words were just words. We weren't just teaching a root; we were teaching them how to reason." The team stopped seeing morphology as a vocabulary task and started seeing it as a thinking tool—the very bridge from decoding to comprehension we had been missing.

Carlisle (2010) described morphological awareness as a bridge skill—the point where word recognition and language comprehension meet. It is what allows readers to move beyond sight recognition to conceptual understanding. Morphological instruction teaches the mind to analyze and predict. When students learn that re- signals repetition or reversal, that bio- relates to life, or that -ology denotes the study of something, they begin to construct meaning dynamically, piece by piece. Each morpheme becomes a clue in an ever-growing network of inference.

The cognitive power of morphology lies in its efficiency. The brain loves patterns—it is designed to recognize and reuse them. When students internalize common morphemes, they dramatically reduce cognitive load. Instead of memorizing thousands of words, they store a few hundred building blocks and learn to combine them. Working memory, now freed from the burden of decoding, can focus on comprehension and reasoning. Morphology, in this way, becomes an economy of thought.

It also becomes a form of equity. Students who are explicitly taught how words work gain access to the language of academia—the vocabulary of science, history, and literature that often separates fluent decoders from confident comprehenders. Nagy and Townsend (2012) call this "academic morphology": the understanding that the same prefixes and roots that construct everyday words also construct disciplinary knowledge. Teaching students to unpack photosynthesis or democracy is not vocabulary work alone; it is teaching them how knowledge itself is organized.

Morphology brings joy to the act of reading. Once students recognize its logic, they begin to see connections everywhere. The word transport suddenly reveals its twin in transcend; benevolent finds its mirror in benefit.

Words stop being strangers and start to form families. This realization transforms curiosity into cognition. The reader who once sought definitions now seeks relationships, discovering that language is not a list but a lineage.

To teach morphology well is to move from recitation to revelation. It means showing that meaning is not something delivered to the reader but something the reader can build. In doing so, we prepare students not only to understand unfamiliar words but to approach complexity itself with confidence. They learn that knowledge—like language—is constructed from parts that make sense once you know how to see them.

Morphology, then, is more than a linguistic skill; it is a cognitive awakening. It teaches readers that every word is an idea assembled from smaller truths—and that they, too, can assemble understanding from the fragments of the unknown.

Section 3: Syntax and the Architecture of Meaning

Every language has its architecture. Beneath the words that fill a page lies a hidden design—a framework that shapes how ideas connect, how emphasis shifts, how meaning unfolds. That framework is syntax. It is what allows the mind to build sense from sound and structure from sequence. Without it, words are materials without form.

Syntax is often introduced to students as grammar, a set of rules to memorize and avoid breaking. But in truth, it is closer to engineering than law. Syntax is the system through which writers construct thought and readers reconstruct it. It tells us who is acting, upon what, when, and how. It gives order to abstraction and clarity to emotion. Understanding syntax means understanding how language builds logic.

At the neural level, syntax engages the same cognitive regions responsible for pattern recognition and reasoning. The brain uses these systems to anticipate what comes next, to identify relationships between phrases, to hold multiple ideas in working memory until coherence emerges. When students encounter a complex sentence—one that winds through clauses and conditions—they are not merely parsing grammar; they are managing complexity. Each successful decoding of structure is an act of cognitive control, a rehearsal for analytical thought.

Myhill (2011) describes syntax as "the architecture of thinking," arguing that grammar instruction, when taught as design rather than correction, becomes a form of metacognition. Students who can identify the subject and predicate of a sentence are learning more than terminology; they are learning to locate the center of meaning. When they examine how a sentence expands or contracts to convey nuance, they are learning to see how writers shape thought through structure. Syntax, then, is not an obstacle to understanding—it is the path to it.

Consider the difference between *The storm destroyed the village* and *The village was destroyed by the storm*. The information is the same, but the emphasis changes. The first sentence places power in the storm; the second places loss in the village. Syntax directs empathy, agency, and tone. When students learn to notice those shifts, they are learning how language shapes perception.

This awareness deepens comprehension far beyond vocabulary. Skilled readers intuitively track syntactic cues—conjunctions that signal contrast, relative clauses that provide detail, punctuation that indicates pause.

These signals help the mind manage information flow. When teachers make those cues explicit, they equip students to handle the increasingly complex texts of secondary and disciplinary literacy. Syntax becomes the scaffolding that supports comprehension under cognitive weight.

Explicit instruction in syntax also strengthens writing. Reading and writing are reciprocal processes; the same structures that help students interpret meaning help them express it. When students manipulate sentence length, vary clause structure, or experiment with inversion, they are not just learning grammar—they are learning control over thought. They begin to see that language can be shaped to mirror intention, that syntax is a form of agency.

Ultimately, syntax teaches students how to inhabit another's thinking and make it their own. It shows that comprehension is not passive reception but active construction. Each sentence becomes a blueprint the reader must interpret, assembling the pieces into coherence.

Syntax is, in every sense, the architecture of meaning. To understand it is to see how thought itself is built—one phrase, one clause, one deliberate connection at a time.

Section 4: Contextual Vocabulary Instruction through Morphology and Syntax

Vocabulary has often been taught as inventory—a collection of words to be learned, defined, and recalled. Lists are made, tests are given, and students memorize meanings that fade as quickly as they are learned. What these practices overlook is that words do not live alone; they exist within systems—morphological, syntactic, and conceptual—that give them depth and permanence. To know a word is not merely to recognize it; it is to understand how it behaves in the company of others.

When instruction treats vocabulary as context rather than collection, it aligns with how the brain naturally learns. Meaning is strengthened through association—by encountering a word in varied settings, noticing its patterns, and connecting it to prior knowledge. Morphology provides the internal structure; syntax provides the external one. Together, they allow students to see words not as static units, but as dynamic elements of thought.

Consider the word transport. A student who understands its root (port = "carry") and prefix (trans = "across") already possesses a conceptual map of its meaning. But when they encounter it in a sentence—The refugees transported their hopes as well as their belongings—syntax and context deepen that meaning. The word takes on emotional resonance, illustrating not only the act of carrying but the burden and beauty of what is carried. Morphology explains the what; syntax and context explain the how and why.

Nagy and Townsend (2012) emphasize that academic vocabulary grows best through what they call morpho-syntactic awareness—the ability to use grammatical and structural cues to infer meaning from unfamiliar words. This awareness turns reading into discovery. Students learn to watch how a word's position, prefix, or suffix alters its function: construct, construction, reconstruct, deconstruct. Each variation becomes an invitation to reason.

Contextual instruction also aligns with what we know about memory. The brain remembers meaning more readily when it is connected to imagery, emotion, or knowledge. When teachers embed vocabulary in rich texts—historical accounts, science phenomena, or stories filled with human complexity—students encounter words not as tasks to memorize, but as tools for understanding. Repetition across disciplines further strengthens this web. A root learned in literature reappears in biology; a word introduced in social studies resurfaces in art. With each reencounter, understanding deepens and the lexicon expands organically.

Teaching vocabulary through morphology and syntax also restores agency to students. They are no longer dependent on a teacher's definitions; they become investigators of language. A student who can dissect photosynthesis into photo- (light) and synthesis (putting together) no longer fears complexity. They know how to approach the unknown with logic and curiosity.

This approach transforms vocabulary instruction from accumulation to construction. It replaces memorization with metacognition—students thinking about how language conveys meaning. As they become attuned to these patterns, comprehension accelerates because each new word arrives preloaded with clues. Syntax and morphology form a partnership: one reveals a word's internal structure, the other its relational function. Together, they make meaning visible.

Ultimately, contextual vocabulary instruction is not about adding words to a student's repertoire—it is about expanding their capacity to think with precision. Every prefix becomes a clue, every clause a context, every new word an opportunity to reason. In that way, vocabulary ceases to be a list to learn and becomes a language to live in.

Section 5: Oral Language and Prosody as Comprehension Accelerators

Long before a child learns to read, they are already learning how language thinks. Every lullaby, every conversation, every shared story becomes a form of cognitive rehearsal—an apprenticeship in meaning. Through oral language, the brain begins to organize the world: distinguishing cause from effect, emotion from intention, statement from question. By the time the first printed word appears, the neural architecture for comprehension is already under construction.

Oral language is not separate from reading; it is its foundation and its accelerant. The same circuits that process speech are repurposed when the brain begins to interpret print. The quality and variety of spoken interactions directly shape the depth of linguistic comprehension a reader can later achieve. When children engage in dialogue rich with vocabulary, syntax, and narrative structure, they are building the schema that will make reading make sense.

Prosody—our natural rhythm, tone, and emphasis in speech—is one of the most powerful yet overlooked tools in this process. It gives language its emotional and logical shape. When a parent pauses for suspense or stretches a vowel for surprise, they are teaching more than expression; they are teaching how meaning moves through sound. The rise and fall of a sentence conveys relationships that no punctuation can capture. Prosody is comprehension made audible.

Scott and Balthazar (2010) describe prosody as "the cognitive melody of language." It reflects understanding before words can explain it. When teachers model fluent, expressive reading, they activate this same melody in their students' minds. The rhythm and phrasing of text signal structure: commas mark clauses, tone distinguishes character, stress highlights importance. Through listening and imitation, students internalize these cues, learning intuitively how written language mirrors the music of thought.

Explicit instruction in oral language and prosody is therefore not ornamental—it is essential. Classroom discussion, storytelling, partner reading, and choral performance all give students opportunities to connect sound to sense. When teachers encourage students to read with feeling, they are cultivating empathy as well as understanding. Expression requires interpretation; to read a sentence with the right emotion is to have grasped its meaning.

Prosody also accelerates comprehension by supporting working memory. The rhythmic grouping of words into phrases reduces cognitive load, allowing the brain to hold and process larger units of meaning. Fluent readers instinctively chunk information this way; struggling readers often do not. Teaching prosody helps students hear the structure that their eyes may not yet see.

In multilingual and linguistically diverse classrooms, oral language instruction becomes even more vital. Discussion and dialogue give all students access to the shared language of schooling—the syntax, vocabulary, and discourse patterns that written texts assume. Oral rehearsal precedes written mastery. The student who can articulate an idea clearly aloud is halfway to capturing it in print.

When we center oral language and prosody, reading instruction becomes holistic again. It reconnects the visual and the auditory, the analytical and the expressive. It reminds teachers that comprehension begins not with silence and print, but with sound and conversation.

Reading, after all, is silent speech. Every good reader hears the text as they see it, and every good teacher helps students find that voice within. Oral language gives thought its rhythm; prosody gives it soul. Together, they transform reading from a mechanical act into a human one—an experience not only of decoding, but of listening, feeling, and understanding.

Closing Reflection: The Bridge That Language Builds

Every word a child learns is a small act of construction. Piece by piece, language forms the bridges that carry thought. At first, those bridges are narrow—one sound joined to one letter, one word connected to one picture. But as vocabulary grows and syntax expands, the bridges lengthen and strengthen. Morphology gives them structure; prosody gives them movement. Together, they form a network through which comprehension can flow.

Language is not only what reading depends on—it is what reading becomes. As students learn to recognize how words are built, how sentences are shaped, and how tone carries meaning, they begin to see that language is both mirror and map: it reflects the world and shows them how to navigate it. The study of morphology teaches them that meaning is layered; syntax teaches them that meaning is ordered; vocabulary teaches them that meaning is infinite. Oral language and prosody teach them that meaning is alive.

These understandings do more than enrich literacy—they democratize it. When we teach students the systems behind words, we give them access to the architecture of knowledge. They no longer rely on memorization or exposure; they possess the tools to reason their way into understanding. Language becomes less a gate to be passed and more a key to be used.

This is the great transformation that follows foundational mastery: the shift from reading words to reading with language, from recognizing print to reasoning through it. The reader begins to hear the cadence of thought within the text—the pulse of logic, the rhythm of emotion, the music of understanding.

As we move into Chapter 6, the bridge becomes a passageway. The focus turns from language to meaning—from how we build sentences to how we build sense. Comprehension and reasoning emerge as the next stage of the continuum, where every earlier skill finds its purpose. What was once sound and symbol now becomes thought. The reader steps onto the bridge they have built, crossing from the world of words into the landscape of understanding itself.

Reflection Questions:

1. This chapter introduces Maryanne Wolf's POSSUM acronym, particularly highlighting the "systemic neglect" of SSM (Semantics, Syntax, Morphology). Where have you observed this neglect in your own context, and what are the potential consequences for student comprehension?

2. David Share's Combinatorial Model describes a "morpho-lexical phase" where readers "unitize meaningful chunks." How does this concept deepen your understanding of why explicit morphology instruction is critical after the initial sub-morphemic (phonics) phase?

3. Section 1 describes the "cognitive leap from decoding to linguistic comprehension." What instructional shifts or changes in emphasis do you believe are necessary to effectively support students in making this leap in your current setting?

4. The chapter emphasizes that morphology is "reasoning through language" and syntax is "the architecture of thinking." How do these framings elevate these often-misunderstood skills beyond mere grammar rules or vocabulary lists?

5. Section 5 highlights oral language and prosody as "comprehension accelerators." How can teachers intentionally integrate robust oral language practices and explicit prosody instruction into their daily routines to build this bridge to meaning?

Application Steps:

1. **Map Your "SSM" Instruction:** Choose a specific grade level (or grade band) and audit current literacy instruction. Where and how are vocabulary, syntax, and morphology currently taught? Identify areas where these "missing links" are strong, and where they might be systematically neglected.

2. **Morpheme Investigation (Collaborative):** Select a short academic text (e.g., from a science or social studies curriculum). In a small team, identify 5-7 key multisyllabic words. Using morphological analysis (prefixes, roots, suffixes), "dissect" these words. Discuss how explicit instruction in these morphemes could dramatically improve students' access to content knowledge.

3. **Syntactic Deconstruction/Reconstruction:** Take a complex sentence from a content-area text. As a team, deconstruct its syntax:
   - Identify the main subject and verb.
   - Highlight clauses and phrases.
   - Discuss how the sentence's structure influences its meaning, emphasis, or difficulty.
   - Then, try rewriting it in simpler terms or rearranging clauses to see how meaning shifts. How could this type of activity be integrated into instruction?

4. **Design Contextual Vocabulary Mini-Lessons:** For an upcoming unit, select 3-5 high-leverage academic vocabulary words. Instead of just giving definitions, design mini-lessons that explicitly teach these words by:
   - Highlighting their **morphological** components (if applicable).
   - Examining their use within complex **syntactic** structures in the text.
   - Connecting them to other known words or concepts.

5. **Elevate Oral Language and Prosody:** Plan a lesson that explicitly incorporates oral language and prosody as tools for comprehension. This could involve:
   - Modeling expressive reading of a complex text.
   - Guided partner reading with a focus on conveying meaning through intonation and phrasing.
   - Structured academic discussions where students articulate their reasoning using precise vocabulary and varied sentence structures.

CHAPTER 6
The Deep Reading Phase — Comprehension and Reasoning

Introduction

When reading becomes fluent, the visible effort fades, but the invisible work intensifies. Beneath the calm surface of comprehension, the mind is performing one of its most intricate dances—retrieving knowledge, predicting outcomes, weighing possibilities, and assembling ideas into coherence. What once demanded attention now invites reflection. The reader is no longer learning to read; they are reading to learn, to analyze, to understand.

This is the deep reading phase—the stage where literacy becomes cognition. It is here that comprehension reveals its true nature: not a skill to be measured, but a process of reasoning to be cultivated. In this phase, the act of reading transcends recognition and becomes relational. The reader engages not only with text, but with thought itself—questioning, connecting, evaluating, and interpreting.

For decades, comprehension has been taught as strategy: make predictions, ask questions, summarize, infer. These routines have value, but they often mistake behavior for understanding. Genuine comprehension is far less mechanical. It is a synthesis of knowledge, language, and experience—a reconstruction of meaning that the reader performs anew each time they encounter a text. Catherine Snow's expanded view of the Simple View of Reading reminds us that comprehension is not the product of one variable, but the interplay of many: decoding, linguistic knowledge, background schema, and reasoning.

At this point in the reading continuum, the earlier architecture—phonology, morphology, syntax, and fluency—has become the reader's subconscious scaffolding. Freed from the burden of decoding, the mind now devotes its full power to constructing and critiquing meaning. The reader's questions grow deeper: not What does this word mean? but What does the author mean? Not How is this sentence structured? but Why was it structured this way? Each new question signals a higher form of thinking.

This chapter explores how comprehension and reasoning develop as a unified act of cognition. It examines how inference transforms information into insight, how background knowledge gives depth to understanding, and how classroom instruction can move beyond strategies toward genuine intellectual engagement. It argues that comprehension is not a finish line, but a discipline—one that teaches students how to think with text and, eventually, beyond it.

The deep reading phase is where literacy meets intellect, where the language of words becomes the language of ideas. Here, reading is not just an academic task—it is how we learn to reason, empathize, and imagine.

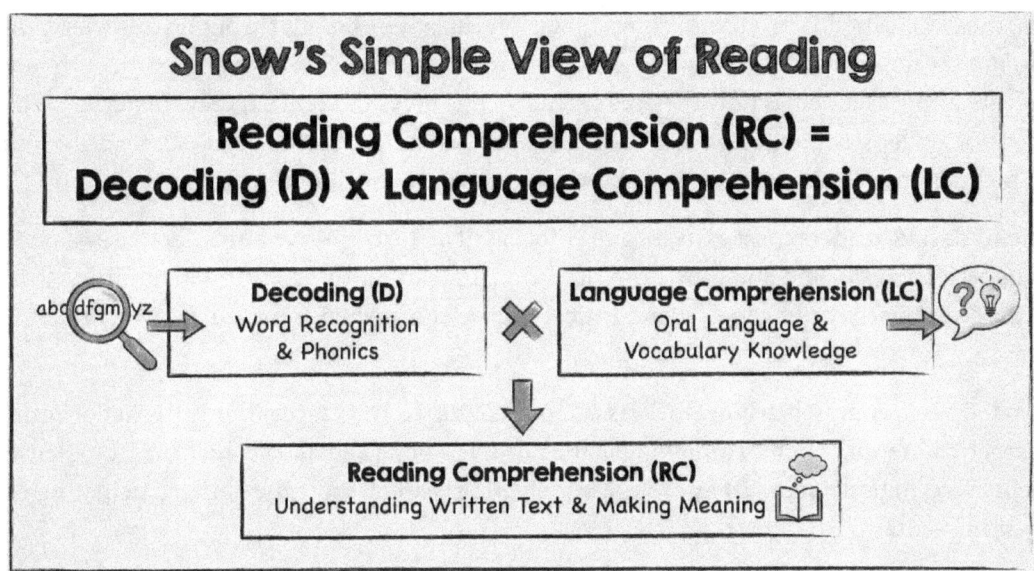

Section 1: What Comprehension Really Is (Snow's Simple View of Reading Expanded)

For much of modern literacy instruction, comprehension has been treated as the summit of the reading process—the point at which decoding and language converge and the reader is declared proficient. Charts are drawn, assessments administered, and growth is measured by how well students can answer questions about a text. Yet comprehension is not a destination. It is an activity—an ongoing negotiation between the reader, the language, and the world the text evokes.

Catherine Snow's interpretation of the Simple View of Reading provides a frame for understanding this complexity. The original model proposed that reading comprehension is the product of two components: decoding and linguistic comprehension. But as Snow and others later emphasized, the relationship is not mathematical—it is dynamic. The reader's ability to construct meaning depends on an ever-shifting network of variables: vocabulary, syntax, background knowledge, motivation, inference, and metacognition. To comprehend is to coordinate all of these systems at once, within the fleeting moment of thought.

Comprehension is not passive absorption; it is active construction. The reader must assemble meaning from clues scattered across the text—linking words and sentences to ideas and experiences stored in memory. This process requires continual prediction and revision. The brain forms a mental model of what the text might mean, tests it against new information, and adjusts as contradictions arise. Understanding is not received; it is built, disassembled, and rebuilt again.

This is why the same text can yield entirely different interpretations. Comprehension is shaped by the reader's knowledge, experiences, and questions. A fifth grader reading Charlotte's Web may grasp friendship and loss; a teacher reading the same book may see themes of mortality, morality, and compassion. The words have not changed—the architecture of understanding has.

For teachers, the implication is profound: comprehension cannot be taught through strategies alone, because strategies do not create knowledge—they organize it. True comprehension instruction must therefore attend to what students know as much as how they read. Knowledge gives inference its raw material; without it, comprehension collapses into guesswork. As Duke and Cartwright (2021) argue, "a reader's ability to understand text depends as much on what they bring to the page as what they find upon it."

To comprehend deeply, readers must also engage emotionally. The cognitive and affective systems of the brain operate in concert; curiosity and empathy drive attention, and attention fuels understanding. A disengaged reader may decode flawlessly but comprehend little, because comprehension requires investment. The text must matter.

In this expanded view, comprehension emerges as both cognitive and cultural. It is the act of connecting text to the larger frameworks of meaning that shape our lives—our beliefs, our histories, our sense of self. When students read to understand, they are not simply processing words; they are participating in the human project of making sense.

The role of the teacher, then, is not to deliver comprehension but to cultivate the conditions in which it can flourish: to ensure students have the linguistic tools, the background knowledge, the curiosity, and the confidence to engage in that act of meaning-making. Comprehension is less an endpoint than a conversation between mind and text—a dialogue that expands each time it is renewed.

When we understand comprehension as construction rather than completion, assessment itself changes. The question is no longer, Can the student recall what the text said? but Can they show how their understanding evolved as they read? In that distinction lies the heart of deep reading.

Section 2: The Role of Inference, Background Knowledge, and Schema

Every time a reader encounters a text, they bring a silent companion: everything they already know. Every experience, every word stored in memory, every conversation and curiosity becomes part of what the brain draws upon to make sense of new language. Reading comprehension is not the extraction of meaning from text—it is the integration of text with what already lives inside the mind. Without that internal framework, the words remain flat, stripped of resonance.

Background knowledge is therefore not enrichment; it is infrastructure. It provides the scaffolding upon which comprehension is built. When a reader recognizes the concept of gravity or justice or migration, they are not merely identifying vocabulary—they are connecting ideas across contexts. Those connections activate what cognitive scientists call schema: mental frameworks that organize knowledge into patterns. Schema allow readers to anticipate, interpret, and infer. They tell the brain, "This makes sense because it fits with what I've seen before."

Inference is the engine that powers this process. It is how the mind fills the spaces between the stated and the implied, how readers bridge what the author writes with what the reader already knows. Kendeou and colleagues describe inference as "the continuous updating of a mental model." Each new sentence confirms, refines, or disrupts the model the reader is building. In this way, comprehension becomes an act of reasoning—one that depends not on perfect recall but on the flexibility of thought.

When a reader infers, they are performing several cognitive acts at once: retrieving relevant schema from memory, mapping it onto the text, identifying what is missing, and constructing a plausible bridge between the two. These bridges are what transform information into insight. Without inference, texts remain literal; with it, they become alive.

Knowledge and inference exist in constant reciprocity. The more a reader knows, the more they can infer; the more they infer, the more they learn. This cycle is what makes reading exponential. Each encounter with text expands schema, which in turn makes future comprehension faster and deeper. This is why content-rich instruction matters so profoundly. Students immersed in knowledge-rich curricula—science, history, literature—are not just learning facts; they are building the background structures that will make all future reading easier.

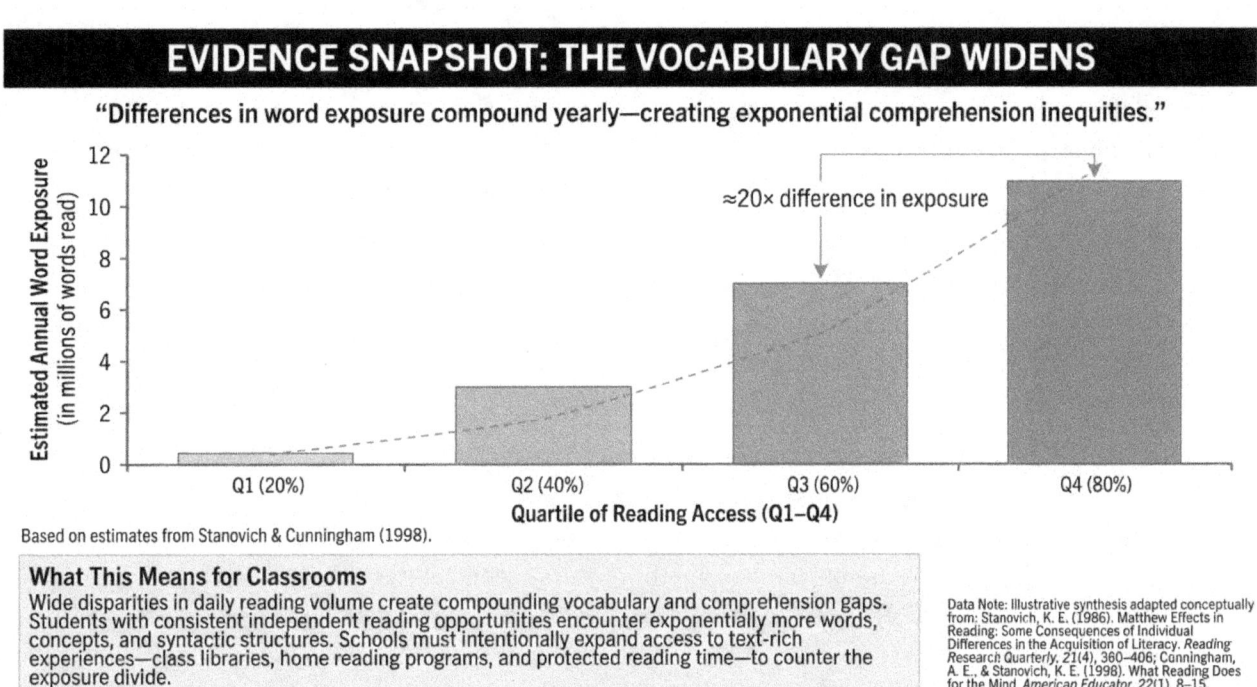

For decades, comprehension instruction focused on generic strategies: predict, summarize, clarify. But without the fuel of background knowledge, these strategies collapse into empty rituals. A student can "predict" the next event in a story only if they understand the world it describes. They can "clarify" a sentence only if they know what the words refer to. Comprehension strategies organize thinking; knowledge provides the substance that thinking manipulates.

Schema also give reading its emotional texture. They allow readers to empathize, to see themselves in others, to connect the abstract to the personal. When students read about injustice and recall times they've witnessed unfairness, comprehension becomes moral as well as mental. The schema that organize thought also organize empathy.

In classrooms that honor this truth, knowledge is not treated as background—it is foregrounded as the very fabric of comprehension. Teachers build it deliberately through conversation, content study, and interdisciplinary learning. They understand that every new topic enriches the reader's capacity to reason about all others.

Inference, background knowledge, and schema form the invisible trilogy of comprehension. They are the silent architecture that allows meaning to rise. When teachers nurture them intentionally, reading transforms from an exercise in recall to an act of reasoning, connection, and reflection. The reader becomes both scientist and storyteller—analyzing evidence, testing hypotheses, and constructing a narrative of understanding that is uniquely their own.

Section 3: Teaching Comprehension through Discussion, Questioning, and Analysis

Comprehension cannot thrive in silence.

It grows in dialogue—between text and reader, teacher and student, student and student. To teach comprehension is not merely to assign reading; it is to create the conditions in which thinking becomes audible. The classroom, in this sense, is not a testing ground for understanding but a rehearsal hall for reasoning.

When students speak about what they read, they externalize thought. They give shape to the invisible processes of inference, evaluation, and synthesis. As they articulate ideas, they also refine them—revising misconceptions, expanding interpretations, and building shared meaning. In this way, discussion is not an accessory to comprehension; it is comprehension made visible.

Research in dialogic teaching, from Pressley and Afflerbach (1995) to Fisher and Frey (2014), shows that comprehension deepens when students are guided to explain their reasoning rather than recite answers. When teachers prompt students with open-ended questions—What makes you think that? What evidence supports your idea? How does this connect to something you've seen before?—they activate the cognitive processes that define deep reading: justification, connection, evaluation. Each question becomes a small invitation to think aloud.

In these moments, the teacher's role shifts from transmitter to conductor. The goal is not to confirm correctness, but to sustain curiosity. Effective comprehension instruction is dialogic, not didactic. It transforms the classroom into a space where texts are not consumed but interrogated—where language becomes a lens for examining complexity.

This approach demands patience. Genuine discussion cannot be scripted. It unfolds organically, guided by the text and by the students' evolving interpretations. Teachers scaffold, model, and redirect, but they also listen. Listening itself is an act of instruction; it signals that student ideas have value, that comprehension is something we build together rather than deliver from above.

Questioning, when used intentionally, sharpens this process. The best questions do not close inquiry—they open it. They ask students to compare, evaluate, infer, and reimagine. Rather than asking, What happened? a teacher might ask, Why did the author choose to reveal this event now? Instead of, Who is the main character? they might ask, How does the character's decision reflect the story's central idea? Such questions invite metacognition; they teach students to monitor how they think as much as what they think.

Analysis, the highest form of discussion, begins when students learn to see a text as a system—of choices, perspectives, and implications. They start to trace patterns, notice structure, and evaluate purpose. This is not a skill reserved for older readers; it begins the moment a child asks, Why did the author say it that way? That simple question signals a shift from comprehension to reasoning.

In classrooms that teach comprehension through discussion, questioning, and analysis, something remarkable happens: students begin to internalize the teacher's voice. The questions once asked aloud become self-directed. As they read, they silently anticipate, What might come next? What does this remind me of? How do I know this is true? The teacher has done more than teach comprehension—they have transferred the habit of inquiry.

This is the essence of deep reading. It is not the accumulation of answers but the cultivation of awareness. Discussion turns comprehension from a private act into a shared exploration. Questioning transforms it from recall into reasoning. Analysis elevates it from understanding text to understanding thought.

In such classrooms, reading is no longer quiet absorption but collective intelligence—voices weaving meaning together, one insight at a time.

Section 4: The Rise of Metacognition: Readers Monitoring Their Own Understanding

Every skilled reader carries an invisible companion: an inner voice that questions, checks, and guides comprehension in real time. Does this make sense? Why did the author say that? Should I reread? These quiet acts of reflection are not accidental; they are the hallmarks of mature literacy. Metacognition—the ability to think about one's own thinking—is what transforms reading from an act of consumption into an act of consciousness.

When a reader monitors their understanding, they become both participant and observer in the learning process. They engage with the text while simultaneously evaluating the success of that engagement. This dual awareness allows them to recognize confusion, deploy strategies, and repair meaning when it falters. It is a kind of internal dialogue between the reader and their reasoning self.

The seeds of metacognition are planted early, long before students can name the process. A child who pauses and asks, What's happening here? or says, That doesn't sound right, is already demonstrating self-monitoring. The teacher's role is to nurture these instincts, to make them explicit through modeling and language. When teachers share their own thinking—I'm not sure what the author means yet, so I'm going to reread that paragraph—they make visible what skilled readers do invisibly.

Pressley and Afflerbach (1995) described this as strategic awareness: the reader's conscious control over the processes of understanding. But metacognition extends beyond strategy; it encompasses the reader's beliefs about themselves as learners. A student who believes that comprehension can be improved through effort is far more likely to engage in self-correction than one who sees confusion as failure. Metacognition, therefore, is as much about mindset as mechanism.

As students mature, metacognition becomes their internal compass. It guides them through unfamiliar genres, complex arguments, and abstract ideas. They begin to anticipate difficulty before it arrives, drawing upon prior knowledge and adaptive strategies. They no longer wait passively for meaning; they pursue it.

Instruction that fosters metacognition does not rely on worksheets or checklists. It grows through conversation, reflection, and modeling. Teachers ask, How did you figure that out? What made you change your mind? What strategy worked best here? These questions prompt students to surface their cognitive processes, turning unconscious skill into conscious control. Over time, readers internalize these prompts, creating a self-sustaining loop of reflection and adjustment.

Fisher and Frey (2014) argue that metacognition is the link between visible learning and visible thinking. It is the moment when students begin to see their own cognition as something they can shape. The teacher's voice becomes the student's inner narrator, guiding attention, reminding them to slow down, to question, to reread. Eventually, the external guidance fades, and the student's self-talk becomes the steady rhythm of comprehension.

Metacognition also transforms assessment. When students can articulate how they approached a text, where they struggled, and how they overcame confusion, they demonstrate a level of understanding deeper than any multiple-choice score could capture. Their awareness becomes evidence of learning.

At its core, metacognition is empowerment. It teaches students that comprehension is not a gift but a craft, that meaning is not given but made. The reader who monitors their own understanding is no longer dependent on direction—they have become their own guide.

This is the rise of agency in literacy—the moment when the reader realizes that thinking is something they can watch, adjust, and ultimately own. And from that awareness, reasoning begins to bloom.

Section 5: Strategies That Cultivate Reasoning and Critical Literacy

When comprehension matures, it begins to ask harder questions. The reader no longer stops at understanding what a text says—they begin to examine how and why it says it, and what that means in the larger world. This is the moment when reading becomes reasoning, when literacy reveals its highest purpose: not only to inform, but to transform.

Reasoning is the natural evolution of comprehension. It grows when students are given the intellectual space to compare ideas, question assumptions, and trace implications. It thrives when they are trusted to think deeply rather than answer quickly. True reasoning in reading instruction is not a checklist of strategies—it is a culture of inquiry that teaches students how to navigate complexity with patience and evidence.

One of the most powerful tools for cultivating reasoning is dialogic reading—structured discussions that invite multiple interpretations and require justification. When students debate the motives of a character, the validity of an argument, or the credibility of a source, they are practicing the same cognitive operations that define critical thinking: analysis, evaluation, and synthesis. The teacher's role is to guide without resolving, to ask questions that stretch interpretation rather than settle it.

Critical literacy extends this reasoning into the moral and social realm. It asks readers to consider whose voice is speaking, whose is missing, and how language shapes perception. When students analyze perspective and bias, they begin to understand that texts are not neutral—they are products of context, culture, and power. This awareness turns reading into an act of discernment. As Paulo Freire wrote, "To read the word is to read the world."

Fisher and Frey (2014) emphasize that reasoning and critical literacy must be taught explicitly. Students are not born skeptical or reflective; they learn these habits through modeling and practice. Teachers can introduce frameworks for analysis—such as claim, evidence, and reasoning—or use comparative reading to reveal how different authors frame the same idea. Over time, students internalize these analytical moves, applying them independently across disciplines.

Reasoning also grows through writing. When students write about what they read—constructing arguments, supporting claims, or synthesizing perspectives—they are required to externalize thought. Writing is reasoning made visible. It reveals gaps in understanding and forces clarity. The interplay between reading and writing, therefore, is not an instructional coincidence—it is the cognitive feedback loop through which critical literacy is refined.

Instruction that cultivates reasoning does not shy away from complexity. It leans into it. Students read challenging texts not to feel overwhelmed, but to feel capable of wrestling with uncertainty. They learn that ambiguity is not confusion—it is evidence of depth. The teacher's task is to normalize struggle, to remind students that meaning worth understanding is meaning worth working for.

Critical literacy also teaches humility. As students encounter texts that challenge their assumptions or present unfamiliar perspectives, they learn that reasoning is not only an intellectual exercise but a moral one. To read critically is to listen—to hold multiple truths long enough to examine them fairly. In doing so, readers develop empathy, the highest form of comprehension.

The strategies that cultivate reasoning are, at their heart, strategies for cultivating humanity: curiosity, discernment, reflection, and respect. They teach students that literacy is not just a way to access information but a way to participate in the shared project of understanding.

When reasoning becomes habitual, reading transcends instruction. It becomes a practice of consciousness—a way of seeing, questioning, and contributing to the world. That is the true destination of comprehension, and the beginning of something greater: transfer, the ability to carry what is learned in one context into every other.

Closing Reflection: Reading as the Practice of Thought

Comprehension, at its deepest level, is not about answers—it is about awareness. Each time a reader encounters a new text, they enter a conversation between what is known and what is possible. They listen, question, test, and build. In doing so, they are not simply decoding language; they are constructing consciousness.

When we teach comprehension as reasoning, we are teaching students how to think in real time—how to connect ideas, weigh evidence, and recognize bias. The skills of deep reading are the same skills that sustain an informed life: discernment, empathy, curiosity, and reflection. The text becomes both mirror and mentor, revealing who we are and who we might become.

In classrooms that nurture this kind of reading, silence feels alive. You can sense the hum of unseen connections, the pause before an insight, the quiet revision of belief. Students are not reading to finish; they are reading to understand—and understanding changes them. That is the work of literacy at its highest form: it transforms comprehension into wisdom.

The Science of Reading, when traced to its culmination, is the science of reasoning. It begins in the tangible—sound, symbol, structure—and ends in the intangible—the mind's ability to think beyond itself. The reader who can analyze a poem, critique an argument, or imagine another's perspective is not displaying a skill; they are exercising humanity.

As we move into the final phase, the focus shifts from what happens within the act of reading to what happens after it. The goal is no longer comprehension alone, but transfer—the reader's ability to apply, adapt, and extend what they have learned across disciplines and into the world.

Reading, at last, becomes reasoning made portable.

Reflection Questions:

1. This chapter distinguishes comprehension as "an activity—an ongoing negotiation between the reader, the language, and the world the text evokes." How does this view differ from (or expand upon) how comprehension is typically understood and taught in your setting?

2. Catherine Snow's expanded Simple View of Reading emphasizes that comprehension is a dynamic interplay of many variables, including background knowledge, motivation, and inference. What implications does this have for moving beyond generic comprehension strategies to more holistic instruction?

3. "Background knowledge is therefore not enrichment; it is infrastructure." How do you currently (or how could you more effectively) build robust background knowledge and schema to support deep comprehension and inference for all students, especially those with limited prior exposure?

4. Section 3 argues that "Comprehension cannot thrive in silence. It grows in dialogue." How might your classroom or school foster more genuine discussion, questioning, and analysis to cultivate reasoning, rather than simply assessing recall?

5. Metacognition is presented as the "invisible companion" of skilled readers, empowering them to monitor and repair their own understanding. What specific instructional practices can teachers implement to explicitly nurture metacognitive awareness and strategic thinking in students?

Application Steps:

1. **Analyze Your "Comprehension" Assessments:** Review a sample of comprehension assessments used in your school (e.g., unit tests, standardized test practice questions, classroom quizzes). To what extent do they measure "active construction" and "reasoning" versus simple recall of information? Discuss how you might revise them to better reflect the definition of deep comprehension.

2. **Schema Activation & Building Protocol:** For an upcoming unit or text, design a structured protocol for building and activating students' background knowledge *before* reading. This could involve:
   - Image analysis and discussion.
   - KWL charts or concept maps.
   - Short videos or expert guest speakers.
   - Pre-teaching key vocabulary and concepts directly related to the text's schema.
   - Focus on how these activities prepare students for inference.

3. **Implement a Dialogic Reading Routine:** Choose a challenging text and plan a lesson around a specific section, focusing on "teaching comprehension through discussion, questioning, and analysis." Instead of asking recall questions, prepare open-ended prompts that encourage students to:
   - Justify their interpretations with evidence.
   - Compare and contrast ideas.
   - Infer author's purpose or unspoken messages.
   - Evaluate the credibility of information.
   - Model your own "thinking aloud" during the discussion.

4. **Metacognitive "Think-Aloud" Modeling:** Select a short, slightly challenging passage. Practice modeling your own metacognitive process as you read it aloud. Articulate your questions, confusions, connections, and strategies for repairing meaning. Then, provide students with opportunities to practice this "inner voice" through turn-and-talks or response journals.

5. **Cultivate Critical Literacy through Juxtaposition:** For a relevant topic, select two texts that present different perspectives, biases, or genres (e.g., a historical account and a fictionalized story, a news article and an opinion piece). Design an activity where students compare and contrast how each text constructs meaning, whose voices are amplified, and what assumptions are made. This helps them move from "what it says" to "how it thinks."

CHAPTER 7
The Transfer Phase — Reading as Reasoning

Introduction

Every learning journey reaches a point when mastery must move beyond the lesson. The skill that was once deliberate becomes intuitive, the strategy that was once practiced becomes instinct. In reading, this moment is called transfer—the capacity to carry what has been learned in one context and apply it freely in another. It is the mark of true understanding, the final expression of literacy as reasoning.

At this stage, the reader no longer asks, How do I decode this? or What does this mean? They ask, How can I use what I understand here to make sense of something new? Transfer is what turns knowledge into intellect, comprehension into wisdom. It is where literacy ceases to be a subject and becomes a habit of mind.

John Hattie's Visible Learning research places transfer at the peak of learning—where surface knowledge and deep understanding combine to form flexible expertise. Transfer is not rote repetition or simple recall; it is the creative recombination of ideas. It is what allows a student who has analyzed character motivation in literature to analyze historical bias in a primary source, or to critique an argument in science. The skill is not confined to its origin; it migrates.

This is where the reader becomes the thinker. The same processes that once built fluency and comprehension now serve reasoning and synthesis. Morphology helps unpack new academic language; syntax helps trace logic across disciplines; metacognition helps regulate complexity. The architecture built in earlier chapters remains in motion, carrying thought forward into new contexts.

The transfer phase is also where reading intersects most directly with identity. When students can apply literacy beyond school—to understand a news article, question a claim, or empathize with another's experience—they are not just demonstrating learning; they are enacting citizenship. Reading becomes a moral act, a way of engaging with the world critically and compassionately.

This chapter explores how to design instruction that makes transfer possible. It examines how disciplinary literacy extends comprehension into analysis, how rhetorical reading connects literacy to writing and civic reasoning, and how educators can design tasks that cultivate independence, synthesis, and agency. It ends where all great learning ends—with students who no longer need the scaffolds we have built, because they have internalized the architecture of thinking itself.

Reading as reasoning is the mind's way of proving that knowledge can travel. It is the moment the bridge becomes a road—the point where the science of reading becomes the art of understanding.

Section 1: The Nature of Transfer: From Visible Learning to Visible Thinking

Transfer is the quiet triumph of learning.

It is the moment when knowledge detaches from its original lesson and finds new life elsewhere—when a strategy taught in a reading workshop surfaces unprompted in a science investigation, or when a student interprets a primary source with the same discernment once used to analyze a poem. Transfer is not the product of instruction alone; it is the evidence that understanding has become internalized, flexible, and alive.

John Hattie describes transfer as the apex of visible learning—the phase where surface and deep learning converge. In the early stages, students acquire skills and facts; in the middle, they integrate and connect them; and in the final phase, they apply them independently, adapting what they know to unfamiliar problems. Transfer, therefore, is not a strategy to be taught, but a condition to be cultivated. It emerges when instruction helps students see patterns that outlive the task.

Reading provides one of the most elegant demonstrations of this process. Every fluent reader, knowingly or not, transfers constantly. The decoding skills developed in phonics are applied automatically to new vocabulary; the syntactic awareness honed in language study supports comprehension in history and science; the reasoning practiced in literary analysis strengthens argumentation in writing. The architecture of literacy, once built, becomes the foundation for every act of thought that follows.

But transfer is fragile. It does not happen by accident or exposure. It requires explicit bridging—moments when teachers make learning visible by naming the connection between skill and application. When a teacher says, The way you traced cause and effect in this story will help you do the same in social studies, they are activating transfer. They are teaching students to see knowledge as portable, not confined to one subject or one day.

Transfer also depends on metacognition. Students must recognize not only what they know, but when and why to use it. This awareness—the ability to abstract the principle from the practice—is what allows learning to travel. The reader who understands how to infer in a narrative can infer in an editorial because they recognize the underlying thinking, not just the surface form.

Hattie reminds us that transfer is visible thinking—the moment when understanding becomes agency. It signals that learning has crossed the boundary from schoolwork to self-work. A student who reads critically in one domain begins to live critically in another: questioning claims, weighing evidence, seeking nuance. Literacy thus becomes not just academic skill but intellectual posture—a way of approaching the world.

The conditions for transfer are coherence, reflection, and challenge. Coherence ensures that learning builds logically from one phase to the next, so students can see the throughline of meaning. Reflection allows them to pause and recognize their own cognitive movement—to name the strategy, the schema, the shift. Challenge provides the reason to apply what they know to something new, something difficult enough to require thinking rather than recall.

Transfer is the culmination of the science of reading because it proves that reading has become reasoning. It shows that knowledge, once scaffolded, can stand on its own—that the learner now carries the framework within. Every act of independent comprehension, every moment of application, every instance of insight is a small act of transfer—the brain confirming that it no longer needs to be told what to do; it has learned how to think.

Section 2: How Disciplinary Literacy Extends Comprehension into Analysis

As students move through the upper grades, the texts they encounter become less about language itself and more about knowledge. Each discipline—history, science, mathematics, literature—uses its own vocabulary, structures, and conventions to build meaning. To read well across these domains is to understand not just what the words say, but how each field thinks. This is the work of disciplinary literacy: the extension of comprehension into analysis, the transformation of reading from a general skill into a specialized form of reasoning.

All comprehension depends on background knowledge, but disciplinary literacy depends on epistemology—an understanding of how knowledge is created and communicated within a field. A scientist reads to evaluate evidence; a historian reads to interrogate perspective; a literary critic reads to interpret language and theme. Each discipline asks its own set of questions and rewards its own forms of proof. The reader who grasps these distinctions can move fluently between worlds, adjusting their stance to match the logic of the text before them.

Shanahan and Shanahan (2012) call this "progressing from generalist to specialist." In the early grades, reading instruction emphasizes universal strategies—predicting, summarizing, questioning. As students mature, they must learn to read as practitioners, not merely as participants. The question shifts from What does this mean? to How does this field make meaning? This is the cognitive leap from comprehension to analysis.

Consider how this plays out in practice. In history, the skilled reader looks for sourcing, context, and corroboration, recognizing that every document is a perspective shaped by time and intention. In science, the reader attends to precision and procedure, distinguishing hypothesis from conclusion, data from interpretation. In mathematics, reading becomes a process of translation—decoding symbolic language into logical sequence. In literature, the reader explores ambiguity, tone, and voice, understanding that truth may reside not in certainty but in complexity. Each domain, when taught through its own literacy, becomes an apprenticeship in thought.

Disciplinary literacy also reveals the full architecture of transfer. The analytical habits cultivated in one discipline reinforce those in another. The skepticism learned in evaluating a historical source strengthens the critique of an argument in a persuasive essay; the reasoning used to interpret a scientific graph sharpens the interpretation of a metaphor. The brain does not compartmentalize expertise—it cross-pollinates it.

Instruction that fosters disciplinary literacy must therefore be intentional. Teachers serve as translators of disciplinary thinking, making visible the ways experts read, question, and reason. A history teacher might model how to compare primary sources; a science teacher might think aloud through an experimental procedure; an English teacher might annotate a text to reveal how syntax shapes tone. Each of these acts is not merely about content—it is about cognition. Students are being shown how to think within a system.

When literacy becomes disciplinary, learning becomes authentic. Students begin to see reading not as a school requirement but as the method by which knowledge itself is built. They discover that texts are not repositories of information but conversations between experts, and that to read critically is to join that conversation.

This is the highest form of comprehension—the moment when reading transcends text and enters the realm of analysis. It is what prepares students not only for college or career, but for citizenship: the ability to weigh claims, recognize reasoning, and understand the nature of truth in a complex world.

Transfer lives here—where comprehension becomes specialized, and specialized understanding becomes universal once again. For when students learn how each field constructs knowledge, they learn how to construct it themselves.

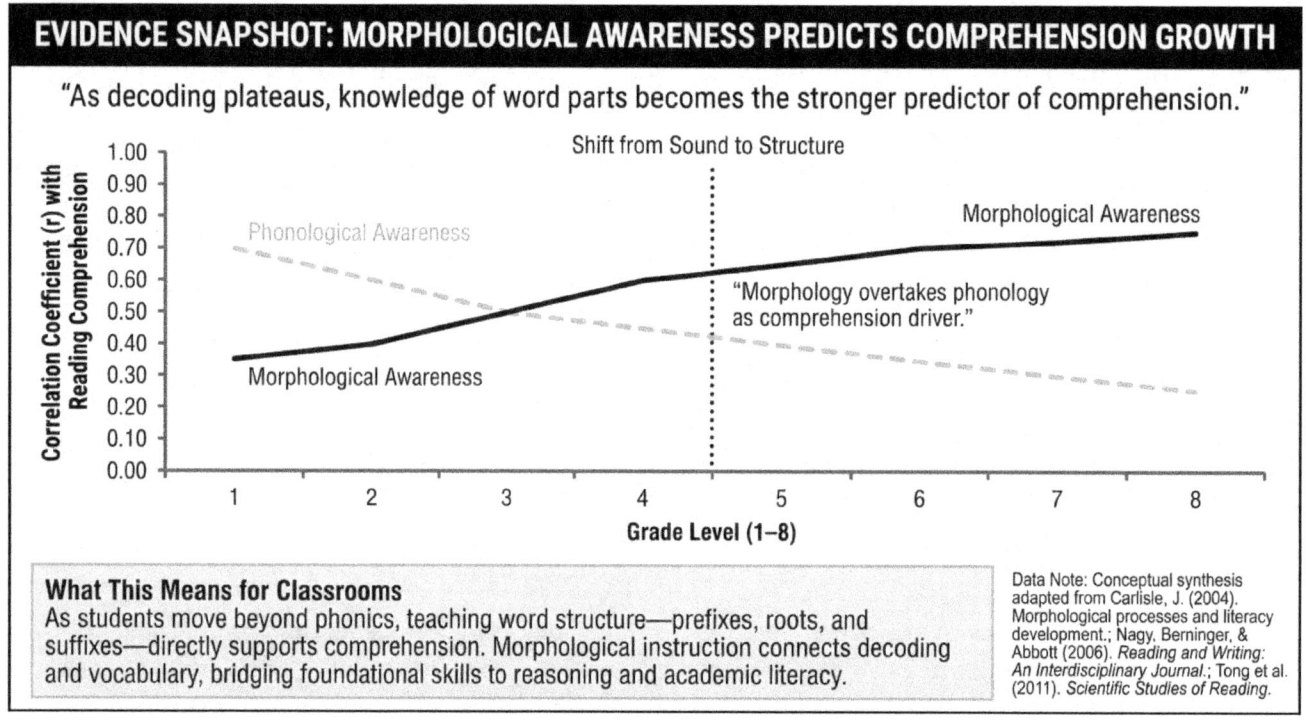

Section 3: Rhetorical Reading — Connecting Literacy to Writing, Argument, and Civic Reasoning

Every text is an argument, whether whispered or declared. It seeks to persuade—to shape thought, evoke emotion, or guide action. When readers learn to see writing rhetorically, they begin to recognize language not as neutral but as intentional. This awareness transforms reading from an act of absorption into an act of discernment. The reader becomes a critic, a thinker, and ultimately, a participant in civic dialogue.

Rhetorical reading is the practice of asking three questions: What is this text trying to do? How is it trying to do it? And what effect does it have on me? These questions connect literacy to writing because they require the reader to reverse-engineer the author's choices—the structure of argument, the tone of appeal, the evidence used to persuade. The reader learns to see the blueprint behind the words.

This kind of reading builds the foundation for argumentation. The student who can identify a claim in another's writing can begin to craft one of their own. The same skills that decode an author's intent—analyzing logic, evaluating evidence, recognizing bias—are the skills that empower students to write and reason effectively. Rhetorical reading thus completes the circuit of literacy: reading feeds writing, and writing refines reading.

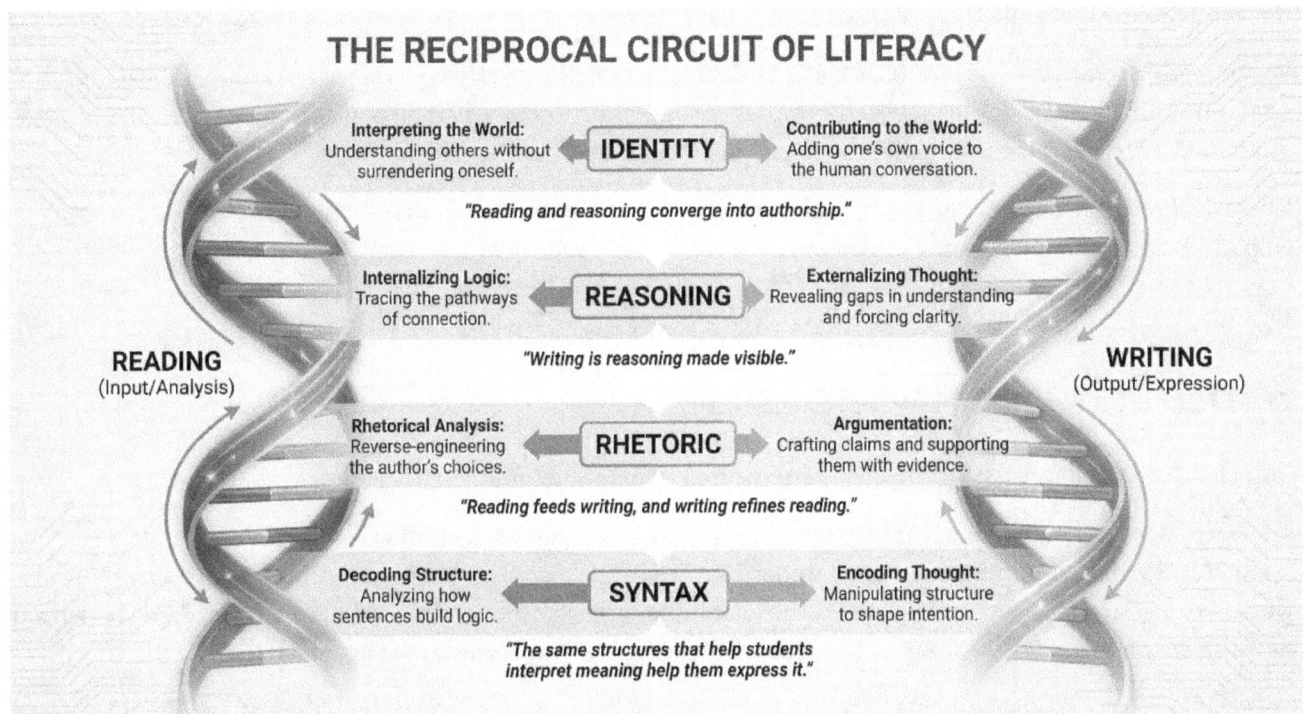

It also grounds comprehension in ethics. To read rhetorically is to engage with perspective. It asks the reader to consider not only what is said, but who is saying it and why. In a world saturated with information, this capacity for discernment is essential. Students who can detect manipulation, question authority, and evaluate sources are not merely literate—they are liberated.

Wineburg's (1991) research on historical thinking underscores this point. Expert readers in history do not simply absorb facts; they interrogate sources, comparing accounts, weighing motives, and contextualizing claims. The same cognitive vigilance applies to all forms of reading in civic life. Whether parsing a news article or a social media post, rhetorical readers resist passivity. They read with skepticism, empathy, and evidence.

Connecting literacy to civic reasoning means teaching students that texts are not static—they are acts of communication within a society. Reading becomes a means of participation, a way to enter the public discourse with awareness and integrity. When students learn to recognize rhetorical intent, they become equipped to navigate the complexities of democracy—to listen critically, to question responsibly, and to contribute thoughtfully.

Rhetorical reading also redefines writing instruction. Instead of treating composition as a separate subject, we can position it as the natural outcome of deep reading. Students read to understand how arguments work, then write to practice that craft themselves. They learn that every rhetorical choice—word, sentence, structure—is a decision about impact. As they internalize these moves, they gain agency not only as readers but as authors of meaning.

In the most profound sense, rhetorical reading teaches perspective-taking. It reveals that no text is universal, no voice omniscient, no meaning fixed. It invites readers to hold multiple truths at once, to recognize complexity as a sign of maturity rather than confusion. In doing so, it restores to literacy its moral dimension: the ability to understand others without surrendering oneself.

When reading reaches this level, transfer has fully occurred. The student no longer distinguishes between academic and civic reasoning, between comprehension and conscience. They read and write as thinkers—aware that every text, including their own, participates in shaping the shared world.

Rhetorical reading is the art of seeing both the text and the intention behind it. It is literacy extended into empathy, argument, and action—the moment when understanding becomes responsibility.

Section 4: Designing Transfer Tasks That Build Synthesis and Independence

Transfer does not happen by chance; it is engineered through design.

The brain does not automatically carry knowledge from one context to another—it needs deliberate opportunities to see connections, to test understanding, and to apply what it knows in new and meaningful ways. The classroom, therefore, must become a laboratory for synthesis: a place where students are challenged to think beyond the text, to use what they have learned as the raw material for insight.

Transfer tasks are not assessments of recall; they are demonstrations of reasoning. They ask students to integrate multiple sources, perspectives, or disciplines into something new. When a student compares a historical event to a modern social issue, writes a scientific explanation in the style of an editorial, or creates a multimedia argument grounded in evidence, they are not repeating information—they are transforming it.

John Hattie's Visible Learning framework reminds us that transfer flourishes under the same conditions that foster deep learning: clarity, challenge, and reflection. Clarity ensures that students understand the purpose of what they are learning and how it connects to what came before. Challenge invites them to stretch their knowledge to unfamiliar contexts, engaging higher-order thinking. Reflection allows them to step back and articulate how their learning moved and why it mattered.

In practice, this means designing tasks that honor complexity. Instead of assigning comprehension questions after reading, teachers might ask students to write a letter from one character to another, compose an op-ed about a scientific discovery, or design a visual metaphor for a historical theme. Each task requires synthesis—the ability to merge understanding from multiple domains into a coherent whole. The form is creative; the function is cognitive.

Synthesis also demands independence. As students move through the learning continuum, the scaffolds that once supported them—sentence frames, graphic organizers, guided questions—must gradually fade. Independence does not emerge from abandonment but from trust: the confidence that students have internalized the structures of thought we have modeled. Teachers guide less not because they care less, but because they have built systems strong enough for students to stand on their own.

Transfer tasks also humanize assessment. They allow teachers to see the learner's reasoning, not just their recall. In a student's argument, design, or reflection, we glimpse the invisible architecture of understanding—the pathways of connection that traditional tests rarely capture. Assessment becomes less about correctness and more about coherence: Can the student use what they know to make meaning in a new situation?

The most powerful transfer tasks are rooted in authenticity. They mirror the kinds of thinking demanded beyond school—analyzing conflicting sources, weighing evidence, considering implications. In this way, students see that literacy is not confined to the classroom; it is the operating system of thought itself.

When we design for transfer, we design for independence. We invite students to step beyond rehearsal and into creation, to see learning not as something that ends with mastery but as something that begins with it. Every synthesis task, every reflective question, every open-ended challenge says to students: You have the tools. Now build something new.

In these moments, reading and reasoning converge into authorship—students no longer echo the voices of others but add their own. That is the essence of transfer: when learning moves freely between disciplines, between ideas, and finally, between people.

Section 5: Reading as Identity — Students as Meaning-Makers and Contributors

At the end of every continuum of learning stands a reader who is no longer simply decoding, interpreting, or analyzing—but becoming.

Reading, once a tool for understanding others, becomes a mirror for understanding oneself. The more students learn to engage with text—to infer, evaluate, and reason—the more they begin to construct an identity as thinkers. They see themselves not as recipients of knowledge, but as participants in its making.

This is the quiet culmination of the Science of Reading: not just cognitive growth, but human growth. When readers recognize that meaning is made, not given, they also recognize their agency in the world. They begin to understand that authors are not distant authorities but fellow meaning-makers—and that they, too, can shape perception through language, argument, and story.

Reading and identity are inseparable. Every act of comprehension carries an echo of self: How does this connect to me? What do I believe about this? Where do I stand within this idea? As students ask these questions, they begin to build an inner framework for judgment and belonging. Reading becomes reflection; literacy becomes self-knowledge.

This is why transfer is ultimately moral as much as intellectual. When students learn to carry ideas from one context to another, they also learn that ideas themselves carry responsibility. A reader who can question a text can question injustice. A student who can analyze bias in a source can recognize it in society. The same cognitive flexibility that makes transfer possible makes empathy possible. Reading teaches discernment, but it also teaches care.

As learners move through this final phase, the boundaries between disciplines dissolve. The student who reads a poem about migration can apply its insight to a history lesson, to a policy debate, to a conversation at home. The thinking that begins in the classroom ripples outward, transforming how they read the world itself. This is reading as identity—the moment when literacy ceases to be academic and becomes existential.

To nurture this phase, teachers must create classrooms where students see themselves reflected in the texts they read and the ideas they explore. Representation is not just inclusion; it is recognition—the affirmation that one's story belongs in the larger story of learning. When students encounter diverse voices, they begin to imagine their own as part of that chorus.

In such classrooms, the final act of reading is contribution. Students write, speak, create, and advocate—not to complete an assignment but to participate in understanding. They carry forward what they have learned, adding to the collective dialogue of humanity. Reading becomes both inheritance and offering.

When we see reading as identity, we restore purpose to the entire continuum of literacy. Phonemic awareness, morphology, syntax, comprehension, reasoning—all of it leads here: to the learner who uses language to make sense, to make change, to make meaning.

The Science of Reading, fully realized, is not a system to master but a way of seeing—how thought moves through words, how knowledge moves through people, and how understanding moves through generations.

Every reader who learns to think becomes a contributor to that movement. That is the ultimate transfer—the transformation of literacy into legacy.

Closing Reflection: The Architecture That Thinks

The story of reading is, at its heart, the story of how thought learns to travel. It begins in the smallest sound and ends in the broadest sense—in the brain's astonishing ability to turn vibration into vision, symbol into understanding, and understanding into wisdom. Every phase of this architecture—foundation, bridge, depth, and transfer—reveals not a staircase to climb, but a spiral that continues upward, each turn drawing strength from what came before.

In the early stages, children learn the patterns of sound and sight, the precision of code. In time, those patterns form language; language gives rise to comprehension; comprehension matures into reasoning; and reasoning, finally, expands into identity. What begins as a neurological process becomes a human one. The Science of Reading, viewed through this continuum, is not only about how the brain learns to read—it is about how people learn to think, to feel, and to belong through language.

Every teacher who helps a child connect sound to symbol is not just teaching reading—they are laying the first beam of a lifelong structure of thought. Every lesson in vocabulary or syntax adds dimension to that structure; every act of discussion, inference, and reflection fills it with light. And when that structure becomes strong enough to hold independent reasoning—to support transfer, analysis, and empathy—it ceases to be a classroom construct. It becomes a part of the learner themselves.

The architecture of literacy is, ultimately, the architecture of freedom. Once students know how to read the world, they are no longer confined by its boundaries. They can question, imagine, and contribute. Reading becomes their way of navigating complexity with courage and grace.

As we move into Part III: The Systemic Design of Literacy, the focus turns outward once more—from the internal architecture of cognition to the external architecture of schools. The question shifts from How does reading develop? to How must our systems evolve to sustain that development? Because just as every reader needs structure to think, every school needs coherence to last.

The architecture now extends beyond the mind. It becomes the blueprint of a system that learns—an ecosystem of teaching, leadership, and design strong enough to hold every learner's growth.

Reflection Questions:

1. This chapter defines transfer as "the capacity to carry what has been learned in one context and apply it freely in another," making it the "final expression of literacy as reasoning." How does this definition elevate the goal of reading instruction beyond simple comprehension?

2. John Hattie's research places transfer at the peak of visible learning. What are the instructional conditions (e.g., clarity, challenge, reflection) that you currently provide, or could provide, to actively cultivate transfer in your students?

3. Section 2 discusses how disciplinary literacy extends comprehension into analysis. In what ways do your current teaching practices or curriculum explicitly help students read "as a scientist," "as a historian," or "as a literary critic"? What more could be done?

4. Rhetorical reading is presented as connecting literacy to writing, argument, and civic reasoning. How can classrooms actively foster the habit of asking "What is this text trying to do? How is it trying to do it? And what effect does it have on me?" to build critical citizens?

5. The chapter concludes by stating that "Reading and identity are inseparable." How can educators intentionally design learning experiences that empower students to see themselves as "meaning-makers and contributors," fostering a sense of agency and purpose through literacy?

Application Steps:

1. **Identify a "Transfer Opportunity":** Look at an upcoming unit or topic in your curriculum. Identify a core literacy skill or concept (e.g., identifying main idea, analyzing cause and effect, evaluating evidence) that students have already learned in one context. Design a specific activity or task that requires them to apply that skill to a *new and different* text or discipline.

2. **Disciplinary Reading Protocol Design:** Choose a specific content area (e.g., science, history). Work with a colleague from that discipline to develop a short, explicit "reading protocol" that models how experts in that field approach a text. This could include specific questions to ask, what to look for, or how to annotate for disciplinary purpose.

3. **Rhetorical Analysis Mini-Lesson:** Select a non-fiction text relevant to your curriculum (e.g., a persuasive essay, an editorial, a primary source document). Design a mini-lesson that guides students through the three rhetorical reading questions: What is it trying to do? How is it trying to do it? What effect does it have on me? Emphasize author's choices and audience impact.

4. **Create a "Synthesis Challenge":** Develop a transfer task that requires students to synthesize information from *at least two* different sources or disciplines. Examples:
   - Compare and contrast two accounts of a historical event.
   - Write an argumentative essay using evidence from both a science text and a social studies text.
   - Create a presentation that connects a literary theme to a current social issue.

5. **Promote "Reading as Identity" through Contribution:** Design an activity where students are invited to "contribute" their understanding or perspective beyond answering questions. This could involve:
   - Writing an opinion piece for a school newspaper.
   - Creating a podcast episode explaining a complex concept.
   - Leading a class discussion on a controversial topic.
   - Developing a project that addresses a real-world problem related to their reading.
   - The goal is to shift from consuming information to producing knowledge and contributing to shared understanding.

PART III
Designing Systemwide Coherence

The most remarkable thing about the human brain is not its capacity for learning, but its capacity for connection. Every new skill, every idea, every act of reasoning strengthens the pathways between neurons until understanding becomes effortless. The science of reading describes this miracle of coherence within the mind. Yet schools, the institutions built to nurture that same learning, often operate without it.

A system that teaches reading across thirteen years of schooling must learn to think as the brain does: vertically, continuously, and cohesively. But too often, the architecture of literacy fragments as it rises—one philosophy in the early grades, another in the middle, another still in the high school years. Foundational instruction thrives in isolation, comprehension strategies live apart from content, and writing becomes detached from reading. The result is not failure, but fatigue. Teachers work harder within their silos while students experience learning as a series of disconnected events rather than a coherent journey.

To fulfill the promise of the Science of Reading, we must build what the brain models so elegantly: a seamless, interconnected system. Systemwide coherence is the organizational equivalent of neural integration—a network in which every grade, every teacher, every initiative contributes to a single developmental continuum. When this happens, learning no longer resets each year; it accumulates.

This part of the book explores how to design that continuum. It begins by outlining how the science of reading can serve as a K–12 spine, guiding everything from curriculum and intervention to professional learning and assessment. It then examines how culture sustains coherence—how clarity, efficacy, and collaboration replace compliance as the drivers of improvement. Finally, it reimagines assessment as a tool for insight rather than inspection, designed to measure not just what students can recall, but how deeply they can think.

To design coherence is to think like both scientist and architect: to ground every structure in evidence, and to build every connection with purpose. When systems function as the brain does—integrating rather than isolating, aligning rather than layering—they achieve what every great reader achieves: fluency, flexibility, and flow.

Systemwide coherence is not the end of reform; it is the condition that makes reform unnecessary. It transforms the science of reading from a series of programs into a living ecosystem—one where knowledge grows upward, clarity flows downward, and every learner, teacher, and leader moves within the same current of understanding.

CHAPTER 8
Building the K–12 Continuum

Introduction

In every strong literacy system, there is a single throughline—a spine of learning that connects the first sound a child blends in kindergarten to the final argument they defend before graduation. This throughline is not a curriculum, nor a checklist of standards; it is a developmental architecture that guides both minds and systems. When built with intention, it allows the science of reading to do what it was always meant to do: grow with the learner.

Most districts, however, are not built this way. They inherit their structure in fragments—different programs for different grades, separate frameworks for intervention and instruction, professional learning plans disconnected from classroom practice. The result is a system that teaches reading in pieces, while the human brain learns it as a whole. Students progress through grades, but not always through understanding; teachers pass the baton without a common map of the course.

A true K–12 continuum solves this problem. It aligns what the science has made clear—that literacy development is continuous, recursive, and cumulative—with how schools are organized. It transforms instruction from a sequence of initiatives into a seamless progression, one that traces the journey from phonemic awareness to reasoning, from recognition to reflection, from reading to transfer. The goal is not uniformity but unity: a system that adapts without fracturing, that evolves without losing its coherence.

In such a continuum, the Science of Reading becomes not an early literacy mandate but a shared developmental language. Kindergarten teachers and high school English teachers speak in the same terms—orthographic mapping, morphology, syntax, inference, metacognition—because they are teaching different expressions of the same cognitive process. Intervention specialists and classroom teachers work in synchrony, supporting the same architecture rather than duplicating efforts.

This chapter explores how to build that spine. It begins by mapping the developmental literacy progression from K to 12, then examines how multi-tiered systems of support (MTSS) can integrate seamlessly with the Science of Reading to serve every learner. It considers how teacher learning must mirror student learning and how explicit skill instruction can coexist with knowledge-rich curriculum.

To build a continuum is to give coherence a structure. It is to design a system that learns as students do—year over year, stage by stage, thought by thought. Because when literacy development and system design move in harmony, reading growth is no longer dependent on a moment in time. It becomes the defining movement of the entire school experience.

Section 1: Mapping the Developmental Literacy Progression

Every effective literacy system begins with a map—a visible representation of how reading develops, what changes in the learner's mind at each stage, and what kind of instruction is needed to support that change. Without that map, schools drift. Each grade level works diligently, but direction is lost in the handoff from one to the next. Teachers know what to teach, but not always how their work connects to the broader journey of reading development.

The Science of Reading offers that map, but it must be translated from research to reality. Decades of cognitive and linguistic study have shown that reading develops in identifiable phases: from phonological awareness and decoding to fluency and automaticity, to linguistic comprehension, reasoning, and transfer. Yet in many districts, these phases remain trapped inside separate programs or grade-level standards. The science is clear; the system is not.

To map a developmental literacy continuum is to chart the growth of the reading brain alongside the growth of the school system itself. It means articulating what students need to master, how those skills evolve across years, and where instructional emphasis should shift. It also means seeing literacy as recursive rather than linear—recognizing that older students may need to revisit foundational concepts, and younger ones can engage in complex reasoning through discussion and play. The continuum is not a staircase; it is a spiral that expands as students mature.

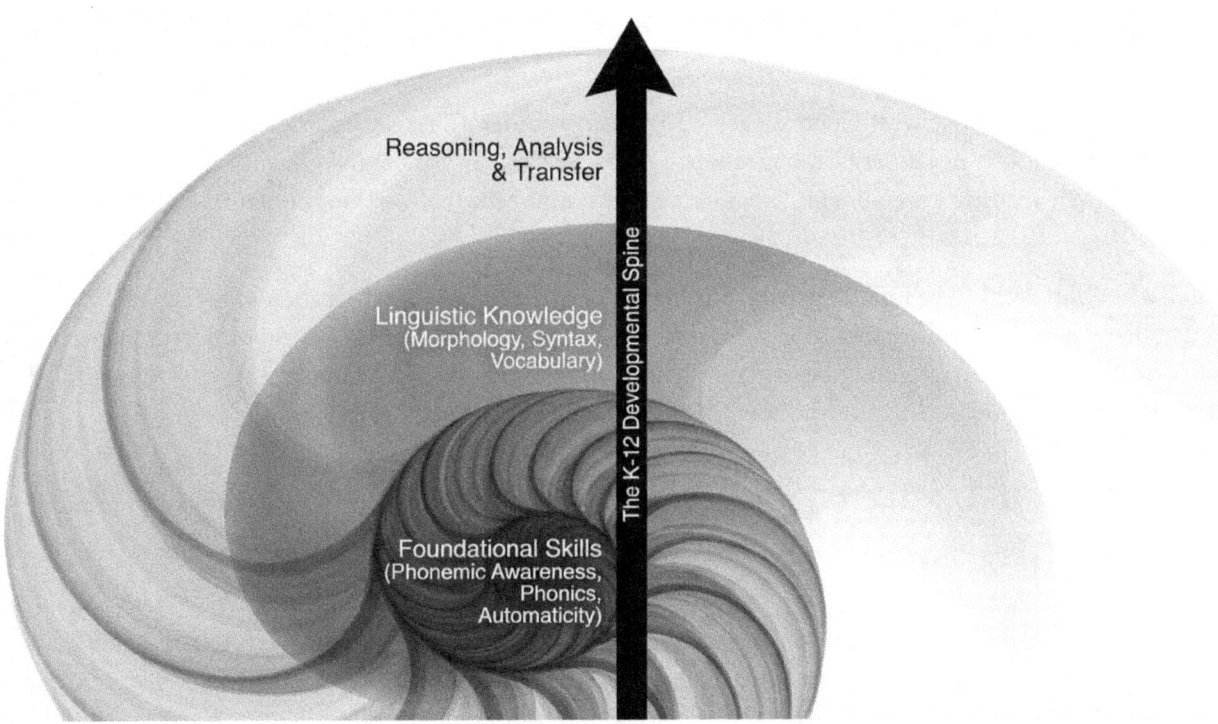

In practice, this mapping process begins by identifying the core pillars that underpin all literacy development:

- Foundational Processing – Phonemic awareness, phonics, and orthographic mapping that make print accessible.
- Linguistic Knowledge – Vocabulary, morphology, and syntax that make language intelligible.
- Cognitive Integration – Comprehension, inference, and reasoning that make ideas meaningful.
- Metacognitive and Transfer Skills – Reflection, synthesis, and application that make learning independent.

When these pillars are placed along a vertical K–12 chart, patterns emerge. We see how early instruction in sound–symbol correspondence becomes middle-grade instruction in morphology, how syntax awareness in elementary years evolves into rhetorical analysis in high school, how fluency develops into prosody and argumentation. The same skills stretch, deepen, and transform—but they never disappear.

This is what system alignment looks like: when kindergarten instruction on letter–sound blending is understood as the first brick in the same wall that supports twelfth-grade comprehension of tone and purpose. Each phase relies on the precision of the one before it and prepares the conditions for the next. Teachers begin to see themselves not as isolated practitioners but as co-architects of a shared structure.

Mapping the developmental progression also clarifies the role of assessment. Instead of measuring only grade-level outcomes, schools begin to monitor movement along the continuum. A student who improves in fluency but stagnates in vocabulary may need linguistic support; another who decodes well but struggles to infer may need targeted reasoning instruction. The continuum becomes both a diagnostic and a design tool—a way of seeing learning as motion rather than moment.

The ultimate goal is coherence without constraint. The map provides a shared direction, not a script. It ensures that everyone—from kindergarten teacher to literacy coach to principal—can articulate where students are in their reading development, what comes next, and how their actions contribute to that progression.

When a district builds this developmental spine, it does more than align curriculum; it aligns belief. It creates a collective understanding that reading is not the domain of a single grade band or department, but the shared work of the entire system. The continuum becomes the connective tissue that holds the school together—the visible evidence that instruction, like learning itself, is designed to grow.

Section 2: Integrating MTSS and SoR for Seamless Tier 1–3 Design

Every school system is built upon two intersecting imperatives: the moral imperative to teach every child and the practical imperative to meet each child where they are. The Multi-Tiered System of Supports (MTSS) exists to reconcile these two truths. It ensures that instruction is not one-size-fits-all, and that intervention is not an afterthought but a continuation of the same learning journey. Yet too often, MTSS and the Science of Reading function as parallel systems—each grounded in evidence, but rarely integrated into one coherent framework.

In many districts, Tier 1 instruction operates on a different logic than Tier 2 or Tier 3. Core classroom instruction emphasizes foundational skills and comprehension strategies, while intervention programs rely on separate materials, separate language, and separate data systems. The result is fragmentation: students experience reading as disjointed, and teachers struggle to see how their efforts align.

True integration begins when MTSS and the Science of Reading are understood not as initiatives, but as architectures of support. Both are rooted in the same principle—progress monitoring and responsive design. The Science of Reading defines what the brain needs to learn; MTSS defines how the system ensures it happens for everyone. When combined, they form a developmental support spine that ensures no learner falls through the gaps between tiers.

Tier 1, the foundation of MTSS, must embody the full scope of reading science. It is not simply "core instruction" but universal access to evidence-based practice: explicit phonics in the early years, morphology and syntax in the middle grades, comprehension and reasoning in adolescence. Tier 1 is where equity begins—not with remediation, but with prevention. When Tier 1 is robust, the number of students needing Tier 2 support diminishes because the system is already teaching the way the brain learns.

Tier 2 interventions then function as extensions, not corrections. They target specific skill deficits within the same architecture of literacy—using consistent language, methods, and measures. A student receiving Tier 2 phonics support should encounter the same letter–sound patterns, routines, and expectations present in the classroom, just intensified and scaffolded. In a coherent system, intervention feels familiar, not foreign.

Tier 3 represents precision, not separation. It is reserved for students with persistent or compounded needs, often requiring specialized instruction and diagnostic insight. But even here, the work remains aligned with the developmental continuum. The same principles of phonemic awareness, orthographic mapping, and linguistic comprehension apply; the difference lies in dosage, pacing, and individualization. Tier 3, when connected to Tier 1 through shared assessment and planning, becomes a bridge back to success rather than a cul-de-sac of isolation.

Integrating MTSS and the Science of Reading also transforms leadership practice. Data teams shift from compliance review to diagnostic inquiry. Instead of asking, How many students are in Tier 2? they ask, What specific component of reading is breaking down, and what instruction will repair it? The focus moves from placement to precision, from counting students to understanding learning.

When alignment reaches this level, the system begins to behave like the brain itself—self-monitoring, adaptive, and continuously responsive. Assessment data becomes feedback, not judgment; intervention becomes instruction, not exception. The tiers cease to be categories and become gradients of intensity, all anchored to the same science and the same belief: that every student can learn to read when the system learns to teach coherently.

This seamless design also strengthens teacher efficacy. When interventionists, classroom teachers, and special educators work from one shared framework, collaboration replaces confusion. Time is no longer spent reconciling programs; it is spent refining practice. Students experience consistency of language and expectation, which accelerates mastery and confidence.

A well-integrated MTSS–SoR framework is not a collection of layers—it is a single system breathing at different depths. Every tier is part of the same continuum, ensuring that equity is not reactive but built into the very structure of instruction.

When schools reach this level of coherence, the question is no longer Who needs intervention? but What does the system need to adjust to ensure everyone learns? That is the shift from response to prevention, from fragmentation to fluency.

Section 3: Aligning Teacher Learning and Student Learning Around the Same Continuum

Systems achieve coherence not when everyone uses the same materials, but when everyone learns within the same logic. The most successful literacy systems recognize that teacher learning and student learning are mirror images of each other—two progressions moving along the same developmental spine. When that alignment occurs, professional growth stops feeling like initiative overload and begins to feel like collective purpose.

Most professional learning models operate on a different timeline than student learning. Teachers attend workshops on phonics while students study comprehension, or they focus on data analysis while students practice fluency. These efforts, while well-intentioned, often create dissonance: teachers are learning about one phase of literacy while teaching another. Coherence collapses because the system's adults and children are not growing in sync.

The remedy lies in reimagining professional development as a parallel continuum—a developmental journey that mirrors how literacy itself unfolds. Just as students move from surface learning (acquisition of skill) to deep learning (application and reasoning) to transfer (independence), teachers should experience professional learning that follows the same trajectory.

- In the Surface Phase, professional learning focuses on explicit knowledge of the Science of Reading—the foundational "what" and "why." Teachers study phonology, orthographic mapping, morphology, and syntax, grounding their understanding in cognitive and linguistic science.
- In the Deep Phase, learning shifts to application—how to implement these practices within authentic lessons, how to differentiate instruction, how to interpret formative data. Teachers engage in modeling, peer observation, and collaborative planning that moves theory into practice.
- In the Transfer Phase, teachers internalize and adapt. They reflect, innovate, and coach others. The goal is not fidelity to a program but fluency with the principles. The science becomes instinctive; decision-making becomes responsive.

When professional learning follows this continuum, instructional improvement stops being episodic and becomes evolutionary. Teachers grow as their students grow. The language of learning becomes consistent across every layer of the system: the same terms—automaticity, morphology, inference, reasoning—appear in student targets and teacher goals. Every PLC conversation, every coaching dialogue, every professional reflection reinforces the developmental model that underpins student progress.

This alignment also transforms culture. Teachers begin to experience the same kind of cognitive journey they are creating for students—one that honors curiosity, reflection, and mastery. Professional learning ceases to feel like an external demand and starts to feel like a shared inquiry. When adults experience the satisfaction of visible growth, they are more likely to replicate that experience for children.

Moreover, aligning teacher learning with student learning creates a feedback loop of insight. As teachers apply what they have studied, they generate classroom evidence that enriches collective understanding. Teams analyze what worked, why it worked, and how to refine it. The system itself becomes a learning organism—adaptive, data-informed, and self-correcting.

Leadership plays a crucial role in sustaining this alignment. Rather than mandating professional development topics from above, leaders design learning sequences that evolve alongside curriculum pacing and student needs. A district introducing morphology instruction in grades 3–5, for instance, schedules teacher learning on morphological awareness months before implementation, followed by observation cycles and reflection sessions that deepen practice. Professional learning becomes anticipatory and responsive—a form of Tier 1 support for educators.

In truly coherent systems, teachers are not only implementers of the Science of Reading; they are scholars of it. They understand how each instructional move connects to brain research, how each phase of reading development demands a corresponding phase of teaching development. Student learning and teacher learning advance together, each reinforcing the other's progress.

When alignment reaches this level, something extraordinary happens: improvement becomes self-sustaining. Teachers no longer wait for directives; they iterate from within. The system stops chasing the next program because it has already found its spine—the shared continuum of learning that unites every reader and every educator in a single, continuous act of growth.

Section 4: Balancing Explicit Skill Instruction with Knowledge Building

Every debate in literacy eventually returns to a familiar tension: skills or knowledge?

Should schools prioritize the explicit teaching of foundational skills, or immerse students in rich, content-driven experiences that build vocabulary, comprehension, and curiosity? For decades, the pendulum has swung between these poles—phonics or meaning, decoding or discovery, structure or story. The truth, however, is far simpler and far more demanding: students need both, and systems must be designed to provide both in balance.

The Science of Reading has clarified beyond doubt that foundational skills—phonemic awareness, phonics, orthographic mapping—are non-negotiable. Without them, access to print remains limited, and the gateway to comprehension never fully opens. But once those gateways are built, the purpose of reading expands. Reading becomes a vehicle for knowledge acquisition, for reasoning, for connection. To teach only skills is to prepare students to climb the staircase without ever letting them see where it leads.

Conversely, to teach only through exposure to rich texts without ensuring automaticity is to mistake access for understanding. Knowledge-building requires cognitive capacity; comprehension depends on fluency.

When the brain labors to decode, it cannot simultaneously construct meaning. Thus, knowledge-building and skill-building must be seen not as opposing forces but as interdependent systems—the mechanical and the meaningful working in synchrony.

Balancing the two requires a structural solution, not a philosophical compromise. A coherent K–12 literacy continuum ensures that explicit instruction and content immersion operate on a shared schedule of development. In the early grades, direct and systematic teaching of foundational skills occupies the foreground, while oral language, read-alouds, and content-rich discussions build background knowledge in the background. As decoding becomes automatic, the ratio shifts: explicit skill work remains, but linguistic and conceptual knowledge move to the center. By the time students reach middle and high school, the emphasis is on disciplinary literacy—using reading to learn, analyze, and create.

This dynamic balance—what Hattie calls surface to deep to transfer learning—requires deliberate orchestration. Leaders must ensure that time, materials, and professional learning reflect the evolving cognitive needs of students. For instance, a kindergarten block that devotes twenty minutes to phonemic awareness and phonics is developmentally essential; a tenth-grade block should devote that same intensity to vocabulary precision, reasoning, and rhetorical reading. The coherence lies not in sameness, but in sequence.

Knowledge-building itself must also be intentional. It is not simply reading "interesting books" or embedding literacy into other subjects; it is designing a curriculum where content deepens understanding of language. A science unit on ecosystems expands domain-specific vocabulary and conceptual schema; a social studies unit on immigration builds empathy and analytical thinking; a literature unit on voice and identity enhances awareness of syntax, tone, and perspective. In each case, knowledge-building strengthens comprehension, which in turn accelerates skill mastery.

When explicit instruction and knowledge-building operate together, they create a feedback loop of literacy growth. Foundational skills grant students access to knowledge; knowledge enriches the language through which skills are practiced. The brain, ever efficient, integrates both processes simultaneously—storing patterns of form and meaning that mutually reinforce each other.

The system's role is to ensure that this integration happens by design, not by chance. Every curriculum decision, every professional learning plan, every assessment system must reflect the belief that skill and knowledge are not stages to be completed but dimensions to be maintained.

In the end, the question is not Which matters more? but How can we ensure that neither is neglected? A coherent literacy system achieves that balance naturally because it is built on the understanding that decoding and discourse, phonics and philosophy, structure and story, all belong to the same human endeavor: learning to think through language.

When that balance is achieved, the pendulum finally stops swinging. It becomes still—its energy transformed into motion forward.

Closing Reflection: The Spine That Holds the System

Every great structure depends on an invisible spine—something that holds its weight, keeps its shape, and allows movement without collapse. In the human body, it is the backbone. In literacy systems, it is coherence.

To build a K–12 continuum is to construct that spine—an unbroken thread that connects what the youngest learner sounds out with what the oldest learner reasons through. When this thread is visible, instruction ceases to feel like a sequence of unrelated moments and begins to feel like one continuous act of learning. A lesson on phonemes in kindergarten and a lesson on rhetoric in high school become chapters in the same story: how thought becomes language, and language becomes understanding.

The power of the Science of Reading lies not only in its precision but in its potential for connection. It gives us a shared developmental language—a way to describe how the reading brain grows and what each learner needs at every phase. MTSS gives that language structure, ensuring every student receives the right support at the right time. Together, they transform literacy from an individual teacher's responsibility into a system's collective design.

When teacher learning mirrors student learning, coherence deepens. When explicit skill instruction meets knowledge-building in balance, coherence expands. And when systems recognize that reading is both a cognitive act and a cultural force, coherence endures.

In the strongest systems, this alignment is not enforced through mandates—it is sustained through meaning. Teachers understand why they teach what they teach, leaders understand how each decision supports learning, and students experience reading as a journey that always moves forward.

The K–12 continuum, once built, becomes more than a structure. It becomes a living rhythm—pulsing with clarity, responsiveness, and shared belief. It allows every learner, teacher, and leader to move in harmony, advancing along a single developmental spine that supports both growth and purpose.

As we turn to Chapter 9: From Curriculum to Culture, the focus shifts from the system's structure to its spirit. Coherence, once designed, must now be lived—through the conversations, relationships, and collective efficacy that give the continuum life beyond the page.

Because a framework, no matter how elegant, is only as strong as the culture that breathes within it.

Reflection Questions:

1. This chapter states, "A true K–12 continuum... transforms instruction from a sequence of initiatives into a seamless progression." How does this ideal compare to the current state of literacy instruction across grade levels in your school or district? Where are the most significant "fragments"?

2. Section 1 highlights the importance of mapping the developmental literacy progression, moving from "a staircase" to "a spiral." How does viewing literacy as a recursive spiral, rather than linear stages, impact your understanding of instruction for both younger and older students?

3. The chapter emphasizes that Tier 1 instruction must embody the *full scope* of reading science, acting as prevention rather than just core instruction. What would it look like for Tier 1 in your context to fully embrace this comprehensive, preventative role?

4. "Teachers grow as their students grow." Reflect on the alignment between professional learning initiatives and student learning needs in your system. In what ways does (or doesn't) your professional development mirror the "surface to deep to transfer" continuum for educators?

5. Section 4 addresses the perennial "skills or knowledge?" debate by advocating for a dynamic balance. How is your system currently balancing explicit skill instruction with knowledge-building across the K-12 continuum? What opportunities exist to improve this integration, especially as students advance through grades?

Application Steps:

1. **Develop a K–12 Literacy Continuum Map (Initial Draft):** As a school or district leadership team, begin drafting a visual K–12 literacy continuum. Use the four pillars (Foundational Processing, Linguistic Knowledge, Cognitive Integration, Metacognitive & Transfer Skills) as headings. For each pillar, brainstorm key skills/concepts and how their emphasis or complexity shifts across different grade bands (K-2, 3-5, 6-8, 9-12).

2. **Audit MTSS Tiers for SoR Integration:** Convene your MTSS team or grade-level representatives. Analyze how the Science of Reading principles are (or are not) explicitly woven into Tier 1 core instruction, Tier 2 interventions, and Tier 3 supports. Look for consistency in language, instructional practices, and assessment. Identify 1-2 key areas for immediate integration improvement.

3. **Align Professional Learning to Student Needs:** Review your professional learning plan for the upcoming year related to literacy. For each PD offering, identify which phase of the student literacy continuum it addresses. Then, assess whether teacher learning is designed to progress from surface to deep to transfer, mirroring the student journey. Propose adjustments to create a more coherent teacher learning continuum.

4. **Balance Audit - Early vs. Later Grades:**
   - **K-2 Focus:** Examine a typical K-2 daily literacy schedule. Where is the balance between explicit foundational skills instruction (phonemic awareness, phonics) and knowledge-building activities (read-alouds, discussions, content connections)?
   - **3-12 Focus:** Examine a typical 3-12 content-area lesson. Where is the explicit instruction in linguistic knowledge (morphology, syntax) and metacognitive/reasoning strategies balanced with the acquisition of content knowledge? Discuss necessary shifts.

5. **Create a Shared Language Glossary:** Begin compiling a shared glossary of key Science of Reading terms (e.g., orthographic mapping, morphology, prosody, schema, metacognition) with common definitions and examples relevant to your school context. Distribute this among all K-12 staff to foster a consistent "developmental language" as advocated in the chapter.

CHAPTER 9
From Curriculum to Culture

Introduction

Every system begins with design, but it endures through culture.

A district can align its curricula, standardize its assessments, and structure its interventions with mathematical precision—but without a shared sense of purpose and belief, coherence remains mechanical. It functions, but it does not flow. True literacy systems breathe; they adapt, evolve, and sustain themselves through the collective understanding that the work belongs to everyone.

Culture is coherence in motion. It is what happens when people internalize the structures we build—when teachers, leaders, and students begin to act not from compliance, but from conviction. In education, culture is not an accessory to instruction; it is its condition. It determines whether professional learning becomes practice, whether collaboration becomes trust, and whether progress becomes permanent.

The Science of Reading provides the knowledge. System design provides the architecture. But only culture provides the endurance. Without it, reforms dissolve with leadership changes, new programs outpace understanding, and the developmental spine we so carefully build loses its tension. Sustainable literacy improvement requires that coherence move beyond documents and frameworks and take root in relationships, language, and shared experience.

This chapter explores how that happens. It examines how professional clarity and collective efficacy turn theory into daily behavior, how coaching conversations anchor adults in the same learning phases that guide students, and how leadership transforms walkthroughs and data meetings into tools for reflection rather than inspection. It ends with a look at feedback—the circulatory system of a learning culture—and how evidence can fuel inquiry rather than fear.

To move from curriculum to culture is to cross the final bridge of coherence. It is the point where systems stop managing literacy and start living it. In these cultures, reading is not just a subject—it is a shared language of thinking, talking, and growing. Every conversation, every decision, every classroom interaction reflects a single conviction: literacy is how we learn, together.

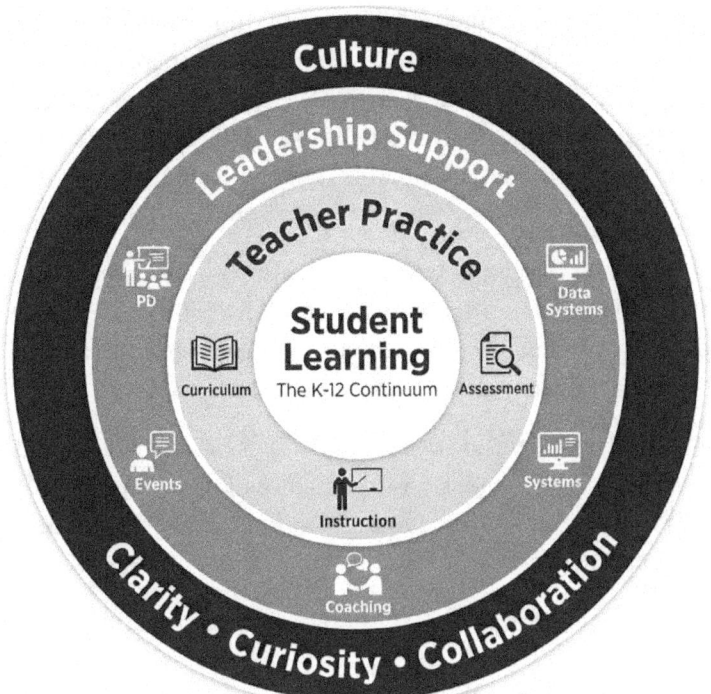

Section 1: Building Professional Clarity and Collective Efficacy

Every strong literacy culture begins with clarity.

Not policy clarity or procedural clarity, but the kind of clarity that lives in the mind of every teacher—the deep, internal understanding of why they teach what they teach, how learning happens, and what impact their instruction has. Without that, coherence collapses into compliance. Initiatives multiply, data accumulates, and energy dissipates. But when professional clarity is paired with collective efficacy—the shared belief that teachers, together, can influence student outcomes—systems begin to move with extraordinary precision.

John Hattie (2018) ranks collective teacher efficacy as one of the most powerful influences on student achievement. But efficacy cannot exist in abstraction. It grows from clarity—the knowledge that what we do matters because we understand how and why it works. In literacy systems grounded in the Science of Reading, this means every educator sees themselves as part of a single developmental continuum, not as an isolated practitioner. The kindergarten teacher decoding phonemes, the reading specialist coaching morphology, and the high school English teacher guiding rhetorical analysis are all engaged in the same pursuit: shaping the mind to read and reason.

When professional clarity is absent, culture fractures. Teams may meet frequently but speak different languages—one using program terminology, another using intervention data, another discussing standards. Without shared conceptual anchors, collaboration becomes translation. But when clarity exists, conversation becomes coherence. Teachers no longer debate methods in the abstract; they refine practice within a common framework of learning science.

Building that kind of clarity requires both intellectual and emotional work. Teachers must not only learn the developmental model of reading but see themselves in it. This happens through modeling, reflection, and dialogue. When leaders invite teachers to map where their instructional focus aligns on the literacy continuum—where phonological awareness transitions into morphology, where fluency gives way to reasoning—they begin to see how their contribution fits into the system's larger story. Ownership replaces obligation.

Clarity also depends on language. A coherent culture speaks in consistent terms, not to standardize thought but to standardize meaning. When teachers across grades and disciplines use the same vocabulary to describe learning—terms like automaticity, linguistic comprehension, metacognition, and transfer—they eliminate semantic noise and amplify collaboration. Shared language turns theory into collective cognition.

From clarity grows efficacy. Teachers begin to witness alignment in action: a second-grade decoding lesson reflected in the fluency of a fourth-grade reader, a middle school focus on morphology enriching the comprehension of high school texts. Each connection reinforces the belief that their collective effort is not only coordinated but consequential. Efficacy thrives on evidence of coherence.

Leaders play a pivotal role in this process. Their task is not to impose certainty but to create transparency. When leaders articulate how every initiative ties to the literacy spine, when they simplify priorities and protect instructional focus, they turn complexity into confidence. Clarity, like trust, cannot be mandated; it must be modeled.

In systems that achieve this synthesis of clarity and efficacy, culture changes texture. Teachers no longer see improvement as a series of reforms to endure but as a shared craft to refine. Professional learning becomes a site of discovery, not compliance. Collaboration becomes energizing because everyone knows the destination and their place along the route.

Ultimately, professional clarity tells teachers what to see; collective efficacy convinces them what they see can change.

Together, they turn literacy from a curriculum to a conviction.

Section 2: Coaching Conversations Anchored in the Learning Phases

Systems become coherent one conversation at a time.

The frameworks may be solid, the continuum precise, the professional learning robust—but without ongoing dialogue that bridges research and classroom reality, coherence remains conceptual. Coaching is the mechanism through which understanding becomes behavior, and behavior becomes culture. The most effective literacy systems treat coaching not as supervision, but as conversation—an evolving exchange that mirrors the very learning process it supports.

In traditional models, coaching often functions as evaluation in disguise. Observations are followed by checklists, data discussions turn into audits, and feedback meetings become more about accountability than growth. But in systems aligned with the Science of Reading, coaching operates on a different frequency. It is developmental, not judgmental. Its purpose is not to monitor teaching, but to deepen learning—both for the teacher and for the coach.

Anchoring coaching conversations in the phases of learning—surface, deep, and transfer—provides a shared structure for that dialogue. This model, drawn from Hattie's Visible Learning framework, gives both parties a way to locate where instruction currently resides and where it needs to go next. It transforms feedback from evaluation ("Did it work?") into inquiry ("What kind of learning was this designed to elicit?").

- At the Surface Phase, coaches focus on clarity and precision. They help teachers refine explicit instruction: modeling, guided practice, corrective feedback. The goal is mastery of foundational skill and cognitive load reduction.

- In the Deep Phase, conversation shifts toward conceptual understanding. Coaches and teachers examine how lessons foster connections—how students apply skills to interpret, infer, and integrate meaning.

- At the Transfer Phase, dialogue centers on independence and synthesis. The question becomes: How are students using what they know to generate something new?

These phases create a developmental map for teacher reflection, mirroring the same continuum students follow. Coaching thus becomes a parallel learning model—teachers experiencing the same cognitive progression they are cultivating in students.

When coaching adopts this lens, it changes tone. Conversations are rooted in shared evidence, not subjective judgment. A coach might say, I noticed that your explicit phonics instruction was strong in modeling and repetition (surface), but I wonder how we might bridge that skill to morphological analysis (deep). What do you think students might need to make that connection? This kind of question positions teachers as partners in inquiry, not recipients of evaluation.

An Example from the Field: A Coaching Conversation in Practice

I recall a post-observation conversation with a 7th-grade ELA teacher in the Delsea Regional district. Her lesson on identifying an author's claim was excellent—it was clear, well-modeled, and students successfully identified the claim in an assigned article. By traditional measures, it was a perfect "Surface" and "Deep" learning lesson.

The conversation started with the teacher's reflection: "I think it went well. They all found the main claim and could point to the evidence."

I agreed, "It was incredibly clear. Your modeling was precise, and the students definitely knew the 'what' and 'how' for this article. I'm wondering, now that they're secure in this 'Deep' phase of understanding, what it would take to push them to 'Transfer'?"

The teacher paused. "What do you mean? Like, have them do it with a harder article?"

"That's one way," I said. "Or, what if 'Transfer' means they see that this move—finding a claim—isn't just an ELA skill? What if we gave them an article from their science class and asked them to find the 'claim' there? Or even better, what if we asked them to compare the type of evidence the ELA author used versus the type of evidence the science author used?"

The teacher's eyes lit up. "So, 'Transfer' isn't just doing the skill again. It's... applying the concept of the skill somewhere new."

"Exactly," I replied. "You've built a strong foundation in this 'Deep' phase. The 'Transfer' phase is just about connecting that foundation to the next one—in this case, disciplinary literacy. It's not a new lesson; it's a new connection."

The conversation wasn't an evaluation. It was an act of co-design, anchored in a shared language of the learning phases. We weren't just talking about a lesson; we were talking about the continuum.

The most powerful coaching cultures thrive on curiosity. Coaches listen as much as they guide; they approach feedback as dialogue, not direction. They know that growth emerges from trust, not compliance. When teachers feel psychologically safe, they are more likely to experiment, reflect, and adjust—the very conditions that define learning itself.

These conversations also strengthen coherence vertically and horizontally. A coach working with early literacy teachers uses the same language of learning phases as a coach supporting secondary ELA. Across the district, every feedback conversation shares a rhythm: Where are students in their learning? What instructional moves best match that phase? What evidence will show they are ready to move forward? The language of phases becomes the language of practice.

Anchored in this framework, coaching becomes a system of mirrors. Each dialogue reflects the same truths up and down the organization: that learning requires clarity, challenge, and reflection; that expertise grows through feedback; and that understanding deepens through conversation.

When done well, coaching transforms culture because it transforms talk. Teachers begin to coach one another, using the same reflective questions in PLCs and informal exchanges. Principals adopt the same inquiry stance in classroom walkthroughs. Dialogue spreads like neural connection—linking people through shared language and purpose.

Coaching, at its highest form, is coherence in conversation. It is how systems think aloud, how collective expertise becomes visible, and how culture moves from curriculum into the daily rhythm of practice.

Section 3: Literacy Walkthroughs: Observing for Transfer, Not Just Task

In a coherent literacy system, observation is not surveillance—it is reflection.

Walkthroughs, when designed with intention, are the connective tissue between system vision and classroom reality. They provide leaders and coaches with a window into instructional patterns, but more importantly, they provide teachers with a mirror—one that reflects not just what is happening, but how learning is unfolding.

Traditional walkthroughs tend to focus on surface-level compliance: evidence of posted objectives, presence of centers, use of programs. They collect data but rarely deepen understanding. The result is what many teachers experience as "drive-by feedback"—momentary visibility without meaningful dialogue. The system learns little, and teachers learn less.

But when walkthroughs are reframed around learning transfer rather than task completion, they become engines of professional growth. The goal shifts from documenting what teachers are doing to understanding what students are thinking. A walkthrough in a Science of Reading–aligned classroom, for instance, might look not for "students engaged in phonics," but for evidence that students are applying phonics knowledge in authentic reading or writing tasks. The observer is not asking, Was instruction delivered? but Is learning transferring?

This perspective changes everything.

When observers enter classrooms asking where on the learning continuum students are working—surface, deep, or transfer—they begin to see instruction as dynamic rather than static. A first-grade classroom might be deeply engaged in surface learning (explicit decoding practice), while a fifth-grade classroom might be navigating the transition to deep learning (morphological analysis and vocabulary reasoning). Both are correct; both are coherent. What matters is not sameness, but alignment—each phase serving its developmental purpose.

To achieve this, walkthroughs must be designed with a shared lens. Observers—principals, coaches, literacy leads—use a continuum-based tool that emphasizes evidence of thinking:

- Surface Evidence: Students accurately practicing foundational skills; clear modeling; guided feedback loops.
- Deep Evidence: Students connecting, comparing, or explaining; using vocabulary to reason about text.
- Transfer Evidence: Students independently applying prior learning to new content, genres, or contexts.

This framework replaces the binary "look-for" checklist with a developmental one. It acknowledges that excellence in a phonics lesson looks different from excellence in an inferential discussion, yet both belong to the same spine of literacy. The purpose of observation is not to rate performance but to recognize progression.

Equally important, walkthroughs must feed dialogue, not data dashboards. The most valuable outcome of observation is conversation—teachers and leaders discussing what they saw, what they wondered, and what might come next. When data from multiple walkthroughs is aggregated, it should not be used to evaluate teachers but to evaluate the system. Are we seeing consistent progression from skill to reasoning? Where does learning appear to stall? How might professional development respond? In this model, walkthroughs function as formative assessment for the adults.

Over time, this approach transforms both trust and transparency. Teachers begin to welcome observers because they see them as thinking partners, not auditors. Leaders begin to see patterns instead of anecdotes. The system begins to self-correct, guided by feedback that is descriptive, developmental, and humane.

Walkthroughs anchored in transfer also model intellectual humility. Observers enter classrooms not to confirm assumptions but to learn—to see how theory lives in practice and how practice refines theory. This stance communicates to teachers that learning is everyone's work, regardless of title.

When systems reach this level of coherence, observation becomes less about oversight and more about insight. Walkthroughs stop being moments of tension and become moments of connection—a shared opportunity to see learning through the same developmental lens that unites the entire continuum.

To observe for transfer is to watch for thinking. It is to measure not motion, but momentum. And in that shift, the culture of literacy begins to sustain itself—not through mandates or measures, but through the collective attention of people who have learned to see learning the same way.

Section 4: The Feedback Loop: How Data Informs Practice Without Narrowing It

In any system that values improvement, feedback is inevitable. But in systems that value learning, feedback becomes something more: it becomes the rhythm of reflection. The healthiest literacy systems pulse with this rhythm—a continuous exchange of evidence, dialogue, and adjustment that mirrors how readers themselves learn.

Too often, however, feedback and data lose their purpose in translation. The desire for accountability turns reflection into surveillance, and assessment into anxiety. Teachers begin to see data as something done to them rather than for them, and the system's focus shifts from insight to compliance. In such environments, data narrows instruction rather than enriching it.

To reclaim its true function, feedback must be understood as the system's circulatory system—the flow of information that keeps professional judgment alive. When feedback loops are well designed, they connect classrooms to leadership and back again, ensuring that every decision remains tethered to evidence without becoming confined by it.

The key is purpose. Feedback should serve learning, not labeling. Stiggins (2017) distinguishes between assessment of learning, which measures what has been achieved, and assessment for learning, which reveals what can improve. A feedback-driven culture prioritizes the latter. It asks: What does this tell us about how students are thinking? What does this tell us about how teachers are teaching? What do we do next?

In literacy systems grounded in the Science of Reading, feedback is multidirectional. Teachers receive insight from leaders, but they also generate it for each other. Students, too, become participants in the loop—reflecting on their own progress and using assessment as a tool for metacognition. In this model, data is democratized; everyone is both contributor and consumer.

To protect feedback from becoming reductive, systems must design it with layers of meaning. Quantitative measures—accuracy rates, fluency scores, comprehension levels—offer essential signals, but they cannot stand alone. Qualitative evidence—student work samples, teacher reflections, observed reasoning—gives data its narrative. The two forms together create a full picture of growth: the visible and the vital.

Effective feedback cycles follow a rhythm of collection, reflection, collaboration, and action.

1. **Collection gathers information intentionally, focused on specific learning goals rather than generic metrics.**
2. **Reflection allows teachers and leaders to interpret the story behind the numbers, identifying both strengths and needs.**
3. **Collaboration transforms individual insight into collective learning—teams discuss patterns, share strategies, and co-design next steps.**
4. **Action closes the loop, translating analysis into practice that is observable and measurable.**

When these steps repeat with consistency, data ceases to feel episodic and begins to feel formative. It stops interrupting instruction and starts informing it. Teachers no longer fear the visibility of results because they understand that visibility is what allows improvement.

Leadership determines whether this rhythm feels liberating or limiting. In coherent systems, leaders model curiosity rather than control. They use data conversations to celebrate growth, ask better questions, and refine support. They understand that feedback is not a verdict—it is a verb.

The true measure of a feedback system is not the number of reports produced, but the quality of reflection it inspires. When educators see assessment as a mirror for learning rather than a microscope for judgment, they reclaim their agency as professionals. Data becomes not a ceiling but a compass, always pointing toward deeper understanding.

Ultimately, the goal of feedback is the same as the goal of instruction: transfer. Teachers, like students, should learn to internalize evidence and use it to guide their own next steps. When that happens, improvement becomes organic. The system no longer needs constant external correction because it has learned to self-correct.

This is how culture sustains itself—through feedback loops that keep learning alive.

In such systems, data does not narrow practice; it nourishes it. It feeds the collective confidence that every piece of evidence, every conversation, and every reflection is part of the same living process: a community thinking together about how to help its learners grow.

Closing Reflection: The Heartbeat of Coherence

Every system has a heartbeat. It is not found in its documents or data dashboards, but in the cadence of its conversations—the pulse of people thinking, reflecting, and learning together. Culture is that heartbeat. It is what keeps coherence alive after the plans are written and the initiatives fade.

When literacy becomes culture, the structures we build stop feeling like mandates and start feeling like shared memory. Teachers no longer implement programs; they inhabit principles. Coaching becomes conversation, walkthroughs become inquiry, and data becomes dialogue. Every adult in the system learns to see reading through the same developmental lens and to speak in the same language of learning—surface, deep, transfer. The system itself begins to think as one mind, moving to one rhythm.

This is what happens when professional clarity meets collective efficacy. Teachers know not only what to do but why it matters. They recognize the throughline from foundational skills to reasoning, from decoding to discussion, from comprehension to contribution. Leaders, in turn, stop managing compliance and start cultivating confidence. The system's center of gravity shifts from policy to people.

Coherence, at this stage, is no longer engineered; it is embodied. It lives in how teams plan, how feedback flows, how reflection feels. It is sustained not by monitoring but by meaning. Every conversation—whether between a teacher and coach, a principal and team, or a student and text—echoes the same shared intent: to help thinking grow.

Culture is what remains when structure does its job. It is the invisible current that carries the work forward even when leadership changes, programs evolve, or priorities shift. It is how a system remembers what it believes.

As we move to Chapter 10: Measuring What Matters, the focus turns to evidence—not as control, but as confirmation that learning is alive. Because when culture is strong, measurement ceases to be a scorecard and becomes a mirror. It reflects the system's heartbeat back to itself, showing not only how much has been accomplished, but how deeply it has been understood.

Coherence begins with structure, but it endures through culture. And when culture learns to measure what truly matters—growth in thinking, connection, and collective purpose—it stops beating for compliance and starts beating for life.

Reflection Questions:

1. This chapter states, "Culture is coherence in motion." How does this definition resonate with your experience of effective (or ineffective) literacy initiatives? Where do you observe culture either strengthening or hindering coherence in your context?

2. The text argues that "professional clarity paired with collective efficacy" is foundational. How would you assess the current levels of professional clarity and collective efficacy around literacy instruction in your school or district? What evidence supports your assessment?

3. "Coaching is the mechanism through which understanding becomes behavior, and behavior becomes culture." How do coaching conversations in your system align with the "surface, deep, and transfer" phases of learning? What shifts could be made to make them more developmental and inquiry-based?

4. Walkthroughs are reframed as "observing for transfer, not just task." How might adopting this lens change the purpose, design, and impact of classroom observations in your school? What new insights might emerge?

5. Section 4 discusses feedback as the "system's circulatory system," advocating for a shift from "assessment of learning" to "assessment for learning." How can your system ensure that data informs practice without narrowing it, fostering reflection and inquiry rather than anxiety and compliance?

Application Steps:

1. **Assess Professional Clarity & Shared Language:** Conduct an anonymous survey or focus group with teachers across grade levels. Ask questions like: "How would you describe the core principles of reading instruction in our district?" "What key terms do we use consistently to talk about student reading development?" Analyze responses for consistency and clarity. Use this as a baseline for targeted communication.

2. **Design a "Phased Coaching Protocol":** For a specific literacy focus (e.g., morphology instruction in grades 3-5, rhetorical reading in high school), develop a coaching protocol that includes prompts and "look-fors" specifically aligned to the surface, deep, and transfer phases of learning. Practice using this protocol in peer coaching or leader-teacher conversations.

3. **Refocus Literacy Walkthrough Tool:** Revise your current literacy walkthrough tool (or create a new one) to explicitly look for evidence of student *thinking* and *transfer* across the learning continuum, rather than just implementation of specific tasks or programs. Include space for qualitative observations and reflective questions for the observer.

4. **Create a Data Reflection Cycle:** Establish a routine for data-driven reflection that moves beyond reporting numbers. This could involve:
   - **Collection:** Identify a specific data point (e.g., a phonics assessment, a fluency score, a comprehension task).
   - **Reflection:** Teachers individually reflect on student performance, identifying patterns and individual needs.

- **Collaboration:** Teams meet to collaboratively analyze the data, sharing insights and discussing potential instructional adjustments.
- **Action:** Teams decide on specific, observable instructional shifts to implement, with a plan for re-collecting data.

5. **Model a "Culture of Inquiry" (Leadership Action):** As a leader, intentionally model curiosity and vulnerability. In a staff meeting or PLC, share a specific instructional challenge you've faced (or are currently facing) and how you are using data and collaboration to refine your approach. Frame it as an inquiry, inviting collective problem-solving and demonstrating that learning is continuous for everyone.

CHAPTER 10
Measuring What Matters

Introduction

Every system measures something.

The question—the defining question—is whether what it measures truly reflects what it values. For too long, literacy systems have confused precision with purpose, reducing the profound work of reading to fluency rates, benchmark cut scores, and percentile ranks. These measures matter, but they do not tell the whole story. They reveal whether students can read, but not whether they can think.

Measurement, at its best, is an act of respect. It acknowledges that learning is real—that it leaves traces in language, reasoning, and identity that deserve to be seen. But when assessment becomes detached from learning, it begins to distort what it seeks to understand. Teachers start teaching to the test instead of teaching through the continuum; leaders begin to manage numbers instead of nurturing growth. The system becomes efficient, but not effective.

To measure what matters is to reclaim the deeper purpose of evidence: insight, not inspection. It is to recognize that growth in literacy is not a single trajectory but a network of development—cognitive, linguistic, and metacognitive—each unfolding at its own pace. Accuracy and rate are necessary, but insufficient. The true markers of reading maturity are flexibility, independence, and transfer: the ability to use knowledge in new contexts, to think with text rather than simply about it.

This chapter reimagines assessment as part of the learning architecture itself, not as a separate layer of accountability. It examines how balanced literacy metrics can capture growth across skill, strategy, and synthesis; how formative assessment can be used for learning rather than merely of learning; how rubrics can make visible the cognitive progression from decoding to reasoning; and how data dialogues can restore inquiry to the heart of leadership.

When systems learn to measure what matters, they stop asking, How well did students perform? and begin asking, How deeply are they thinking? They stop using data to justify and start using it to understand.

Ultimately, the goal is coherence between what we teach, what we value, and what we measure. Because when evidence aligns with learning—and learning aligns with life—the system's numbers begin to tell a new kind of truth: that literacy, at its core, is not about speed or score, but about the steady expansion of thought.

Section 1: Designing Balanced Literacy Metrics (Accuracy, Fluency, Reasoning)

Every measure carries a message. It tells the system what to notice, what to value, and ultimately what to reproduce. When our metrics focus narrowly on accuracy and speed, we teach students that reading is a race.

When we expand our measures to include reasoning and transfer, we teach them that reading is thinking. The design of assessment is therefore an ethical act—it defines what we consider to be success.

The Science of Reading has illuminated the importance of precise, explicit instruction in foundational skills. Accuracy and automaticity are essential; they are the mechanical base that allows comprehension to flourish. But when assessment stops there, we mistake readiness for mastery. A student who reads every word correctly may still misunderstand every idea. Accuracy measures decoding, not discernment. Fluency measures flow, not depth. Reasoning measures the mind in motion—how a reader uses knowledge, context, and inference to construct meaning.

A balanced literacy metric acknowledges all three dimensions as parts of one developmental continuum:

- Accuracy confirms that the student can access print—mapping sounds to symbols with efficiency and precision.
- Fluency confirms that the student can sustain that access over time—reading with rhythm, phrasing, and prosody that reflect comprehension in real time.
- Reasoning confirms that the student can integrate, infer, and interpret—using language and background knowledge to generate insight.
- Together, they tell a fuller story of literacy growth: one that moves from mechanical precision to cognitive agility.

A Data Story: How Balanced Metrics Changed the Conversation

I vividly remember a data meeting with a 5th-grade team that was drowning in numbers. Their data wall was covered with fluency scores (words-per-minute) and benchmark pass-rates. The conversation was stuck. "His fluency is 110 wpm, which is green," one teacher said, "but he's failing science. I don't get it." The metrics they had weren't wrong; they were just incomplete. The data told them that students could pronounce words, but not how they were thinking.

Our first move was to introduce a "Balanced Metrics" dashboard. We kept the fluency data, but added two columns: "Morphological Awareness" (from a simple 10-word analysis task) and "Written Reasoning" (from a rubric scoring one common writing prompt).

The very next meeting, the conversation transformed.

The same teacher pointed to the same student's row. "Okay, now this makes sense. His fluency is high, but look—he scored 2 out of 10 on the morphology task. He doesn't see word parts. He's trying to memorize photosynthesis as one giant word. He's not failing science because he can't read; he's failing because he can't reason with the language of science."

By balancing the metrics, the team's diagnosis shifted from "He's a mystery" to "He needs morphological instruction." The data stopped being a grade and became a map.

Designing metrics around this balance requires rethinking both tools and timelines. Accuracy and fluency can be captured through brief, frequent assessments that provide actionable data for instruction. Reasoning, however, requires observation over time—through written responses, discussions, annotations, and transfer tasks. A truly balanced assessment system therefore includes both quantitative indicators (what can be counted) and qualitative evidence (what can be interpreted).

In early grades, this might look like pairing phonics screeners and timed fluency passages with oral retellings that reveal comprehension. In middle grades, it might involve combining vocabulary assessments with open-ended reading analysis or constructed responses that require synthesis. In high school, it might mean tracking not only reading levels but also reasoning levels—the student's ability to critique sources, identify bias, and apply ideas across disciplines.

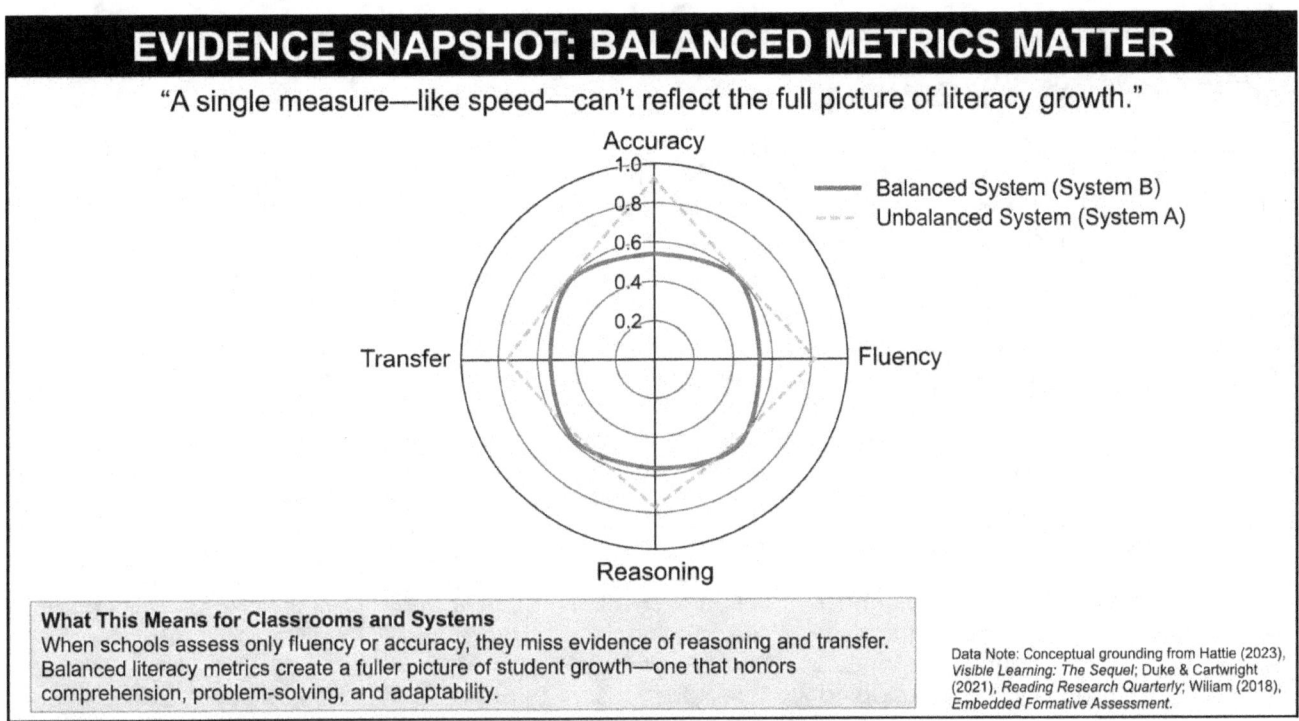

Hattie (2018) reminds us that what gets measured gets valued, and what gets valued gets taught. Balanced metrics send a clear signal to the system: reading is not finished at fluency; it matures into reasoning. When teachers and leaders see data that reflect this continuum, they begin to design instruction that mirrors it. Interventions evolve from decoding-only drills to integrated practice that includes morphology, syntax, and comprehension. The system begins to teach—and measure—the full act of reading.

Balanced metrics also protect against inequity. Over-reliance on speed and accuracy often penalizes multilingual learners, neurodiverse students, and others who process language differently but reason deeply. When reasoning becomes part of the evidence, every student has a path to demonstrate understanding. Accuracy measures access; reasoning measures agency. Both are essential to equity.

Finally, balanced literacy metrics return assessment to its rightful place: as feedback, not judgment. They show growth in multiple dimensions, allowing teachers to celebrate progress rather than chase perfection. They provide leaders with insight into how instruction and development interact, turning data into dialogue rather than directive.

The goal is not to replace one form of measurement with another, but to harmonize them—to create a dashboard that reflects the full spectrum of reading as both science and art. Because when accuracy ensures access, fluency ensures flow, and reasoning ensures meaning, assessment stops fragmenting literacy and starts reflecting it.

A system that measures in balance teaches in balance. And when we measure what the brain truly does when it reads—decode, integrate, and reason—we begin to see learning as it actually lives: precise, fluid, and profoundly human.

Assessment Crosswalk: Balanced Measures for the Science of Reading

Construct Measured	Example Assessment / Task Type	Diagnostic Use (Pre-assessment / Screener)	Formative Use (Progress Monitoring)	Summative Use (Outcome / Mastery)	Sample Thresholds & Interpretive Notes	Con-nection to Balanced Metrics
Phonemic Awareness	Phoneme segmentation, blending, deletion tasks; Elkonin box dictations	Identify specific sound manipulation gaps before phonics instruction	Weekly oral drills or digital probes to monitor automatic blending	Benchmark checklists (e.g., 90 % accuracy in segmenting multisyllabic words)	80 % + proficiency = secure phonemic foundation; below 60 % = targeted intervention	Early auditory analysis feeds later fluency and decoding; do *not* discontinue once phonics begins.
Phonics / Alphabetic Principle	Decodable word reading list; non-sense-word fluency	Diagnose grapheme–phoneme mapping mastery by pattern	Quick-check grids during small-group lessons	End-of-unit word-analysis quiz or timed decoding passage	Accuracy ≥ 95 % and automaticity ≥ 70 cwpm = secure	Links *code to accuracy* — not to comprehension yet.
Morph-ology	Prefix/suffix probe; morphemic word sort; derivational matching	Determine morphological awareness beyond phonics stage	Monthly "word dissection" tasks in vocabulary notebooks	Cumulative morpheme test (20 roots + affixes)	80 % correct decomposition = ready for disciplinary texts	Extends decoding efficiency → reasoning efficiency.
Syntax	Cloze sentence completion; scrambled-sentence reconstruction	Identify sentence boundary or clause-relation issues	Writing samples analyzed for syntactic variety; mini cloze checks	End-of-term writing rubric: syntactic control criterion	3 or more varied sentence types per 100 words = developing syntactic control	Syntax accuracy predicts comprehension phrasing & fluency.

100   The Evolving Science of Reading

Domain	Measurement Tool	Diagnostic Use	Formative Application	Summative Application	Proficiency Indicator	Balanced-Metrics Rationale
Fluency	Oral reading rate, accuracy, prosody rubric (NAEP or WIF-R)	Establish baseline automaticity	Bi-weekly one-minute readings with phrasing feedback	Trimester oral reading benchmark	≥ 95 % accuracy and phrasing score ≥ 3 / 4 = automatic	Balanced view: fluency = *evidence of comprehension*, not speed contest.
Foundational Comprehension	Literal recall, main-idea, sequencing tasks	Diagnose comprehension strategy deficits	Comprehension exit slips; guided-reading anecdotal notes	Benchmark comprehension passages with evidence-citation rubric	80 % literal + 60 % inferential accuracy = proficient	Core bridge from decoding → reasoning.
Deep Reasoning & Analysis	Text reasoning rubric; short constructed response (claim + evidence + analysis)	Identify level of analytical thinking	Feedback cycles using color-coded reasoning strands	End-of-unit writing or discussion rubric (3 criteria: claim clarity, evidence, reasoning)	Level 3 / 4 on reasoning rubric = proficient analytical comprehension	Represents upper end of Balanced Metrics—reasoning as the goal.
Oral Language & Discussion	Academic discourse rubric; recorded small-group talk	Identify expressive/receptive gaps	Weekly structured talk or partner reasoning checks	Presentation / debate rubric	80 % accurate evidence + clarity indicators = proficient	Oral reasoning reflects cognitive comprehension depth.
Working Memory / Processing Speed	Timed recall sequences; multi-step instruction follow tests	Screen for cognitive load limits	Strategy use logs (chunking, rehearsal)	Inclusion in cognitive fluency composites	Span ≥ 4 items = average working memory; < 3 = support needed	Underpins all literacy behaviors—must balance against over-weighting speed.
Disciplinary Transfer (Application)	Multi-text synthesis essay; concept map from 3 sources	Identify cross-domain application ability	Interdisciplinary project journals	Capstone or research paper scoring (integration + citation)	Rubric score ≥ 3 / 4 on "integration" = transfer evident	Culmination of Balanced Metrics—students apply comprehension as reasoning.

Section 2: Using Formative Assessment for Learning, Not of Learning

Every act of assessment reveals a choice about what we believe learning to be. When assessment is used of learning, it closes the book—it defines what has been achieved and records it for accountability. When it is used for learning, it opens the conversation—it reveals what is emerging, what is possible, and what to do next. The difference is not procedural; it is philosophical. It is the difference between measuring performance and nurturing growth.

Paul Black and Dylan Wiliam (2018) describe formative assessment as the process of eliciting evidence of learning and using it to adjust instruction in real time. It is, in essence, feedback that thinks. In a system aligned with the Science of Reading, formative assessment functions as the nervous system—it senses where students are along the developmental continuum and signals what support is needed to move forward.

In the early grades, this might mean quick phonemic awareness checks, word-reading inventories, or fluency passages analyzed not only for speed but for prosody and self-correction. In middle and upper grades, formative assessment might take the form of vocabulary notebooks, morphological analysis tasks, or short written responses that reveal how students interpret meaning. At all levels, the goal is not to grade comprehension but to understand cognition.

The most powerful formative practices are woven into instruction rather than appended to it. A teacher listening to a child read aloud, noting where decoding falters or phrasing improves, is conducting formative assessment. A class discussion that surfaces misconceptions about a text is formative assessment. A student who pauses to annotate, summarize, or ask a clarifying question is self-assessing in the moment. When these micro-assessments are intentional and consistent, they create a continuous feedback loop between teaching and learning.

Formative assessment also changes the emotional landscape of literacy instruction. When students see evidence as a tool for improvement rather than evaluation, anxiety diminishes and agency grows. Teachers can model this stance by using language that focuses on progress ("You've moved from sounding out each word to recognizing patterns—what helped that happen?") instead of deficiency ("You still need to work on accuracy"). Over time, students begin to internalize that mindset. They monitor their own comprehension, notice when meaning breaks down, and use strategies to repair it. In this way, formative assessment builds not only skill but self-regulation.

At the system level, formative assessment prevents the narrowing of curriculum. When leaders prioritize real-time evidence over summative benchmarks, teachers feel empowered to teach responsively. Data meetings become conversations about learning trajectories rather than charts of red, yellow, and green. The focus shifts from Who met the target? to What is the next step for this learner? The system becomes adaptive rather than reactive.

The challenge for many schools is time. Formative assessment feels intangible, and leaders under pressure to report results often default to what is easiest to quantify. But the very nature of formative evidence—its nuance, immediacy, and contextual depth—is what makes it transformative. To honor that value, systems must redesign their rhythms. Short cycles of instruction, observation, and reflection can replace long intervals of testing. A single well-facilitated discussion about student work can yield more insight than hours spent entering scores.

Stiggins (2017) called this shift "assessment literacy"—the ability to interpret evidence in ways that advance learning. It requires professional development, yes, but more importantly, it requires trust. Teachers must trust that formative evidence will be used to guide, not to judge. Leaders must trust that when teachers respond to that evidence with skill and empathy, learning will accelerate. Trust is the precondition for every formative act.

In a coherent literacy culture, assessment becomes indistinguishable from instruction. Every feedback loop, every reflective pause, every student strategy check is a form of formative data. When systems view assessment through this lens, they begin to capture the living process of learning rather than its residue.

To assess for learning is to keep curiosity alive. It reminds everyone—teacher, student, and leader alike—that growth is not something to be proven, but something to be pursued.

Section 3: Rubrics for Reading Transfer — Independence, Metacognition, Synthesis

At its best, a rubric is not a score sheet; it is a mirror.

It allows both teachers and students to see thinking made visible—to trace how comprehension evolves into reasoning, and how reasoning becomes transfer. But too often, rubrics in literacy are reduced to static scales, describing what students did rather than what they are learning to do. They measure the product instead of illuminating the process. A well-designed rubric, grounded in developmental literacy and cognitive science, does something different: it maps how thought matures.

The Science of Reading gives us the content of that progression; Visible Learning gives us its movement. Together, they create a structure for describing not only what students know, but how independently and flexibly they can use it. The purpose of a reading transfer rubric is not to reward proficiency, but to guide growth from dependence to autonomy—from surface understanding to deep synthesis.

A developmental rubric for reading transfer typically spans three intertwined dimensions:

1. **Independence — The Visible Evidence of Agency**

   Students begin by relying on modeling and scaffolds to comprehend or analyze text. Over time, they learn to deploy strategies autonomously, selecting and adapting them to fit the task. Independence does not mean isolation; it means intentionality. The independent reader does not wait for cues—they generate their own.

2. **Metacognition — The Awareness of Thought in Motion**

   As readers internalize strategies, they begin to monitor their understanding. They can explain why they reread a passage, how they inferred a character's motive, or which context clues guided vocabulary interpretation. This self-awareness signals that learning has moved from unconscious reaction to conscious control.

3. **Synthesis — The Integration of Knowledge Across Contexts**

   The highest form of transfer occurs when students use reading as a tool for thinking across disciplines. They connect information from multiple texts, identify themes that transcend genre, and apply insight from reading to new problems. Synthesis marks the moment when comprehension becomes creation.

4. **When these dimensions are placed along a continuum, the rubric becomes a developmental roadmap rather than a rating scale. Instead of labeling students as "basic" or "advanced," it describes the pathway they are on—what cognitive and strategic shifts characterize each phase and what comes next.**

For example:

- A surface-phase reader may recall details but require guidance to infer.
- A deep-phase reader makes inferences independently and begins to evaluate the author's purpose or bias.
- A transfer-phase reader extends meaning beyond the text—using it to build arguments, draw parallels, or generate new ideas.
- Such rubrics bring coherence to the instructional conversation. Teachers across grades can use shared descriptors to discuss student progress without reducing it to numbers. Coaches can analyze patterns across classrooms—where independence plateaus, where metacognition lags, where synthesis emerges—and align support accordingly. Leaders can use aggregated rubric evidence not as performance data but as a portrait of system learning.

For students, rubrics of transfer foster agency. When learners can see where they are and what growth looks like, motivation shifts from compliance to curiosity. They stop asking, What did I get? and start asking, What did I learn? What's next for me as a reader? Rubrics become tools for reflection, not reward.

Designing such rubrics requires courage. It asks systems to measure what cannot be captured in a single sitting: reasoning, reflection, connection. But when rubrics are treated as conversations rather than verdicts, they honor the complexity of reading and the humanity of learners.

Rubrics for transfer remind us that literacy is not static mastery but evolving awareness. They measure the invisible—the capacity to think, to connect, to create meaning beyond the page. And when systems choose to see that growth, they begin to measure not just reading achievement, but reading maturity.

Because in the end, what matters most is not whether a student can repeat what a text says, but whether they can use what it means.

Section 4: Leading Data Dialogues That Inspire Inquiry, Not Fear

Every school has data meetings. Far fewer have learning meetings.

The difference lies not in the numbers on the table, but in the questions around them. Fear-based data cultures ask, Who isn't meeting the benchmark? Learning cultures ask, What does this tell us about how students are thinking, and what can we adjust to help them grow? The data itself hasn't changed; the system's stance has.

In the healthiest literacy systems, data dialogue becomes a disciplined form of curiosity. Teachers and leaders gather not to justify results, but to make sense of them—to interpret evidence through the same cognitive lens they use to study student learning. This is the ultimate expression of coherence: the system learning about itself in the same way it teaches its learners.

Fear narrows, but inquiry expands. When educators feel scrutinized by their data, they play small—teaching to the measure rather than to the mind. But when they feel safe to explore patterns and possibilities, they engage in genuine diagnosis. They look beyond numbers to the thinking behind them: Why are students decoding accurately but struggling to infer? What does this trend suggest about our instruction in background knowledge or vocabulary? These are not defensive questions; they are developmental ones.

Leadership determines which kind of culture takes root. In inquiry-driven systems, leaders use data to create dialogue, not directives. Meetings begin with shared analysis—reviewing evidence of learning from multiple sources: fluency metrics, comprehension rubrics, writing samples, student reflections. The conversation focuses on movement, not ranking: Where have we seen growth along the literacy continuum? What instructional conditions produced it? What barriers remain? The intent is not evaluation, but understanding.

This approach reframes accountability as collective responsibility. When everyone sees data as a mirror rather than a microscope, collaboration replaces competition. Teachers begin to share strategies instead of scores, identifying practices that work across classrooms and adapting them for context. The system becomes less about compliance to benchmarks and more about coherence of practice.

Wiliam (2018) reminds us that "data should be the beginning of the conversation, not the end of it." The best data meetings leave educators with better questions than they started with—questions that lead directly to changes in instruction. For example, after noticing that fluency growth has plateaued in upper elementary grades, a team might explore how morphology instruction could enhance automaticity with multisyllabic words. Data reveals the symptom; inquiry uncovers the cause.

To sustain this culture, leaders must model vulnerability. They must be willing to admit uncertainty, to say, I don't know yet, but let's find out together. This simple stance—humble, transparent, collaborative—signals psychological safety, the condition under which inquiry thrives. In such spaces, teachers no longer hide their challenges; they surface them. The system learns because its people do.

The structure of the dialogue matters, too. Effective data meetings follow a rhythm that mirrors formative assessment:

1. **Analyze the evidence together.**
2. **Interpret what it suggests about learning processes.**
3. **Plan targeted instructional responses.**
4. **Revisit the results to see what changed.**
5. **When repeated consistently, this rhythm turns data analysis into professional metacognition—the system thinking about its own thinking.**

Inquiry-based data leadership also models empathy. It reminds everyone that behind every number is a learner, and behind every learner is a story. Growth in literacy is rarely linear, and metrics must be interpreted with that truth in mind. When data conversations honor both rigor and humanity, they produce not anxiety, but agency.

Ultimately, the goal of data dialogue is not to prove effectiveness but to improve it. A system that uses evidence to learn instead of judge becomes both smarter and kinder. It replaces fear with focus, uncertainty with curiosity, and isolation with collaboration.

When that happens, the numbers begin to mean something different. They no longer measure compliance; they measure coherence—the degree to which a system's actions align with its purpose.

The best data cultures, like the best classrooms, end their meetings not with verdicts, but with commitments: Here's what we've learned. Here's what we'll try next. Here's how we'll know.

In that moment, data becomes what it was always meant to be: not an endpoint, but an invitation—to think again, to teach better, to learn together.

Closing Reflection: When Systems Learn to See

The truest measure of a system is not what it counts, but what it notices.

When a district learns to notice thought—to see growth in reasoning, reflection, and relationship—it begins to understand itself not as an organization that delivers instruction, but as one that learns. The numbers on the page become more than indicators; they become reflections of a shared mind at work.

Balanced metrics, formative evidence, developmental rubrics, and inquiry-based dialogue are not separate tools; they are parts of a single feedback system—the circulatory system of coherence. Each sends signals through the organization, ensuring that learning remains alive and responsive. Together, they allow the system to see itself with accuracy and empathy, with rigor and grace.

In such systems, measurement no longer flattens learning—it illuminates it. Teachers recognize growth not only in speed or score, but in the subtler dimensions of cognition: a student explaining a strategy, monitoring confusion, connecting ideas. Leaders read data not as verdicts, but as voices—each one a piece of evidence in the conversation of improvement. Students, too, begin to see evidence differently; they use it to track their own growth, to witness their own becoming.

When evidence becomes inquiry, data becomes dialogue.

When dialogue becomes culture, systems begin to think.

And when systems begin to think, coherence becomes self-sustaining.

This is the transformation at the heart of visible learning and visible leadership: a shift from measuring outcomes to measuring understanding. It is the point at which the Science of Reading matures into the art of system learning—where the same principles that guide cognition now guide collaboration, reflection, and renewal.

As we move to Part IV: Sustaining the Science of Reading in Practice, the work turns from building coherence to preserving it—from structure to stewardship. Because even the most elegant system, left unattended, can drift back into fragmentation. Sustainability is not a state; it is a practice—the disciplined habit of alignment, reflection, and reinvention.

The ultimate measure of success, then, is not how much we have implemented, but how deeply we have learned to see.

For when systems learn to see, they learn to grow. And when they learn to grow, the work of literacy becomes what it was always meant to be: a living science of connection, continuity, and hope.

Reflection Questions:

1. The introduction states that systems often "confuse precision with purpose," reducing reading to narrow metrics. In what ways do your current assessment practices risk valuing speed and accuracy over depth of reasoning and transfer?

2. Section 1 proposes "balanced literacy metrics" including accuracy, fluency, and reasoning. How would incorporating explicit measures of "reasoning" change your school's approach to literacy assessment and instruction, particularly in middle and high school?

3. The "Assessment Crosswalk" table provides concrete examples. Reviewing this, which "Constructs Measured" do you feel are most consistently and effectively assessed in your system? Which are most neglected, and what might be the impact of that neglect?

4. Black and Wiliam's distinction between "assessment of learning" and "assessment for learning" is crucial. How much of your current assessment practice is genuinely *for* learning (informing instruction in real-time) versus *of* learning (summing up achievement)? What steps could shift the balance?

5. "Leading Data Dialogues That Inspire Inquiry, Not Fear" is a critical cultural component. What specific leadership behaviors or meeting structures could transform data meetings in your context from compliance-focused to inquiry-driven?

Application Steps:

1. Create a matrix of the main literacy assessments used in your school/district (both formal and informal). Map each assessment to the "Construct Measured" categories from the chapter's "Assessment Crosswalk" (e.g., Phonemic Awareness, Phonics, Morphology, Syntax, Fluency, Foundational Comprehension, Deep Reasoning, Oral Language, Working Memory, Disciplinary Transfer). Identify significant gaps or over-representation.

2. **Develop a "Reasoning Evidence Collection Plan":** For an upcoming unit or grade level, brainstorm 3-5 ways to intentionally collect qualitative evidence of student "reasoning" and "transfer" that go beyond traditional multiple-choice or short-answer questions. This could include:

   - Discussion rubrics (for critical thinking, evidence use).
   - Annotation protocols for complex texts.
   - Short constructed responses requiring synthesis across texts.
   - Student reflection journals on their own problem-solving processes.

3. **Refine Formative Assessment "Look-Fors":** Choose one literacy skill or concept that is currently a focus for instruction. Work with a team to identify 3-5 specific, observable "look-fors" that teachers can use during instruction to quickly gauge student understanding *in the moment*. Discuss how this real-time evidence will be used to adjust teaching (e.g., regrouping students, reteaching, extending a concept).

4. **Create a "Reading Transfer Rubric" Draft:** Select a challenging reading task or project (e.g., a research paper, a multi-text analysis, a science lab report). Draft a rubric that specifically measures "Independence," "Metacognition," and "Synthesis" as described in Section 3, using developmental language rather than static labels. Discuss how this could be used with students for self-assessment.

5. **Reframe a Data Meeting Agenda:** Take an agenda for an upcoming data meeting (PLC, grade-level team, leadership team). Rewrite it to prioritize "inquiry" over "inspection." Start with open-ended questions about student thinking, incorporate time for collaborative interpretation of diverse data sources, and conclude with concrete commitments for instructional adjustments rather than just reporting results.

PART IV
Teaching for Transfer and Agency

The ultimate purpose of coherence is freedom.

Every structure we have built—the continuum, the culture, the systems of feedback—exists not to contain learning, but to release it. The Science of Reading, when fully realized, does not end in accuracy or automaticity. It ends in agency—the learner's ability to think independently, apply knowledge across contexts, and act with discernment and empathy in the world.

When the science is strong, instruction no longer serves the text alone; it serves the mind behind it. The goal of reading becomes not replication but reasoning, not recall but reflection. Transfer is the moment when the cognitive and the human converge—when students begin to use what they have learned to shape how they see, question, and contribute.

This phase of the journey demands a shift in purpose. Teaching for transfer and agency means moving beyond teaching what to think toward teaching how to think. It means honoring the brain's natural design for connection—the way it links new learning to prior knowledge, language to experience, skill to identity. It means trusting that comprehension, once internalized, can expand into curiosity, analysis, empathy, and imagination.

The science remains essential, but here it becomes art. Fluency evolves into reflection. Morphology and syntax become instruments of precision and voice. Reading comprehension merges with reasoning, argument, and civic awareness. Instruction no longer builds capacity for literacy alone; it builds capacity for humanity.

Part IV explores this evolution in two final movements.

Chapter 11, "From Reading to Thinking," examines how transfer transforms literacy from a set of skills into a form of consciousness—how reading develops empathy, identity, and agency, and how secondary literacy can be reimagined as an apprenticeship in thought.

Chapter 12, "Leading the Literacy Evolution," turns to the horizon of leadership—how systems sustain this transformation through coherence, curiosity, and clarity; how data, AI, and human judgment can coexist; how literacy leadership becomes the architecture of wisdom.

Together, these final chapters complete the continuum. The work that began with decoding ends with discernment; what began in sound ends in sense; what began in the science of reading culminates in the science of being human.

Because the goal of literacy has never been mastery—it has always been meaning. And meaning, once found, must move.

CHAPTER 11

From Reading to Thinking

Introduction

The final promise of literacy is not accuracy, but awareness.

To teach a child to read is to give them access to knowledge; to teach them to think is to give them access to themselves. The Science of Reading, understood deeply, has never been only about the efficient conversion of print to sound—it is about the gradual awakening of the mind to meaning. Reading begins as perception, becomes cognition, and ultimately matures into reflection.

When reading reaches this level, it ceases to be a school subject and becomes a way of being. The proficient reader can navigate the text; the independent reader can navigate the world. Through transfer, what was once a skill becomes a stance—an orientation toward knowledge that is analytical, empathetic, and ethical.

This is the transition the education system so often misses. Too frequently, instruction ends at comprehension—as though understanding a text were the destination rather than the doorway. In truth, comprehension is the threshold of reasoning. It is the moment when literacy turns from recognition into agency, when the reader begins to ask not only What does this mean? but What does this mean for me, for others, for the world?

Cognitive science calls this transfer, but its emotional dimension is just as profound. The act of applying knowledge beyond its original context requires courage, curiosity, and imagination. It is how students learn to think with what they know—to move from repeating ideas to generating them, from interpreting to integrating, from consuming information to contributing to understanding.

In this chapter, we explore how that transformation occurs—how the reading brain becomes the thinking brain. We examine why cognitive transfer defines true literacy, what neuroscience reveals about independent thought, how reading fosters empathy and identity, and how secondary literacy can become an apprenticeship in reasoning and humanity.

Ultimately, this chapter argues that reading and thinking are not sequential but symbiotic. Reading provides the raw material for thought; thinking gives reading its purpose. The two evolve together until they become indistinguishable. The reader, having mastered the code and the comprehension, now becomes something larger: a maker of meaning, a builder of wisdom, a participant in the human conversation.

Because literacy, at its highest expression, is not about what we know—it is about how we choose to think with it.

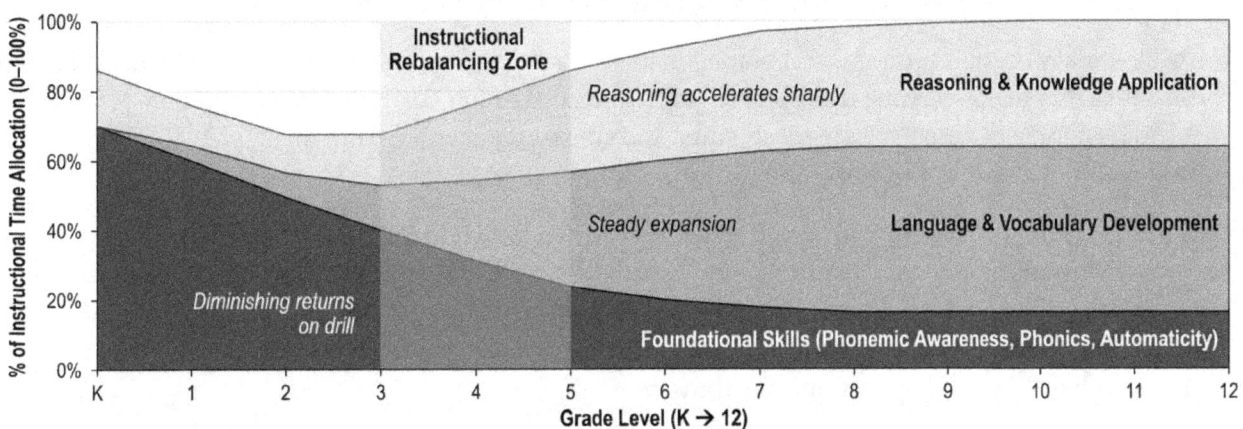

Section 1: Why Cognitive Transfer Defines True Literacy

The measure of learning is not what remains in memory, but what moves into use.

In the same way, the measure of literacy is not what readers can recall, but what they can transfer—the capacity to take knowledge, strategies, and insights from one context and apply them flexibly in another. Cognitive transfer is the invisible line between competence and comprehension, between comprehension and consciousness. It is where reading ceases to be the reproduction of information and becomes the production of understanding.

When the Science of Reading first took hold in schools, its focus on explicit skill instruction corrected a long-standing imbalance. For decades, classrooms overemphasized exposure to text and underemphasized the cognitive infrastructure required to access it. Phonemic awareness, decoding, orthographic mapping—these were not optional skills but neural prerequisites. Yet once those foundations are established, the purpose of instruction must evolve. The brain, like the system, must learn to think across boundaries.

Transfer is the sign that learning has generalized.

Cognitive scientists describe transfer as the moment when neural networks, once activated in specific tasks, begin to link across domains. The same brain circuits that decode patterns of letters can later decode patterns of logic; the same reasoning applied to analyze a text can be applied to interpret data, evaluate arguments, or imagine possibilities. Each act of reading rewires the architecture of thought, strengthening connections between language, attention, and executive function.

In the classroom, this movement is often subtle but profound. A student who learns to infer the author's intent in a story may later infer the bias in a media article. A student who practices summarizing informational text may later use that same structure to synthesize evidence in a science lab report. Transfer is the mind's way of saying, I know how to think here because I have thought somewhere like this before.

This is why literacy is not just one subject among many—it is the condition of all subjects. Reading builds the very capacities that make learning transferable: inference, abstraction, analysis, and integration. It teaches students to recognize patterns, manage ambiguity, and construct meaning from incomplete information—all cognitive operations essential to reasoning in any discipline.

But transfer does not occur automatically. It must be designed for. Hattie's (2018) Visible Learning research reminds us that transfer emerges when students are taught not only what to learn but how to think about their learning. Instruction that stops at strategy tells students what to do; instruction that emphasizes reflection helps them understand why it works and when to use it. This metacognitive awareness—"I can take this thinking elsewhere"—is the key that unlocks transfer.

For educators, this means teaching reading as both process and principle. The same explicitness that defined phonics instruction must extend to reasoning: modeling how inference looks, how synthesis feels, how interpretation functions. Students should see the teacher not only decoding words, but decoding thought—making visible the reasoning that turns comprehension into cognition.

Cognitive transfer is also the foundation of equity. When students can think flexibly, they become less dependent on context, curriculum, or circumstance. They gain intellectual mobility—the ability to use what they know to navigate what they don't. Transfer is what turns literacy into liberation; it ensures that understanding learned in one setting can empower action in another.

In the end, the truest test of reading is not whether students can answer questions about a text, but whether they can ask better questions of the world. Transfer is that bridge—from skill to insight, from learning to life. It is the moment when the reader's knowledge begins to think for itself.

Section 2: The Neuroscience of Independent Thought

Every time a reader engages with text, the brain performs a quiet miracle. It converts marks on a page—shapes that carry no intrinsic meaning—into sound, then into sense, then into reflection. Each stage requires a distinct neural collaboration: visual regions recognizing symbols, auditory regions mapping phonemes, linguistic regions constructing meaning, and prefrontal regions monitoring coherence. Reading is not one act; it is a symphony of cognition.

What begins as a mechanical process—decoding—quickly becomes a cognitive orchestra. Over time, as neural pathways strengthen through practice, the act of reading shifts from effortful to automatic. But the real transformation comes later, when those same pathways begin to serve a higher function: connecting ideas, evaluating perspectives, generating original thought. The neuroscience of independent thinking begins in the circuitry of literacy.

Maryanne Wolf (2008) describes this transformation as the emergence of the "deep reading brain." When foundational processes become fluent, the brain is free to redirect its energy toward abstraction and empathy. The neural economy changes: working memory once devoted to decoding now supports analysis, synthesis, and imagination. This shift—automaticity giving way to agency—is the biological basis of cognitive transfer.

In imaging studies, proficient readers exhibit coordinated activation across multiple brain networks:

- The temporo-parietal region, responsible for phonological processing, continues to operate in the background, maintaining accuracy.
- The occipito-temporal region, home of the "visual word form area," recognizes words instantly, freeing attention.
- The inferior frontal gyrus and prefrontal cortex engage in higher-order reasoning—evaluating evidence, managing ambiguity, integrating new information.
- Together, these regions form a neural model of learning itself: precision at the base, flexibility at the top. The Science of Reading provides the foundation for that precision; independent thought is its summit.

This neural design explains why explicit instruction in foundational skills enhances—not inhibits—creative and critical thinking. Fluency is not the opposite of reflection; it is its precondition. When decoding becomes effortless, cognitive resources are liberated for inference, evaluation, and empathy. The most fluent readers are not those who read fastest, but those whose brains read freely.

Neuroscience also reveals the power of connectional learning—the brain's tendency to reuse existing circuits for new purposes. When readers analyze structure in text, they activate the same networks used for causal reasoning in science and problem-solving in mathematics. Reading literally builds the brain for transfer. It is not a discrete skill but a generative one, continually creating new neural linkages across domains.

Independent thought, then, is not an innate gift; it is a learned neurological state. It develops when instruction is sequenced to mirror how the brain builds connections—from explicit skill, to integrated language, to conceptual reasoning. Each layer strengthens the next, until students no longer depend on prompts or scaffolds to guide comprehension. Their thinking becomes self-propelled.

This is what the brain seeks: efficiency that leads to exploration. Once the mechanics of reading stabilize, curiosity takes over. The prefrontal cortex begins to simulate possibilities, to imagine perspectives, to predict outcomes. Reading activates not only the language network but the default mode network—the region associated with introspection and empathy. To think independently is also to feel expansively.

In essence, reading is the rehearsal hall for the mind's independence. It trains the brain to hold multiple ideas in working memory, to test them against prior knowledge, and to synthesize something new. Each time a student engages with text, they are practicing the neural choreography of thought itself.

The Science of Reading gave us the blueprint for how literacy is built. Neuroscience completes the picture by showing what that literacy allows the brain to become: an organ capable of reasoning, reflection, and self-awareness.

The ultimate purpose of reading instruction, then, is not simply to activate the reading circuits—but to cultivate the thinking circuits. For when the brain learns to read, it learns the deeper lesson that all knowledge teaches: how to think for itself.

Section 3: How Reading Builds Empathy, Civic Reasoning, and Identity

Every time a reader enters a text, they step into another consciousness. They imagine a voice, a perspective, a world that is not their own. The act of comprehension, at its deepest level, is also an act of empathy—the ability to think and feel with another mind. Neuroscience confirms what literature has always known: reading does not just inform us; it transforms us.

Functional MRI studies show that when readers engage with narrative, the same neural regions used for real-world social cognition—the medial prefrontal cortex, temporoparietal junction, and precuneus—light up as if the reader were experiencing those events themselves. This is sometimes called "neural coupling": the reader's brain mirrors the author's or character's mental states. In this way, reading becomes rehearsal for empathy. It allows us to practice perspective-taking safely, repeatedly, and richly.

But empathy is only the beginning. When reading moves from story to society—from imagining others to understanding systems—it becomes the foundation for civic reasoning. This is the cognitive and ethical ability to interpret evidence, weigh competing claims, and recognize bias or manipulation. In an age saturated with information and argument, civic reasoning is not an enrichment skill; it is a survival one.

The Science of Reading teaches us how language is learned; civic reasoning teaches us what language does. Every text, whether literary, informational, or digital, carries an intention. Skilled readers recognize that intention, evaluate its credibility, and place it in context. They understand that comprehension without critique can lead to persuasion without awareness. Reading thus becomes both shield and bridge—protecting us from deception while connecting us to shared truth.

Sam Wineburg (2018) describes this as "reading like a historian"—sourcing, corroborating, contextualizing. But the same principles apply to all forms of literacy. Whether analyzing a poem, a political speech, or a post on social media, readers use the same critical capacities to separate evidence from emotion, fact from framing, truth from noise.

Empathy and reasoning together shape identity.

As readers encounter diverse voices—some affirming, some unsettling—they assemble an internal library of perspectives. Each new text challenges or confirms who they are, inviting reflection on values, culture, and worldview. The adolescent reader, especially, uses books to test possible selves. Through fiction, they explore belonging; through nonfiction, they confront reality; through argument, they construct belief. The process of reading becomes the process of becoming.

This identity-building function of literacy has profound implications for equity. When students see themselves reflected in texts, they experience affirmation—the recognition that their stories matter. When they see lives unlike their own, they experience expansion—the realization that human experience is plural. Both are essential to a complete education. Representation, therefore, is not just inclusion; it is instruction in empathy.

At the classroom level, teaching for empathy and civic reasoning means treating texts as dialogues rather than documents. Teachers can invite students to ask:

- Whose voice is speaking, and whose is silent?
- What claim is being made, and what evidence supports it?
- How does this perspective challenge or enrich my own?
- Such questions turn comprehension into consciousness. They teach students that reading is not passive absorption but active participation in the moral and intellectual life of a society.

Reading builds empathy by expanding imagination.

It builds civic reasoning by disciplining interpretation.

And it builds identity by giving shape to reflection.

When all three dimensions converge, literacy becomes the most human of sciences. It teaches not only how to think, but how to care. It reminds us that every act of understanding is also an act of connection—that the words we decode are, ultimately, the voices of one another.

In this light, the goal of reading instruction is not simply to produce proficient readers, but compassionate thinkers—people who can hold complexity, listen deeply, and act wisely in the world. Because to read well is to imagine well, and to imagine well is the beginning of justice.

Section 4: Reimagining Secondary Literacy as Intellectual Apprenticeship

By the time students reach adolescence, the mechanics of reading have often been mastered, yet the meaning of reading begins to fade. What was once a process of discovery can become a process of compliance—chapters assigned, questions answered, grades earned. In too many secondary classrooms, reading becomes something students do for school rather than something they use for life. The system has taught them to decode and comprehend, but not to inquire and create.

The challenge is not that older students have outgrown the Science of Reading; it is that systems have outgrown their imagination for it. The cognitive architecture that begins with phonemic awareness and decoding matures into reasoning, synthesis, and judgment. In secondary literacy, that architecture must now be harnessed for intellectual apprenticeship—the deliberate mentoring of students into the habits of mind that define disciplinary and civic thought.

An apprenticeship model reframes literacy instruction as participation in a community of thinkers. Students are not recipients of information but apprentices in interpretation. Each discipline—history, science, literature, mathematics—has its own ways of reading the world, its own conventions for constructing evidence and argument. The secondary classroom becomes the workshop where these ways of thinking are made visible, modeled, and practiced.

To apprentice readers into thought, teachers must first make their own thinking transparent. This begins with cognitive modeling: narrating how they analyze a claim, question an assumption, or trace logic across paragraphs. It continues with guided practice, where students attempt the same reasoning with support, and culminates in independent inquiry, where students apply those cognitive tools to new texts and contexts. The structure mirrors the developmental continuum itself: explicit, supported, transferred.

This model transforms the role of the teacher. No longer the sole source of knowledge, the teacher becomes a master thinker—one who demonstrates not certainty, but inquiry. Their power lies not in providing answers, but in modeling how to ask better questions. As the apprenticeship deepens, authority shifts: the thinking once externalized by the teacher becomes internalized by the student. They begin to conduct the dialogue of reasoning on their own.

Such apprenticeship also requires authentic text work.

Secondary students crave relevance. They must see that reading and reasoning are not separate from the real world but continuous with it. Texts drawn from journalism, science, social commentary, and literature should invite them to grapple with genuine ambiguity—issues that demand evidence, empathy, and discernment. When adolescents are trusted with complexity, they rise to meet it.

This reimagining of secondary literacy also aligns with what Hattie and Fisher & Frey (2021) describe as surface, deep, and transfer learning. In the surface phase, students practice discipline-specific comprehension: close reading, evidence gathering, vocabulary precision. In the deep phase, they analyze relationships—between texts, ideas, and contexts. In the transfer phase, they synthesize insight across genres, disciplines, and even generations. The secondary classroom becomes both laboratory and launch pad for this evolution.

At its core, intellectual apprenticeship restores purpose to literacy. It reconnects reading to thinking, thinking to identity, and identity to contribution. Adolescents begin to see literacy not as a test of recall, but as a practice of reasoning—how knowledge is built, contested, and advanced. They begin to experience themselves not as students completing assignments, but as thinkers entering an ongoing human conversation.

This model also dignifies the teacher's role. It elevates secondary educators from deliverers of content to cultivators of intellect. Their classrooms become the places where the next generation learns to weigh truth, construct argument, and imagine possibility—where the mind learns both discipline and freedom.

Reimagined in this way, secondary literacy becomes the final proving ground of the Science of Reading's purpose. The early years build access; the middle years build fluency; the later years build agency. When reading instruction evolves into apprenticeship, it fulfills its original promise: to equip learners not just to decode the world, but to interpret, challenge, and change it.

Section 5: A Vision for Reading as a Social, Moral, and Cognitive Act

To read is to think—but also to belong.

Every act of reading situates a mind within a conversation: between author and reader, between self and society, between what is and what could be. Reading is thus not only a cognitive act—it is a profoundly social and moral one. It shapes how we see others, how we interpret the world, and how we choose to live within it.

The Science of Reading explains how the brain learns language; what it cannot explain alone is what language makes of us. The neural circuits that allow comprehension also enable compassion. The same executive functions that manage inference also govern moral reasoning. Literacy is the meeting point of intellect and empathy—a human technology that allows thought to move from the private to the collective.

Every time a student decodes a word, they are participating in a larger inheritance: centuries of human effort to record, remember, and reason. To read well is to join that continuum—to recognize that words are not just symbols but social acts. They carry histories, biases, hopes, and values. The literate person learns to read not only what the text says but what it does—how it positions, persuades, includes, or excludes. Reading is therefore a moral practice: it demands discernment, humility, and care.

In the classroom, teaching reading as a social and moral act begins with perspective. When teachers treat texts as living dialogues rather than static documents, students learn to engage as participants, not consumers. They consider how voices interact, how power operates, and how meaning shifts with context. They learn that understanding a text is inseparable from understanding the world that produced it—and the world it seeks to shape.

This approach also transforms literacy from competition to collaboration.

Reading together becomes an act of community building: shared inquiry, shared reflection, shared humanity. A discussion about a character's choices becomes a rehearsal for ethical reasoning; analyzing an argument becomes practice for civic participation. Through dialogue, students learn that interpretation is both personal and collective—that understanding deepens when it is tested against the perspectives of others.

In this sense, reading is also an act of hope. It presupposes that meaning exists, that communication is possible, that empathy can bridge difference. Each time a student engages a text with curiosity and openness, they reaffirm the fragile but essential faith that human understanding can be built—and rebuilt—through words.

Cognitive science gives this vision its foundation: comprehension as an integrated process of attention, memory, and reasoning. But it is through the moral and social dimensions of literacy that this comprehension finds its purpose. The ultimate outcome of reading instruction is not accuracy or even analysis—it is wisdom. It is the capacity to hold complexity without despair, to discern truth without arrogance, to act with understanding rather than reaction.

When reading is taught in this spirit, the classroom becomes a microcosm of democracy itself. Students learn to listen, to reason, to disagree constructively, and to revise their views in light of evidence. They experience literacy not as performance, but as participation. The page becomes a mirror, a window, and—most powerfully—a meeting place.

To teach reading as a social, moral, and cognitive act is to affirm that literacy is how humanity survives its own complexity. It is how we remember who we are and imagine who we might still become.

In the end, the goal of reading instruction is not mastery of text but mastery of thought—and the courage to use that thought for good.

Closing Reflection: The Thinking Heart of Literacy

Every child who learns to read begins by imitating sound. Yet somewhere along the way, that sound becomes sense, and sense becomes self. Reading, in its deepest form, is the mind learning to hear its own thought. It is the quiet conversation between language and consciousness that turns knowledge into meaning and meaning into wisdom.

The Science of Reading has taught us how this miracle begins—how the brain builds pathways from phoneme to word, from word to world. But it is transfer that reveals where the path leads: toward agency, empathy, and identity. When decoding becomes fluent and comprehension becomes reflective, literacy reaches its highest function—not simply to interpret the world, but to transform it.

This transformation is not theoretical; it is neurological and moral. The same circuits that once decoded letters now link reasoning to compassion, logic to imagination. Reading teaches the brain to hold multiple ideas at once, to test truth against experience, to imagine the unseen. It rehearses empathy by allowing us to inhabit other minds, and it sharpens judgment by teaching us to evaluate ideas. In this way, literacy becomes both the architecture and the conscience of thought.

In adolescence, these capacities deepen through apprenticeship—the gradual handover of intellectual authority. When teachers make their thinking visible, students learn not only content but cognition. They inherit the tools of inquiry, the discipline of reasoning, and the humility of uncertainty. This is how literacy matures from comprehension to contribution. The student who once asked What does this mean? begins to ask What can I make of it?

To read, then, is to join the human project of understanding. It is to participate in the collective construction of meaning that binds generations together. Each text we encounter becomes both mirror and map— reflecting who we are and guiding who we might become.

This is why literacy, at its core, is not an academic subject but a moral practice. It demands awareness, empathy, and courage. It invites us to think beyond ourselves, to reason with others, and to act with conscience. When we teach reading as thinking, we are not only shaping minds; we are shaping citizens capable of discernment and hope.

The journey from reading to thinking is, ultimately, the journey from instruction to humanity. It completes the cycle of the Science of Reading—not as a method to master, but as a mirror of how the mind and heart learn together.

And yet, this transformation cannot sustain itself without leadership—leadership that understands coherence as culture, assessment as inquiry, and literacy as the architecture of freedom. The final chapter turns to that challenge: how systems evolve, not just to implement science, but to embody it.

Because to lead literacy in this century is not merely to manage instruction. It is to guide an evolution of thought.

Reflection Questions:

1. The chapter opens by stating, "The final promise of literacy is not accuracy, but awareness." How does this perspective reshape your ultimate goals for reading instruction, moving beyond basic comprehension to fostering a deeper "awareness" in students?

2. Section 1 argues that "Cognitive transfer is the invisible line between competence and comprehension, between comprehension and consciousness." What specific instructional shifts might be necessary in your context to more deliberately design for and measure this kind of transfer?

3. "The Neuroscience of Independent Thought" explains how fluency liberates cognitive resources for higher-order thinking. How can educators explicitly communicate this connection to students, helping them understand *why* foundational skills are crucial for developing independent thought?

4. The chapter eloquently connects reading to building empathy, civic reasoning, and identity. How explicitly do your current literacy lessons invite students to engage with texts in ways that cultivate perspective-taking, critical evaluation of claims, and reflection on their own worldview?

5. Reimagining secondary literacy as "intellectual apprenticeship" shifts the teacher's role from knowledge-provider to master thinker. What would this look like in practice in a secondary classroom you know well, and what support would teachers need to embrace this role?

Application Steps:

1. **"Beyond Comprehension" Lesson Redesign:** Choose a text or unit that you currently teach. Redesign a lesson or activity to explicitly foster *transfer* or *independent thought* beyond basic comprehension. For example, instead of summarizing, ask students to:
   - Apply a concept from the text to a new, real-world scenario.
   - Critique the author's argument using external evidence.
   - Create a new product (e.g., a persuasive speech, a design proposal) based on the text's insights.

2. **Explicit "Why" for Foundational Skills:** For a specific foundational skill you teach (e.g., phonics patterns, morphology, sentence structure), design a short, explicit mini-lesson that explains *to students* how mastering this skill will liberate their brain for deeper thinking, analysis, and creativity. Use analogies or examples that resonate with their experiences.

3. **Integrate Empathy & Civic Reasoning Prompts:** For an informational or literary text, develop a set of discussion prompts or writing tasks that explicitly encourage empathy, civic reasoning, and identity reflection. Examples:

- "How might a character's decision be viewed differently by someone from a different background?"
- "What biases might be present in this historical account, and how does recognizing them change your interpretation?"
- "How does this text connect to current events, and what responsibility do we have as citizens to engage with this issue?"

4. **Model "Thinking Aloud" for Apprenticeship:** As a teacher (or leader coaching teachers), prepare to model "thinking aloud" with a challenging text for secondary students. Focus not just on what you're reading, but *how* you're thinking as an expert in that discipline: questioning, connecting, inferring bias, evaluating evidence, or synthesizing ideas. Make your cognitive process visible and explicit.

5. **"Literacy for Life" Student Showcase:** Design a culminating project or showcase where students demonstrate how they use reading and thinking skills *beyond* the classroom. This could involve presentations on personal reading journeys, projects connecting text to community issues, or arguments for social change based on research. The goal is to celebrate reading as an act of agency and contribution.

CHAPTER 12
Leading the Literacy Evolution

Introduction

The future of literacy will not be determined by programs, policies, or even research alone. It will be determined by leadership—by the people who have the courage to align science with purpose, coherence with culture, and knowledge with hope. The Science of Reading began as a movement of evidence; it must endure as a movement of understanding.

In every generation, education stands at a crossroads between reform and evolution. Reform changes practice; evolution changes perspective. Reform rearranges what exists; evolution reimagines what is possible. The Science of Reading has given schools the most powerful framework for understanding how the brain learns to read. But what will determine its lasting impact is how leaders choose to translate that framework into systems, relationships, and beliefs that outlive any initiative cycle.

Leadership in this moment demands a new literacy of its own—a literacy of systems thinking, of coherence, of collective efficacy. It requires leaders who can see connections where others see silos, who can turn research into rhythm, and who understand that alignment is not uniformity but unity of purpose. True literacy leadership is not managerial; it is generative. It creates the conditions under which expertise grows naturally and sustainably across the organization.

The challenge is no longer to prove that the Science of Reading works; it is to ensure that it works everywhere and for everyone. That requires more than fidelity—it requires philosophy. Leaders must cultivate a systemwide vision in which instruction, intervention, and professional learning form one developmental continuum. They must recognize that coherence is not built through compliance, but through shared meaning.

This chapter explores how to lead that evolution.

Section One reframes literacy leadership as the art of moving from fragmentation to coherence—creating systems that think as clearly as they act.

Section Two introduces three leadership mindframes—clarity, curiosity, and collaboration—that serve as the compass for sustaining momentum.

Section Three demonstrates how visible results, when communicated transparently and humanely, build both confidence and continuity.

Section Four looks toward the horizon—where artificial intelligence, analytics, and human expertise intersect—and considers how the next generation of literacy leaders can ensure that technology amplifies, rather than replaces, the teacher's intellectual craft.

To lead the literacy evolution is to hold a paradox: to honor evidence while embracing empathy, to seek precision without losing purpose, to pursue coherence without constraining creativity. It is to recognize that leadership itself is a form of literacy—the ability to read complexity, interpret meaning, and write a future that others can believe in.

In the end, the Science of Reading can transform instruction.

Only leadership can transform systems.

And when both are aligned, they can transform lives.

Section 1: Moving from Fragmented Initiatives to Coherent Design

Every school system is full of good intentions. Each initiative begins with urgency, research, and a promise of impact. Yet, over time, even the most promising reforms begin to fragment. Programs multiply faster than understanding; professional development becomes event-driven rather than developmental; coherence gives way to complexity. What began as innovation becomes noise.

This fragmentation is not born of carelessness but of compassion—leaders trying to meet too many needs too quickly. But when systems layer initiative upon initiative without a unifying design, they exhaust their people and dilute their purpose. The result is what Michael Fullan calls "motion without movement." Teachers are busy, yet directionless; leaders are active, yet impact stalls.

Coherent design begins with a different premise: that systems, like readers, must be taught how to think. Fragmented systems focus on doing more; coherent systems focus on understanding better. Fragmented systems accumulate; coherent systems align. The Science of Reading provides the map for this alignment because it gives the system a clear developmental logic—how literacy grows from perception to reasoning, from skill to synthesis. When leaders adopt that same developmental mindset for the organization itself, coherence becomes inevitable.

To move from fragmentation to coherence, leaders must first ask: What story does our system tell about how students learn to read? If that story changes from classroom to classroom, or from grade to grade, fragmentation has already taken root. Coherence begins when everyone—teacher, coach, principal, superintendent—can describe literacy as one evolving process, not a collection of disconnected programs.

In coherent systems, professional learning, assessment, and intervention are not parallel tracks but concentric circles, each reinforcing the other. Foundational skills, language development, comprehension, and reasoning are understood as parts of one continuum, so Tier 1 instruction naturally anticipates the needs of Tier 2 and Tier 3. Coaches use the same vocabulary as teachers; administrators use the same conceptual framework as instructional teams. The entire organization speaks one dialect of learning—the dialect of development.

This alignment requires design thinking.

Leaders must view the system as an ecosystem rather than a hierarchy. Every element—curriculum, PD, data systems, interventions—must function as an interdependent organism that grows toward a shared purpose.

The Science of Reading provides the anatomy; leadership provides the physiology—the flow of energy, communication, and renewal that keeps the system alive.

Creating such coherence also demands courage. Fragmentation feels comfortable because it creates the illusion of responsiveness—every need met by a new initiative. Coherence feels demanding because it requires restraint: the discipline to say no to what is interesting in order to protect what is essential. Yet coherence is the only way to move from short-term success to long-term transformation.

In practice, this means designing around principles, not products. Instead of anchoring the system to a program, leaders anchor it to processes: explicit instruction, formative feedback, collaborative inquiry. Programs can be swapped; principles endure. When every decision passes through the filter of Does this strengthen our continuum?, fragmentation loses its foothold.

Coherence is not a finish line; it is a habit. It must be renewed constantly through reflection, data, and dialogue. The system, like the learner, must become self-aware—able to diagnose its own strengths and gaps, to course-correct in real time. When leaders model this metacognitive stance, they teach their organization how to think systemically, not just act strategically.

When a system reaches this state of coherence, it begins to move as one organism. Every classroom decision aligns with district vision; every professional learning session reinforces instructional purpose; every data meeting feeds improvement rather than anxiety. Fragmentation gives way to flow.

This is the hallmark of leadership in the literacy evolution: designing systems that learn.

Because just as the reading brain builds meaning by connecting neurons, a literate organization builds impact by connecting people.

Section 2: Leadership Mindframes for Literacy: Clarity, Curiosity, Collaboration

Every great literacy system begins not with a program but with a perspective.

The most successful leaders do not simply implement frameworks—they embody them. They understand that literacy reform, like literacy itself, is a cognitive process: it requires awareness, reflection, and continual meaning-making. Systems grow in the direction of their leaders' thinking. When leaders think with clarity, curiosity, and collaboration, coherence becomes not just an outcome, but a culture.

These three mindframes form the invisible architecture of sustainable leadership. They are not strategies to be applied; they are stances to be lived.

1. Clarity: The Compass of Coherence

Clarity is the antidote to initiative fatigue. It gives shape to the system's story and ensures that every action connects back to purpose. Without clarity, even good ideas fragment; with it, even modest initiatives can have exponential impact.

In the context of literacy, clarity means more than knowing what the Science of Reading entails—it means being able to articulate why it matters, how it functions, and where it lives in every phase of the learning continuum. Leaders who think with clarity make invisible learning visible. They translate research into reason, showing how each instructional move connects to the brain's architecture and to the learner's journey.

Clarity also brings calm. When teachers understand not only what to do but why it works, anxiety gives way to agency. They can adapt practice without losing coherence because they carry the system's principles internally. In this sense, clarity is both compass and contract—it orients people toward the same destination and binds them to the same purpose.

Clarity-driven leadership sounds less like directives and more like narratives:

> "Here's how this connects to what we already know."
>
> "Here's the next phase in our learning journey."
>
> "Here's what it will look and feel like when it's working."

These are not slogans; they are acts of coherence-building in language. Every word a leader chooses either amplifies or obscures meaning. Clarity is precision with empathy—it informs without overwhelming, and it inspires without oversimplifying.

2. Curiosity: The Engine of Improvement

Curiosity is what keeps clarity alive. It transforms leadership from maintenance to learning. Without curiosity, even coherent systems stagnate; they become museums of past reforms rather than laboratories of evolving understanding.

Curiosity-driven leaders see data not as proof, but as possibility. They treat evidence as dialogue—signals to interpret, not verdicts to enforce. When scores rise, they ask, Why? What conditions created this growth? When progress stalls, they ask, What can this teach us about the system's next need? This stance shifts accountability from inspection to inquiry.

In literacy leadership, curiosity also manifests as humility. The Science of Reading is vast, and no leader can master it all. But the most effective leaders are those who remain fascinated by it—who read research not to confirm what they know, but to expand what they understand. They model the intellectual behaviors they hope to cultivate in others: asking better questions, seeking disconfirming evidence, and remaining teachable in the face of complexity.

Curiosity breeds innovation. It encourages teams to pilot, reflect, and iterate rather than adopt, abandon, and replace. When leaders protect the space for inquiry, teachers begin to see themselves as researchers in their own classrooms. The system becomes a learning organism—adapting through wonder rather than fear.

3. Collaboration: The Architecture of Collective Efficacy

Clarity gives direction, curiosity gives energy, but collaboration gives strength.

No literacy system can sustain itself on individual brilliance; it requires collective intelligence. Collaboration turns understanding into action and isolates insight into systemwide improvement.

True collaboration is not coordination—it is co-construction. It occurs when teachers, coaches, and leaders think with one another, not merely around one another. In coherent systems, professional learning communities function less as meeting structures and more as ecosystems of shared reasoning. Teachers analyze student work together, connect patterns across classrooms, and design next steps in unison.

Collective efficacy, as Hattie (2018) and Donohoo (2017) remind us, is the single most powerful influence on student achievement. But it does not emerge from slogans or trust falls; it emerges from shared success in solving meaningful problems. When teachers witness that their collaboration leads to visible gains in student learning, confidence becomes collective.

Leaders cultivate this by flattening hierarchy and elevating expertise. They make it safe to share uncertainty, and they treat vulnerability as the birthplace of insight. They replace top-down evaluation with side-by-side reflection. Over time, the system develops distributed cognition—multiple minds thinking as one, connected by shared language and mutual respect.

These three mindframes—clarity, curiosity, and collaboration—form a recursive cycle. Clarity sets direction. Curiosity deepens understanding. Collaboration amplifies impact. Together, they create a culture in which learning flows upward, outward, and inward simultaneously.

When leaders internalize these mindframes, they cease to manage change and begin to model it. They embody the very learning they hope to sustain. In their presence, systems become less reactive, more reflective; less mechanical, more mindful.

Leadership Mindframes

The literacy evolution, in the end, is not led by policy. It is led by thought.

And thought, when shared through clarity, curiosity, and collaboration, becomes culture.

Section 3: Building System Momentum Through Visible Results

Momentum is coherence in motion.

It is the point at which alignment becomes acceleration—when shared understanding begins to produce shared progress. In a healthy literacy system, momentum is not created by mandates or slogans but by results that are visible, meaningful, and shared. When educators can see the impact of their collective effort, belief turns into energy, and energy becomes movement.

The Science of Reading gives leaders the blueprint for instructional precision; visible learning gives them the framework for sustaining improvement. Together, they teach us that progress is not what happens after learning—it is what makes learning possible. The key is visibility: ensuring that growth is seen, understood, and celebrated at every level of the system.

1. Making Learning Visible to Teachers

Teachers build confidence through evidence. When they can trace the link between instructional practice and student growth, efficacy flourishes. This means leaders must create systems that make learning visible in real time—using formative data, student work, and classroom observation as mirrors for reflection rather than as measures of control.

A literacy team reviewing running records, for example, should not be analyzing compliance with a phonics routine; they should be studying patterns in student reasoning. Where are readers self-correcting? Where are they monitoring meaning? What instructional moves preceded improvement? When teachers can connect cause and effect between teaching and learning, professional learning stops feeling abstract and starts feeling alive.

Momentum grows when evidence feels personal. A teacher who sees her students decoding independently for the first time or reasoning through a complex text experiences motivation more powerful than any external incentive. Visible success creates psychological safety—it confirms that effort leads to impact.

2. Making Learning Visible to Students

Systems sustain energy when students share ownership of their growth. This means helping them see the same evidence their teachers see, but through a lens of agency rather than evaluation. Simple visual tools—progress graphs, reflection journals, success criteria written in student-friendly language—transform assessment into affirmation.

When a student can say, "Last month I was sounding out every word; now I can read this paragraph smoothly," or "I used to summarize without explaining why; now I connect ideas," the abstract concept of learning becomes tangible. Visibility breeds motivation, and motivation sustains momentum.

More importantly, visible learning cultivates metacognition. Students who track their progress begin to think like learners—they monitor comprehension, adjust strategies, and set goals. They internalize the very processes that make literacy transfer possible.

3. Making Learning Visible to the System

For leadership, visibility is both strategy and safeguard. Transparent data sharing—done thoughtfully and humanely—prevents drift and reinforces coherence. When schools use common indicators of progress aligned with the reading continuum, improvement becomes collective rather than competitive.

Leaders can use "learning dashboards" not as compliance trackers but as storytelling tools—living narratives that show how literacy development unfolds across classrooms and years. When principals and teachers review this evidence together, the focus shifts from accountability to alignment: What practices are producing the most growth? What conditions support that success? How can we scale them without losing context?

Momentum is sustained through this rhythm of recognition. Regular cycles of reflection and celebration remind educators that progress is happening—that the system is moving, not merely acting. Even small victories, when made visible, generate a sense of agency that fuels the next step forward.

4. Protecting the Integrity of Evidence

For results to build momentum, they must be authentic. Systems falter when they prioritize optics over insight—when data is used to display success rather than to deepen understanding. Visible learning does not mean constant visibility; it means purposeful transparency. Leaders must protect the integrity of evidence by ensuring that data remains diagnostic, not performative.

This balance requires humility. Leaders must be willing to say, "This part of our system is strong; this part needs attention," and model comfort with imperfection. When leaders view setbacks as feedback, they normalize reflection as a strength, not a weakness. The message becomes clear: progress is not proof of perfection but evidence of persistence.

5. Turning Visibility into Velocity

Momentum builds when feedback becomes motion. Each cycle of visibility—evidence, reflection, adjustment—propels the system forward a little faster, a little smarter. Teachers refine practice, students refine thinking, leaders refine design. Over time, coherence becomes kinetic.

Visible results, however, must always serve purpose. The goal is not to move quickly but to move wisely—to let progress follow learning, not precede it. When systems chase speed over substance, momentum becomes burnout. When they anchor motion in meaning, momentum becomes mastery.

In the literacy evolution, visible results are not the finish line; they are the fuel. They remind educators that their collective effort is working, that the science they study translates into success for every learner.

Leadership, then, is less about creating momentum and more about sustaining it—keeping the system's attention on the evidence of learning, not the noise of initiatives. Because when teachers, students, and leaders can all see progress, they stop needing to be pushed. They begin to move together, pulled forward by the proof of their own impact.

Section 4: The Next Frontier: Integrating AI, Analytics, and Human Expertise

Every era of education inherits both a question and a promise.

The question before us now is whether technology will narrow or expand our humanity.

The promise—if we lead wisely—is that it can do both: sharpen what we know, while deepening who we are.

Artificial intelligence and advanced analytics are transforming the landscape of literacy instruction and system design. For the first time in history, schools have the capacity to analyze learning patterns at scale—to see, in real time, how students acquire phonemic awareness, vocabulary, fluency, and comprehension. Algorithms can identify gaps faster than humans can calculate them; predictive tools can anticipate risk before it appears in the classroom. These capabilities hold enormous potential to enhance equity, precision, and personalization.

But potential without philosophy is peril.

Without human wisdom to interpret, contextualize, and apply what machines reveal, data becomes noise, and technology becomes distraction. The future of literacy will not belong to systems that collect the most data, but to those that understand it best.

1. Analytics as Amplifier

Data analytics, when guided by pedagogy, can extend the visibility of learning far beyond what observation alone can offer. It can reveal patterns too subtle for the eye to see: a student whose comprehension improves only when text complexity aligns with background knowledge, a school where fluency accelerates when morphology is taught explicitly.

Yet analytics must serve as mirror, not microscope. The goal is not to inspect every move a teacher makes, but to illuminate the relationships between instruction and learning that are otherwise invisible. Leaders who frame analytics as a tool for reflection, not evaluation, turn data into dialogue and insight into improvement.

When analytics amplify understanding, they dignify practice. They allow teachers to see the impact of their craft in sharper detail—and to adjust instruction not reactively, but responsively.

2. Artificial Intelligence as Partner

Artificial intelligence, used with ethical and instructional intention, can become a partner in both teaching and leadership. AI can generate adaptive texts, scaffold comprehension for multilingual learners, analyze reading fluency with precision, and offer personalized practice that mirrors a student's current zone of development. For teachers, it can automate the mechanical to preserve time for the meaningful: conferring, questioning, connecting.

But the essential shift lies not in automation—it lies in augmentation.

AI should extend human expertise, not replace it. The best use of machine intelligence is to handle pattern recognition at scale so that human intelligence can focus on judgment, empathy, and creativity—the uniquely human capacities no algorithm can replicate.

This partnership requires new literacies of its own. Teachers and leaders must learn to "read" algorithms critically—to question biases, validate insights, and understand how the technology interprets learning. Just as the Science of Reading taught us to look beneath the surface of comprehension, the science of AI demands that we look beneath the surface of data.

3. Leadership in the Age of Insight

As AI and analytics become embedded in education, leadership must evolve from information management to meaning management. The modern literacy leader's task is not to keep up with technology, but to ensure that technology keeps faith with learning.

This means creating ethical frameworks that prioritize transparency, privacy, and equity. It means ensuring that the algorithms we use reflect the diversity of the learners we serve. And it means maintaining a moral compass that keeps humanity at the center of innovation.

Leadership in this frontier is not defined by technological fluency alone, but by philosophical clarity.

Leaders must ask:

- Does this tool deepen understanding or distract from it?
- Does it empower teachers or reduce them to operators?
- Does it expand students' agency or simply monitor their behavior?
- The answers to these questions will define not only the future of literacy but the future of education itself.

4. The Human Future of Literacy

The real revolution in literacy will not come from machines, but from meaning.

AI can process information; only humans can assign value to it.

Analytics can predict patterns; only teachers can inspire potential.

Technology may accelerate learning, but it is human connection that gives learning purpose.

The Science of Reading has shown us how the brain learns to read. The next chapter of that science will show us how minds, human and artificial, can collaborate to teach more wisely. But wisdom will remain the province of the teacher—the one who interprets data with empathy, who turns insight into instruction, and who reminds every learner that understanding is not a transaction but a transformation.

In the age of AI, the most advanced systems will not be those that think for us, but those that think with us.* They will allow educators to see learning more clearly and to act more compassionately. The promise of technology, like the promise of literacy itself, is not to make humans obsolete, but to make them more fully human.

When leaders integrate AI, analytics, and human expertise with intention, they complete the circle of the literacy evolution.

The Science of Reading taught us how learning begins.

Leadership taught us how systems sustain it.

Technology now offers us the means to see it more fully—but only if we remember what it is for.

Because the future of literacy will not be written by machines.

It will be written by those who still believe that words—and the wisdom they carry—belong to us.

Closing Reflection: Leadership as the Literacy of Systems

Leadership is the final literacy.

It is the ability to read a system, to interpret its strengths and weaknesses, and to compose a future worthy of its people. Like all literacies, it depends on fluency and empathy—on knowing how to translate complexity into clarity, and evidence into action. But the highest form of leadership, like the highest form of reading, is not mechanical. It is moral. It is the act of making meaning in public, for the good of others.

The literacy evolution demands this kind of leadership: steady enough to hold coherence, humble enough to invite inquiry, and visionary enough to see beyond compliance to contribution. Leaders in this movement are not just administrators of reform—they are architects of understanding. They build systems that think, cultures that learn, and communities that believe again in the possibility of progress.

Each mindframe—clarity, curiosity, and collaboration—finds its culmination in this purpose.

Clarity ensures that every decision aligns with principle.

Curiosity keeps the system alive, turning reflection into renewal.

Collaboration transforms individual insight into collective intelligence.

Together, they create an ecology of thought where improvement becomes the natural consequence of understanding.

The integration of technology and analytics now adds another layer to this literacy of leadership. The leader of the future must not only interpret words and numbers, but also patterns and ethics. They must read the code as carefully as the classroom. Yet amid these advances, the essence of leadership remains unchanged: to connect people through purpose. The tools may evolve, but the calling endures.

In the end, the measure of a leader is not how many initiatives they have launched, but how many minds they have liberated. A coherent system does not follow orders; it follows understanding. And when understanding is collective, it becomes unstoppable.

This is the literacy evolution's final truth: systems learn as people do—through reflection, feedback, and courage. When leaders model that process, they turn organization into organism, structure into story, and policy into practice that breathes.

As this journey moves toward its close, we return to the beginning: the child, the teacher, the text. Every decision made at the leadership level exists for that moment of connection—when a reader encounters words that awaken thought, empathy, and possibility. The purpose of leadership is to make that moment universal.

And so the arc of this work bends back toward its essence.

From research to practice.

From coherence to culture.

From reading to thinking.

From science to humanity.

Reflection Questions:

1. The introduction states, "Leadership in this moment demands a new literacy of its own—a literacy of systems thinking, of coherence, of collective efficacy." How does this definition resonate with the challenges and opportunities you face as a leader in your school or district?

2. Section 1 highlights that "coherent design begins with a different premise: that systems, like readers, must be taught how to think." What specific "story" does your system currently tell about how students learn to read, and how might you assess its coherence across grade levels and departments?

3. The three leadership mindframes (Clarity, Curiosity, Collaboration) are presented as "stances to be lived." Which of these mindframes do you feel is strongest in your leadership practice, and which offers the greatest opportunity for growth to further the literacy evolution?

4. "Momentum is coherence in motion." How do you currently make learning visible to teachers, students, and the system as a whole to build and sustain momentum? What strategies could you implement to enhance this visibility without creating "optics over insight"?

5. Reflecting on "The Next Frontier," how do you envision AI and analytics being ethically and pedagogically integrated into your literacy system to *amplify* human expertise rather than replace it? What philosophical questions must your leadership team address regarding technology's role?

Application Steps:

1. **"System Story" Narrative Audit:** Convene a small cross-sectional team (e.g., K-2 teacher, 3-5 teacher, secondary content teacher, interventionist, administrator). Ask each person to independently write a brief narrative (3-5 sentences) describing "how a student learns to read and think in our school/district from K-12." Then, compare the narratives. Identify areas of coherence and fragmentation, using this as a starting point for dialogue.

2. **Leadership Mindframe Self-Assessment & Action Plan:**
   - **Self-Assess:** Rate yourself (and invite your leadership team to rate themselves) on a scale of 1-5 for Clarity, Curiosity, and Collaboration in relation to literacy leadership.
   - **Action Plan:** For the lowest-scoring mindframe, identify 1-2 concrete actions you will take in the next month to strengthen it (e.g., **Clarity:** Craft a concise, shared "why" statement for your literacy work; **Curiosity:** Schedule a "learning walk" with a specific inquiry question; **Collaboration:** Design a PLC meeting around co-creating a lesson).

3. **Design a "Visible Learning Dashboard" Prototype:** Work with a team to design a simple visual "dashboard" that makes a specific aspect of literacy learning visible to teachers and students. This could be a progress tracker for a foundational skill, a rubric tracker for reasoning development, or a visual representation of class-wide growth on a specific comprehension strategy. Focus on how it communicates progress, not just performance.

4. **Facilitate an AI/Analytics Ethics & Pedagogy Discussion:** Organize a discussion with your leadership team and a few key educators about the role of AI and analytics in literacy. Use the chapter's guiding questions: "Does this tool deepen understanding or distract from it? Does it empower teachers or reduce them to operators? Does it expand students' agency or simply monitor their behavior?" Document key agreements and questions for further exploration.

5. **Develop a "Momentum Communication Strategy":** Create a plan for how you will regularly communicate visible results and celebrate successes in literacy throughout the year. This should go beyond data reports and include stories, teacher testimonials, student work showcases, and acknowledgments of collaborative efforts. The goal is to build collective efficacy through shared evidence of impact.

EPILOGUE
From Science to Humanity

The Literacy of Understanding

The Science of Reading began as an effort to explain how the brain learns to read. But as its reach has deepened, its implications have expanded far beyond decoding and comprehension. It has revealed something more essential: that learning to read is the first rehearsal for learning to think—and that teaching someone to read is the most profound act of faith in what humans can become.

Every insight in this book—the cognitive architecture of literacy, the coherence of systems, the clarity of leadership—points toward a single truth: the purpose of science is understanding, and the purpose of understanding is connection. We study the reading brain not to reduce it to mechanism, but to recognize the miracle of meaning it makes possible.

The Science of Reading has given us the structure of this miracle. It has shown how neural networks knit together to translate print into thought, and how explicit instruction and systematic design ensure that every learner can access that power. But beyond the science lies the humanity—the way reading becomes a bridge between minds, a means of empathy, a mechanism for moral imagination.

When a child learns to read, they inherit the accumulated wisdom of the species. They gain access to stories that outlive their authors, to ideas that transcend time and geography. They also learn, implicitly, that thought is shareable—that understanding can move from one mind to another through the fragile, miraculous medium of language. This is the foundation of civilization itself: literacy as the collective act of remembering and reasoning together.

But this inheritance is not automatic. It depends on teachers who understand the science and honor the soul of their work; on leaders who build systems where equity and excellence are not opposites but allies; and on communities that recognize that literacy is not just an academic goal but a moral responsibility. To teach a child to read is to participate in the continuation of human possibility.

As we move deeper into the century of artificial intelligence and cognitive acceleration, this truth becomes even more urgent. Machines will increasingly read faster, analyze deeper, and predict better. But they will not understand. They will not feel the weight of meaning or the grace of connection. The power to interpret—to see ourselves in words and others through them—will remain singularly human.

Our task, then, is not to compete with machines, but to cultivate what makes us irreplaceable: judgment, empathy, imagination, and wisdom. The Science of Reading gives us the foundation; the science of being human gives us the future.

In this way, literacy is more than a discipline—it is a declaration.

It declares that every mind is worth teaching, that every learner can think, and that every community can grow through understanding. It declares that reading is both an individual act and a collective covenant—that we are bound together by the words we learn to share.

And so, as we close this work, we return to the image with which it began: a teacher and a learner, one sound at a time, one word at a time, constructing meaning together. It is in that moment—humble, ordinary, miraculous—that science becomes humanity.

Because when we teach reading, we are not only teaching children to make sense of the world.

We are teaching the world to make sense of itself.

APPENDICES

How to Use These Tools

The appendices that follow are not checklists—they are tools for thinking. They are designed to help leaders and teams move from the "why" of the Science of Reading to the "how" of coherent system design.

In a complex system, no single tool can capture the whole story. These appendices are therefore designed to work together as a dynamic toolkit for diagnosis, mapping, and continuous improvement.

A Note to Leaders: The greatest risk in systemic work is to mistake the tool for the work itself. These frameworks are not designed for compliance, ranking, or evaluation. They are designed to create clarity and spark the professional conversations that drive genuine, sustainable coherence. Use them as instruments of inquiry, not inspection.

Here is the intended workflow for using these tools:

1. **Start with Diagnosis (Appendix C):** The **Literacy System Audit Tool (Appendix C)** is your starting point. It is a diagnostic instrument, not a scorecard. Use it with your leadership team to hold a mirror up to your current system, identify areas of coherence and fragmentation, and build a shared understanding of your most urgent leverage points.

2. **Consult the Map (Appendix A):** Once you've diagnosed "where you are," the **K-12 Pillar Continuum (Appendix A)** serves as your map. This is the most comprehensive tool in the book, detailing the developmental spine of literacy. When your audit reveals a gap (e.g., in "Linguistic Knowledge"), this map shows you what that pillar looks like in practice across every grade band. It is your primary reference for curriculum alignment and ensuring vertical coherence.

3. **Power the Engine (Appendix D):** The **PLC Reflection Framework (Appendix D)** is the engine of implementation. After using the audit (Appendix C) to identify a problem and the continuum (Appendix A) to define the instructional goal, this tool guides the collaborative work of your PLCs. It provides the structure for teams to test, refine, and reflect on the instructional shifts needed to move the work forward.

In short: **Appendix C** helps you decide *what to fix*. **Appendix A** helps you understand *what it should look like*. **Appendix D** provides the *process to get there*.

Appendix A: The K–12 Pillar Continuum
The Developmental Spine of Literacy Learning

The following continuum illustrates how the **twelve pillars** of literacy evolve across the full span of schooling—how each domain develops from foundational skill to flexible cognition, and how the instructional focus shifts as students progress from learning to read toward reading to learn and, ultimately, reading to think.

This continuum serves as a spine for coherence: a reference for curriculum design, intervention planning, and professional learning alignment. It reminds us that reading development is not a set of discrete stages, but a continuous process of increasing efficiency, integration, and independence.

Visible Learning Phases Applied to Literacy

Phase	Instructional Purpose	Learner Outcome
Surface (Acquired)	Introduce and model new skills explicitly and systematically.	Accuracy, decoding, initial fluency.
Surface (Consolidated)	Reinforce and connect known skills for automaticity.	Efficiency, pattern recognition, confidence.
Deep (Acquired)	Apply foundational skills to meaning-making and analysis.	Integration, inference, comprehension.
Deep (Consolidated)	Extend comprehension into reasoning and reflection.	Flexibility, synthesis, critical thinking.
Transfer	Apply learning independently across contexts and disciplines.	Agency, adaptability, intellectual autonomy.

The 12 Pillars of Literacy

Pillar	K–2	3–5	6–8	9–12
1. Phonemic Awareness	Recognize and manipulate individual phonemes in spoken words through explicit, playful oral practice.	Apply phonemic awareness to spelling and decoding multisyllabic words; connect sound patterns to morphology.	Maintain fluency through automatic sound-symbol recognition; support orthographic efficiency for vocabulary growth.	Use etymology and phoneme-grapheme knowledge to decode academic and technical vocabulary.
2. Phonics	Systematic instruction in sound-letter correspondence and blending; decoding one-syllable words.	Apply advanced phonics to multisyllabic and morphologically complex words; bridge to spelling.	Integrate decoding with morphology and syntax for comprehension of domain-specific texts.	Use structural analysis of word parts for academic and disciplinary literacy.
3. Fluency	Develop accuracy, pacing, and prosody through repeated and guided oral reading.	Build automaticity and expression in connected text; connect fluency to comprehension.	Emphasize phrasing and tone as evidence of understanding; internalize silent reading fluency.	Read flexibly and strategically across genres; adjust fluency to purpose and text type.
4. Vocabulary	Acquire oral and print vocabulary through context-rich instruction and wide exposure.	Study morphology, roots, prefixes, and suffixes to unlock meaning; connect words to content knowledge.	Expand academic vocabulary; analyze word relationships and connotations across contexts.	Apply nuanced vocabulary for rhetorical effect and disciplinary precision.
5. Morphology	Introduce simple inflectional endings (-s, -ed, -ing) in context.	Teach derivational morphology to expand vocabulary and comprehension.	Analyze morphological structure for decoding and meaning in complex texts.	Use morphological awareness to unpack abstract, technical, and multisyllabic words.
6. Syntax	Recognize sentence boundaries and parts of speech through oral language and modeled writing.	Analyze sentence structure to understand relationships between ideas.	Study complex syntax to enhance comprehension and written reasoning.	Manipulate syntax for tone, emphasis, and argumentation.
7. Foundational Comprehension	Retell and sequence; identify main ideas and supporting details.	Infer, summarize, and compare; use text structure to understand meaning.		
8. Deep Reasoning & Analysis			Evaluate, connect, and synthesize across sources.	Analyze argument, perspective, and theme; construct interpretations with evidence.

9. Oral Language Development	Engage in dialogic reading, storytelling, and structured conversation.	Participate in academic talk; paraphrase and explain reasoning.	Use discussion to explore multiple perspectives; extend oral argumentation.	Lead and sustain discourse that integrates evidence, logic, and empathy.
10. Alphabetic Principle	Understand that letters represent sounds; connect print to speech.	Apply the principle in spelling, word analysis, and fluent reading.	Reinforce automatic recognition; bridge to morphological and syntactic analysis.	Use orthographic and morphological understanding to decode complex academic text.
11. Working Memory	Strengthen memory for sounds and sequences through phonological games and repetition.	Use note-taking, rehearsal, and visualization strategies to manage information.	Employ graphic organizers and summarization to sustain comprehension over longer texts.	Integrate multiple sources in extended reasoning and writing tasks.
12. Processing Speed	Build automatic recognition of letters, sounds, and sight words.	Increase efficiency of decoding and word retrieval for comprehension.	Strengthen cognitive flexibility for multi-text analysis and annotation.	Manage complex literacy tasks fluidly across time, media, and modalities.

The K-12 Pillar Prominence Matrix

Focus Status Legend
- **A** Acquisition (Primary Focus)
- **R** Review / Application
- **M** Mastery / Integration (Pillar Absent)

Instructional Pillar	K-2 Status	3-5 Status	6-8 Status	9-12 Status	Longitudinal Trajectory
Phonemic Awareness	A	R	M	M	Scaffold and Fade
Phonics	A	R	R	M	Scaffold and Fade
Alphabetic Principle	A	R	R	R	Acquire and Evolve (to Orthography/Etymology)
Morphology	A (Basic)	A (Advanced)	A (Advanced)	A (Advanced)	Emerge and Dominate
Syntax	A (Basic)	A (Advanced)	A (Advanced)	A (Advanced)	Emerge and Dominate
Info. & Arg. Comp.	A (Basic)	A (Advanced)	A (Advanced)	A (Advanced)	Emerge and Dominate
Metacognitive Thinking	A (Basic)	A (Advanced)	A (Advanced)	A (Advanced)	Emerge and Dominate

Cross-Phase Integration

Across all pillars, the instructional trajectory mirrors cognitive development:

- **Surface Learning** ensures access.
- **Deep Learning** ensures understanding.
- **Transfer Learning** ensures independence.

The goal of the continuum is not to isolate skills but to integrate them into the brain's natural progression—from sound to sense, from structure to story, from comprehension to contribution.

Using the Continuum

- **Curriculum Design:** Anchor units and lessons to specific phases within each pillar.
- **Professional Learning:** Align teacher development to the same progression students follow.
- **Assessment Planning:** Measure growth in both accuracy (surface) and reasoning (deep/transfer).
- **Leadership Coherence:** Use as a systemwide reference for language, planning, and communication.

In sum:

The K–12 Pillar Continuum provides the framework for coherence, ensuring that every learner, teacher, and leader shares the same developmental map. It transforms the Science of Reading from an early literacy movement into a lifelong learning architecture—one that connects the neural, linguistic, and human dimensions of literacy into a single, continuous act of understanding.

Table – 12 Pillars x Phase x Observable Look-Fors

Pillar	Surface – Acquired	Surface – Consolidated	Deep – Acquired	Deep – Consolidated	Transfer
1. Phonemic Awareness	T: Leads oral blending & segmenting with manipulatives. S: Identifies beginning and ending sounds.	T: Links sound manipulation to print. S: Applies segmenting when spelling new words.	T: Connects phonemes to morphemes in decoding. S: Explains how sound changes shift meaning.	T: Prompts analysis of complex sound patterns. S: Self-monitors pronunciation during decoding.	T: Integrates phonemic reasoning into vocabulary work. S: Transfers sound awareness to new orthographic patterns.
2. Phonics	T: Models explicit letter-sound mapping. S: Blends simple words aloud.	T: Uses cumulative review in decodable. S: Applies phonics rules independently.	T: Connects phonics to syllable & morpheme study. S: Decodes multisyllabic academic words.	T: Demonstrates etymology–phonics links. S: Justifies decoding by structure & meaning.	T: Encourages flexible decoding in content texts. S: Transfers phonics strategies to novel vocabulary.
3. Fluency	T: Models phrased, prosodic reading. S: Echo-reads with expression.	T: Guides repeated reading & rate tracking. S: Self-assesses pacing.	T: Connects fluency to comprehension checks. S: Adjusts tone to reflect meaning.	T: Coaches expressive oral reading. S: Interprets tone & mood through fluency.	T: Uses fluency to demonstrate understanding across genres. S: Reads unfamiliar text smoothly & accurately.
4. Vocabulary	T: Pre-teaches key words with visuals. S: Matches word ↔ definition.	T: Reinforces morphology for word families. S: Infers familiar meanings from context.	T: Builds semantic maps & word relationships. S: Explains shades of meaning.	T: Highlights academic vs disciplinary nuance. S: Chooses precise terms in discussion.	T: Promotes vocabulary transfer across subjects. S: Appropriates academic language independently.
5. Morphology	T: Introduces common affixes orally. S: Identifies base + prefix/suffix.	T: Conducts morpheme sorts. S: Groups words by shared parts.	T: Teaches derivational patterns. S: Deconstructs words for meaning.	T: Connects morphology to spelling consistency. S: Generalizes morphemic rules to new words.	T: Integrates morphology in research & disciplinary reading. S: Applies analysis to decode technical terms.

6. Syntax	T: Highlights simple sentence frames. S: Combines short clauses orally.	T: Models compound & complex patterns. S: Experiments with varied syntax.	T: Analyzes how syntax affects emphasis. S: Manipulates clauses for precision.	T: Facilitates syntactic revision in writing. S: Uses syntax to craft argument or voice.	T: Promotes syntactic adaptation by genre. S: Transfers syntactic control to new contexts.
7. Foundational Comprehension	T: Teaches literal questioning & retell. S: Recalls explicit details.	T: Models summarizing main ideas. S: Uses graphic organizers.	T: Guides inference and prediction. S: Cites evidence from text.	T: Facilitates cross-text comparison. S: Synthesizes multiple sources.	T: Prompts compre-hension in novel settings. S: Applies strategies independently to real-world texts.
8. Deep Reasoning & Analysis	T: Introduces why/how questions. S: Articulates simple cause ↔ effect.	T: Scaffolds compare/contrast and viewpoint shifts. S: Evaluates differing perspectives.	T: Models analytical writing from text evidence. S: Justifies reasoning with data or quotes.	T: Coaches synthesis across texts & media. S: Builds conceptual generalizations.	T: Encourages transfer of reasoning to new problems. S: Applies analytic habits in argument and research.
9. Oral Language Development	T: Models turn-taking & listening cues. S: Uses sentence frames orally.	T: Prompts elaboration & clarity. S: Expands utterances using conjunctions.	T: Connects oral rehearsal to writing. S: Plans ideas aloud before composing.	T: Facilitates structured academic talk. S: Uses evidence and disciplinary vocabulary orally.	T: Promotes flexible discourse across audiences. S: Applies oral reasoning in presentations & debate.
10. Alphabetic Principle	T: Links symbols ↔ sounds explicitly. S: Matches letters to phonemes.	T: Reinforces letter patterns in context. S: Reads/writes decodable words fluently.	T: Connects alphabetic understanding to morphology. S: Explains spelling through sound + meaning.	T: Demonstrates cross-language letter–sound logic. S: Analyzes unfamiliar orthographies.	T: Encourages encoding/decoding in new languages or scripts. S: Transfers principle to technological and linguistic contexts.
11. Working Memory	T: Breaks tasks into manageable steps. S: Rehearses information aloud.	T: Embeds retrieval practice in lessons. S: Recalls and applies prior learning.	T: Uses cumulative reasoning prompts. S: Integrates multiple ideas during discussion.	T: Designs multitier tasks for sustained thinking. S: Manages several information sources.	T: Encourages strategic memory tools (e.g., annotation, chunking). S: Transfers memory supports to independent study.

12. Processing Speed	T: Provides timed automaticity drills. S: Reads known patterns with increasing rate.	T: Monitors fluency & automatic recall. S: Demonstrates accuracy and efficiency.	T: Designs complex tasks within time frames. S: Balances pace with comprehension.	T: Encourages flexible pacing for text type & purpose. S: Self-adjusts speed strategically.	T: Transfers efficient processing to novel challenges. S: Demonstrates automaticity in real-world literacy tasks.

APPENDIX B
Visible Learning Phases in Literacy Instruction

Turning Cognitive Science into Classroom Clarity

The Visible Learning model (Hattie & Donoghue, 2016) identifies three recursive phases of learning. In literacy instruction, these phases describe how readers move from acquiring skills to applying them autonomously. Each phase demands different teacher moves, student behaviors, and forms of assessment—but all are connected by feedback and reflection.

1. Surface Learning – Acquisition and Consolidation

Dimension	Description
Purpose	Establish foundational knowledge and accuracy; reduce cognitive load so that working memory can focus on meaning.
Teacher Moves	• Explicit modeling of phonemic, phonics, and vocabulary skills. • Direct instruction with immediate corrective feedback. • Guided practice in short, focused bursts. • Cumulative review to strengthen automaticity.
Student Behaviors	• Listen, repeat, and apply discrete skills. • Ask clarifying questions ("Did I read that correctly?"). • Track improvement in accuracy and fluency. • Demonstrate confidence with scaffolded support.
Assessment Focus	• Accuracy and rate (decoding, word recognition). • Short-cycle formative checks (dictation, oral reading, phonics probes). • Immediate feedback loops rather than delayed grading.
Leadership Lens	Surface learning requires structural support: protected time for explicit instruction, alignment of materials, and coaching that models gradual release.

2. Deep Learning – Application and Integration

Dimension	Description
Purpose	Connect ideas, analyze language and structure, and construct meaning that extends beyond recall.
Teacher Moves	• Use guided inquiry and strategic questioning ("Why does the author…?"). • Model thinking aloud to show inference and synthesis. • Facilitate text-to-text and text-to-world comparisons. • Encourage metacognitive reflection: How did you know that?
Student Behaviors	• Explain reasoning and cite textual evidence. • Collaborate in dialogue that tests ideas. • Revise interpretations when confronted with new information. • Monitor comprehension and self-correct breakdowns.
Assessment Focus	• Comprehension tasks that require explanation and justification. • Analytic rubrics measuring inference, vocabulary use, and reasoning. • Performance-based tasks (discussion, written analysis).
Leadership Lens	Deep learning grows where teachers have time to plan collaboratively and analyze student reasoning, not just accuracy. Leadership ensures PD bridges skill and strategy.

3. Transfer Learning – Independence and Innovation

Dimension	Description
Purpose	Apply and adapt literacy knowledge across new contexts, disciplines, and media; demonstrate agency and creative reasoning.
Teacher Moves	• Design authentic, interdisciplinary tasks. • Provide minimal scaffolds; emphasize student choice and self-direction. • Model how to generalize strategies to novel problems. • Facilitate reflection on learning processes and outcomes.
Student Behaviors	• Select appropriate strategies independently. • Synthesize across multiple texts and perspectives. • Generate arguments, products, or solutions using evidence. • Reflect on how literacy skills support thinking and citizenship.
Assessment Focus	• Rubrics measuring independence, metacognition, and synthesis. • Portfolio assessments, capstone projects, or performance exhibitions. • Student self-assessment and goal setting.
Leadership Lens	Transfer learning thrives in cultures of trust. Leaders emphasize inquiry, celebrate innovation, and align accountability to growth in reasoning rather than repetition of routine.

Phase Interdependence

The phases are recursive, not linear. Readers revisit surface skills to strengthen deep reasoning; transfer performances reveal where surface or deep learning needs reinforcement. Effective systems design assessments that track movement among all three phases rather than treating them as separate benchmarks.

Guiding Principles for Implementation

1. **Align Language:** Use the same phase terminology in teacher coaching, PLCs, and student goal setting to strengthen coherence.

2. **Balance Time:** Ensure instructional minutes reflect cognitive need—more explicit time early, more inquiry later, continual review always.

3. **Feedback as Fuel:** Across phases, feedback is the bridge from effort to insight; it must be descriptive, timely, and actionable.

4. **Equity Through Design:** When every learner moves through the full cycle—skill, understanding, transfer—opportunity gaps close naturally.

5. **Conclusion**

    The Visible Learning phases translate the Science of Reading from a body of research into a rhythm of practice. They allow teachers to teach with precision, students to learn with awareness, and leaders to see growth as a dynamic process rather than a static score.

    When systems internalize these phases, literacy ceases to be an initiative and becomes a living habit of mind—one that mirrors how the brain learns, how knowledge deepens, and how understanding moves from science to humanity.

APPENDIX C
The Literacy System Audit Tool
A Framework for Coherence, Alignment, and Sustainability

The purpose of this audit is not compliance but clarity.

It invites districts, schools, and teams to look at their literacy systems through one lens: Do our structures help every learner move from skill to understanding to transfer?

Each domain below corresponds to one layer of a coherent system—Curriculum, Instruction, Assessment, Professional Learning, and Leadership.

Scores should be used descriptively (to identify priorities and patterns) rather than judgmentally. The scale is:

1 = Emerging 2 = Developing 3 = Operational 4 = Sustaining 5 = Exemplary

1. Curriculum Coherence

Indicator	1–2 Emerging	3 Operational	4–5 Sustaining
Developmental Alignment	Literacy materials fragmented by grade or program; no clear continuum.	Some vertical alignment; early literacy emphasized but later phases unclear.	A documented K–12 continuum connects foundational skills, language, comprehension, and reasoning.
Integration of Science of Reading	Isolated phonics programs or strategy lists without explicit sequence.	Foundational instruction present in K–3; upper-grade integration inconsistent.	The five linguistic pillars and their extensions (syntax, morphology, etc.) appear across all grade bands.
Knowledge Building	Reading curriculum divorced from content learning.	Some cross-disciplinary units.	Reading and knowledge building intentionally intertwined through all subjects.

2. Instructional Practice

Indicator	1–2 Emerging	3 Operational	4–5 Sustaining
Explicit Instruction	Teacher talk unfocused; little modeling or feedback.	Explicit routines in early grades; inconsistent application later.	System-wide use of modeling, guided practice, and gradual release matched to learning phase.
Learning Phases	No shared understanding of surface, deep, transfer learning.	Terms recognized but not applied.	Teachers plan and reflect using the phase model; lessons target cognitive purpose.
Differentiation & MTSS Integration	Intervention disconnected from Tier 1.	Some shared assessments; separate planning.	Tier 1–3 form one continuum with common language, tools, and goals.

3. Assessment and Feedback

Indicator	1–2 Emerging	3 Operational	4–5 Sustaining
Balanced Metrics	Over-reliance on speed/accuracy tests.	Combination of fluency and comprehension data.	Balanced evidence of accuracy, fluency, reasoning, and transfer.
Formative Practice	Summative tests drive decisions.	Some short-cycle formative checks.	Continuous formative feedback informs instruction daily.
Data Culture	Data used for ranking.	Data discussed in teams but inconsistently analyzed.	Inquiry-based data dialogue focuses on learning, not labeling.

4. Professional Learning

Indicator	1–2 Emerging	3 Operational	4–5 Sustaining
Alignment to Continuum	PD topics isolated from classroom focus.	Some alignment by grade level.	PD mirrors student learning phases—surface knowledge, deep application, transfer reflection.
Coaching & Collaboration	Coaching evaluative or absent.	Instructional coaching present but uneven.	Coaching conversations anchored in learning phases; PLCs use shared evidence of impact.
Collective Efficacy	Staff morale low; limited shared language.	Some team planning.	Strong culture of collaboration; teachers believe their joint practice changes outcomes.

5. Leadership and Culture

Indicator	1–2 Emerging	3 Operational	4–5 Sustaining
Vision & Clarity	Multiple conflicting initiatives.	A stated literacy goal but unclear rationale.	Clear, communicated vision linking reading science, coherence, and equity.
Feedback Loops	Top-down mandates.	Periodic reflection meetings.	Regular cycles of evidence → reflection → action across all levels.
Sustainability Mindset	Reform viewed as temporary.	Some succession planning.	Leadership pipeline and structures ensure longevity beyond individuals.

Using the Audit

1. **Collect Evidence** – Gather curriculum maps, lesson plans, PD agendas, and student work.

2. **Rate Collaboratively** – Teams discuss and agree on scores to surface shared understanding.

3. **Identify Leverage Points** – Highlight two indicators with highest leverage for systemic impact.

4. **Plan Next Steps** – Convert insights into 90-day action plans with clear outcomes.

5. **Revisit Quarterly** – Treat the audit as formative assessment for the system itself.

6. **Interpreting Results**

- Scores 1–2 (Emerging): Prioritize foundational alignment; focus on clarity of purpose and language.
- Scores 3 (Operational): Consolidate consistency; embed feedback loops and shared tools.
- Scores 4–5 (Sustaining): Document practices; mentor other schools; codify learning for scalability.
- Reflection Prompts for Leadership Teams
- Where is our system coherent? Where is it fragmented?
- How well does our professional learning mirror student learning?
- What evidence shows that reading instruction leads to reasoning and transfer?
- How do we protect coherence through transitions in leadership or policy?
- Audit to Action Planner – Appendix C: Evolving Science of Reading Implementation

Audit Indicator	Current Score (1–4)	Evidence / Data Source	90-Day Outcome (Target Condition)	First 3 Actions	Owner / Date for Completion
1. Foundational Skills Alignment (Phonemic Awareness → Automaticity)	2 = Developing	Walk-throughs show inconsistent explicit phonics lessons.	By 90 days, 100% of K–2 ELA blocks include explicit phonemic → phonics link lessons 3× weekly.	1: Map core phonics sequence to curriculum 2: Provide PD on blending/segmenting moves 3: Implement lesson look-fors rubric	Literacy Coach / Feb 15
2. Language and Vocabulary Integration	3 = Approaching	Lesson plans include tier 2 words but few morphology connections.	Teachers embed morphological analysis in ≥ 2 content lessons per week.	1: Co-plan morphology mini-lessons 2: Create affix anchor charts 3: Monitor through student writing samples	Grade 4 Team / Mar 1
3. Syntax and Sentence Reasoning	1 = Initiating	Writing samples show limited sentence variety.	80% of students use compound/complex sentences in writing samples by end of quarter.	1: Introduce sentence-combining protocol 2: Add syntax mini-lesson in grammar block 3: Analyze weekly writing for growth	ELA Dept Chair / Apr 5
4. Reading–Writing Connections and Text Reasoning	2 = Developing	Students can summarize but rarely synthesize sources.	Students use evidence + analysis in short responses with rubric avg ≥ 3.	1: Adopt reasoning rubric from Ch. 10 2: Model claim/evidence construction 3: Provide peer feedback sessions	Dept PLC Lead / Mar 20
5. Balanced Metrics System in Use	3 = Approaching	Fluency data collected weekly; few morphology/syntax checks.	Implement Balanced Metrics dashboard tracking fluency, morphology, and reasoning monthly.	1: Create shared data sheet 2: Add morphology probe to formative cycle 3: Review triangulated data each month	Data Coach / Apr 30
6. Collective Efficacy and Coaching Cycle	2 = Developing	PLC notes show limited inter-grade collaboration.	Cross-grade study teams analyze one student work sample per month using Audit rubric.	1: Schedule vertical PLC dates 2: Use Audit tool for shared calibration 3: Track impact via student samples	AP Instruction / May 15

Usage Guidance

- **Cadence:** Reviewed every 30 days within PLC or leadership meeting.
- **Scoring Scale:** 1 = Initiating 2 = Developing 3 = Approaching 4 = Sustaining.
- **Evidence Examples:** lesson plans, walk-through notes, student work, assessment data.
- **Output:** Each indicator's "First 3 Actions" feed directly into the 90-Day Plan dashboard for accountability.

Conclusion

The Literacy System Audit Tool transforms accountability into awareness. It provides a mirror for coherence—revealing not only where a system stands, but how it thinks. Used annually, it becomes a feedback mechanism for continuous learning, ensuring that the Science of Reading is not merely implemented but internalized—woven into the habits, structures, and shared beliefs that define a literate system.

APPENDIX D
PLC Reflection

Collaborative Inquiry for Continuous Literacy Growth

Professional Learning Communities (PLCs) are the heartbeat of coherent literacy systems. When they function as spaces of reflection rather than reporting, they transform collaboration into collective efficacy. This tool provides a framework for literacy-focused PLC conversations aligned with the developmental logic of the Science of Reading and the Visible Learning phases (Surface → Deep → Transfer).

The goal is simple but profound: to help teams think as learners about learning—to analyze evidence of impact, refine practice, and build shared understanding of what works, for whom, and why.

PLC Reflection Framework

PLC Element	Description	Guiding Questions
1. Clarify the Focus	Identify a specific literacy pillar or learning phase for the cycle. Use system data or classroom observations to determine the focus area.	• What skill, strategy, or reasoning process are we targeting? • How does this connect to our continuum or system goals? • Where do students currently sit along the Surface–Deep–Transfer continuum?
2. Examine the Evidence	Review recent formative data, student work samples, and observation notes. Look for patterns, strengths, and gaps.	• What does the evidence reveal about students' current thinking? • What misconceptions or barriers appear consistently? • How do we know if instruction is meeting the intended learning phase?
3. Analyze Instructional Impact	Reflect on the relationship between teaching moves and learning results. Move beyond "Did students get it?" to "What helped them get it?"	• What instructional routines or feedback practices supported success? • Where might our teaching have overloaded or under-challenged working memory? • Which practices fostered reasoning, synthesis, or transfer?

4. Plan the Next Move	Identify one actionable step to test or refine before the next PLC. Anchor it to evidence and clarify expected outcomes.	• What will we adjust or amplify in the next cycle? • How will we know if the change works? • What support or resources are needed?
5. Reflect and Revisit	After implementation, analyze results, document learning, and share across grade bands. Reflection completes the feedback loop for the team and the system.	• What shifted in student performance or engagement? • What did we learn about instruction, not just results? • How does this inform our broader system coherence?

PLC Reflection Template

Cycle Dates: _____

Focus Pillar/Phase: _____

Team Members: _____

1. **Evidence of Student Learning:**

    Summarize current data (quantitative and qualitative) that sparked this focus.

2. **Observed Instructional Patterns:**

    Identify the practices, routines, or scaffolds currently being used.

3. **Strengths to Amplify:**

    List successful approaches that produced measurable or observable growth.

4. **Opportunities to Improve:**

    Describe specific areas where instruction or support needs refinement.

5. **Next Instructional Step:**

    Define a single, observable action the team will implement collectively.

6. **Expected Indicators of Impact:**

    Describe what success will look like in both student behavior and learning evidence.

7. **Reflection After Implementation:**

    Capture results, surprises, and insights for ongoing documentation.

Example in Practice

Focus: Deep Learning in Vocabulary and Morphology (Grades 4–5)

Evidence: Students accurately decode multisyllabic words but misinterpret meaning in context.

Instructional Analysis: Explicit decoding strong (surface); limited application of morphological reasoning (deep).

Next Step: Implement "morpheme mapping" mini-lessons linking roots to content vocabulary.

Expected Impact: Students infer word meaning independently and use roots in writing.

Reflection Outcome: Within two weeks, formative checks show improved comprehension in content reading; teachers report increased student confidence and curiosity about word origins.

Tips for High-Impact PLCs

1. **Start with Evidence, Not Opinion.** Anchor dialogue in real data or student work.
2. **Use Shared Language.** Refer to phases (Surface–Deep–Transfer) and pillars to maintain coherence across teams.
3. **Keep the Cycle Manageable.** Focus on one change at a time; small wins sustain big systems.
4. **Document and Disseminate.** Summaries of learning feed leadership decisions and future PD.
5. **Reflect Upward.** Each PLC's insights should inform system-level reflection—the organization's own metacognition.

Leadership Role in PLC Sustainability

Leaders sustain reflection by creating the conditions for psychological safety and intellectual risk-taking. They protect time, simplify expectations, and model curiosity. When leaders regularly ask, "What did you learn from your last cycle?" instead of "Did you finish the form?", they reinforce a culture where learning, not compliance, drives improvement.

PLC Evidence Menu – Appendix D: Evolving Science of Reading

PLC Step	Purpose / Guiding Question	Acceptable Evidence Artifacts	Quick Collection Techniques	Interpretive Lens (Balanced Metrics Link)
1. Identify Essential Literacy Focus	What pillar or construct needs attention?	• Lesson plans highlighting phonics ↔ morphology ↔ syntax alignment • Curriculum map excerpts	• 5-minute "artifact walk" of recent plans • Highlight visible pillar connections	Ensures instructional coherence across Foundational → Comprehension continuum.
2. Establish Success Criteria	What would proficiency look like in student work?	• Rubric exemplars from Ch. 10 • Student samples annotated for morphology, syntax, reasoning	• PLC calibration of 3 work samples • Color-code features of success criteria	Builds shared expectations; aligns formative checks to Balanced Metrics thresholds.
3. Gather Classroom Evidence	What are students showing us right now?	• Morphology: prefix/suffix exit slips • Syntax: color-coded sentence reconstruction tasks • Fluency: phrasing audio clips • Reasoning: annotated text maps or claim-evidence charts	• 10-minute evidence sweep (collect one artifact per construct) • Quick digital upload or gallery walk	Diversifies evidence beyond rate or accuracy; captures reasoning in real time.
4. Analyze Patterns & Trends	What does the evidence reveal about learning progress?	• Error analyses of morpheme confusions • Syntax highlight reads (students mark clause types) • Reasoning tallies (talk-moves frequency)	• Use discussion protocols (e.g., "I notice/I wonder") • Score 3–5 samples using rubric strands	Anchors analysis in language growth, not surface correctness.
5. Plan Next Instructional Moves	What small adjustments will accelerate progress?	• Updated lesson adaptations • Revised mini-lesson plan drafts	• "Next-step carousel": each PLC member lists one shift for next cycle	Converts analysis to action, sustaining iterative improvement.
6. Monitor Impact & Reflect	Did our change move the learning needle?	• Comparative student samples (before/after) • Data dashboard snippet from Balanced Metrics Tracker	• Side-by-side comparison protocol • 3-minute written reflection per teacher	Reinforces cyclical evidence use—auditing, acting, and adapting within 90 days.

Conclusion

The PLC Reflection process completes the feedback loop that holds a literacy system together.

It ensures that the Science of Reading remains visible in practice, that collaboration deepens into collective expertise, and that every cycle of learning—teacher or student—moves closer to transfer.

When teams engage in reflection this way, coherence becomes not a structure imposed from above, but a rhythm that lives within the daily conversations of educators working together to make thinking visible and literacy inevitable.

References

Alammary, A. (2022). Educational technology integration and student engagement: A synthesis of empirical research. Computers & Education, 188, 104567. https://doi.org/10.1016/j.compedu.2022.104567

Black, P., & Wiliam, D. (2018). Inside the black box: Raising standards through classroom assessment. Phi Delta Kappan, 92(1), 81–90. https://doi.org/10.1177/003172171109200119

Bryk, A. S., Gomez, L. M., Grunow, A., & LeMahieu, P. G. (2015). Learning to improve: How America's schools can get better at getting better. Harvard Education Press.

Carlisle, J. F. (2010). Morphological awareness and reading achievement. Reading Psychology, 31(1), 1–30. https://doi.org/10.1080/02702710902733554

Donohoo, J. (2017). Collective efficacy: How educators' beliefs impact student learning. Corwin Press.

Duke, N. K., & Cartwright, K. B. (2021). The science of reading progress monitoring: Beyond phonics and decoding. Reading Research Quarterly, 56(S1), S25–S44. https://doi.org/10.1002/rrq.411

Duke, N. K., & Pearson, P. D. (2002). Effective practices for developing reading comprehension. In A. Farstrup & S. J. Samuels (Eds.), What research has to say about reading instruction (pp. 205–242). International Reading Association.

Ehri, L. C. (2005). Learning to read words: Theory, findings, and issues. Scientific Studies of Reading, 9(2), 167–188. https://doi.org/10.1207/s1532799xssr0902_4

Fisher, D., & Frey, N. (2014). Better learning through structured teaching: A framework for the gradual release of responsibility (2nd ed.). ASCD.

Fisher, D., & Frey, N. (2021). How learning works: Research-based strategies for smart teaching. ASCD.

Fullan, M. (2020). Nuance: Why some leaders succeed and others fail. Corwin Press.

Fullan, M. (2021). The right drivers for whole system success. Center for Strategic Education.

Hattie, J. (2018). Visible learning: A synthesis of over 1,500 meta-analyses relating to achievement. Routledge.

Hattie, J., & Donoghue, G. M. (2016). Learning strategies: A synthesis and conceptual model. npj Science of Learning, 1(1), 16013. https://doi.org/10.1038/npjscilearn.2016.13

Kendeou, P., McMaster, K. L., & Christ, T. J. (2014). Reading comprehension: Core components and processes. Educational Psychologist, 49(2), 109–127. https://doi.org/10.1080/00461520.2014.907562

Moats, L. C. (2020). Speech to print: Language essentials for teachers of reading (3rd ed.). Brookes Publishing.

Myhill, D. A. (2011). The ordeal of understanding grammar. English Teaching: Practice and Critique, 10(3), 38–54.

Nagy, W., & Townsend, D. (2012). Words as tools: Learning academic vocabulary as language acquisition. Reading Research Quarterly, 47(1), 91–108. https://doi.org/10.1002/RRQ.011

OECD. (2020). Deeper learning and 21st-century competencies. Organisation for Economic Co-operation and Development.

Perfetti, C. A. (2007). Reading ability: Lexical quality to comprehension. Scientific Studies of Reading, 11(4), 357–383. https://doi.org/10.1080/10888430701530730

Pressley, M., & Afflerbach, P. (1995). Verbal protocols of reading: The nature of constructively responsive reading. Erlbaum.

Scott, C. M., & Balthazar, C. H. (2010). The role of complex syntax in written expression. Topics in Language Disorders, 30(1), 65–83. https://doi.org/10.1097/TLD.0b013e3181d0f460

Shanahan, T., & Shanahan, C. (2012). What is disciplinary literacy and why does it matter? Topics in Language Disorders, 32(1), 7–18. https://doi.org/10.1097/TLD.0b013e318244557a

Snow, C. E. (2002). Reading for understanding: Toward an R&D program in reading comprehension. RAND Corporation.

Stiggins, R. (2017). The perfect assessment system. ASCD.

Torgesen, J. K. (2004). Avoiding the devastating downward spiral: The evidence that early intervention prevents reading failure. American Educator, 28(3), 6–19.

Wineburg, S. (2018). Why learn history (when it's already on your phone). University of Chicago Press.

Wolf, M. (2008). Proust and the squid: The story and science of the reading brain. HarperCollins.

Wiliam, D. (2018). Embedded formative assessment (2nd ed.). Solution Tree Press.

Additional Conceptual and Leadership References

- Bryk, A., & Schneider, B. (2002). Trust in schools: A core resource for improvement. Russell Sage Foundation.
- Hattie, J., & Zierer, K. (2019). 10 mindframes for visible learning: Teaching for success. Routledge.
- Moje, E. B. (2015). Doing and teaching disciplinary literacy with adolescent learners. Harvard Educational Review, 85(2), 254–278.
- Wolf, M., & Ullman-Shade, C. (2023). Deep reading in the digital age. Mind, Brain, and Education, 17(2), 80–94.
- Zins, J. E., Weissberg, R. P., Wang, M. C., & Walberg, H. J. (2004). Building academic success on social and emotional learning. Teachers College Press.
- Digital and Ethical Literacy References
- International Literacy Association. (2018). Standards for the preparation of literacy professionals 2017.
- International Society for Technology in Education (ISTE). (2022). ISTE standards for educators and leaders.

- UNESCO. (2023). Futures of education: Reimagining our futures together.
- Neuroscience and Cognitive Science Foundations
- Dehaene, S. (2009). Reading in the brain: The science and evolution of a human invention. Viking Press.
- Immordino-Yang, M. H. (2016). Emotions, learning, and the brain: Exploring the educational implications of affective neuroscience. W. W. Norton.
- Share, D. L. (2025). Blueprint for a Universal Theory of Learning to Read: The Combinatorial Model. Reading Research Quarterly, 60(e603). https://doi.org/10.1002/rrq.603
- Wolf, M. (2023). "Elbow Room": How the Reading Brain Informs the Teaching of Reading. UCLA/CSU Collaborative for Neuroscience, Diversity and Learning.
- Wolf, M., & Barzillai, M. (2009). The importance of deep reading. Educational Leadership, 66(6), 32–37.
- System and Implementation Research
- Bryk, A., Gomez, L., Grunow, A., & LeMahieu, P. (2015). Learning to improve. Harvard Education Press
- Fullan, M., Quinn, J., & McEachen, J. (2018). Deep learning: Engage the world, change the world. Corwin Press.
- Sharratt, L. (2019). Clarity: What matters most in learning, teaching, and leading. Corwin Press.
- Note:

This reference list combines germinal research, contemporary scholarship, and leadership literature cited explicitly and conceptually across the book. It intentionally integrates works from literacy science, educational neuroscience, and systems design to model the book's central premise: that literacy is both cognitive architecture and cultural infrastructure.

Glossary of Key Terms

A

- **Alphabetic Principle:** The understanding that there are systematic and predictable relationships between written letters and spoken sounds. It is foundational to decoding.
- **Automaticity:** The ability to perform a task (like word recognition) accurately, quickly, and effortlessly, freeing up cognitive resources for higher-level processes like comprehension.

C

- **Combinatorial Model (Share's):** A developmental theory of reading acquisition proposed by David Share, describing how reading expertise evolves through a progression of additive cognitive phases (sub-morphemic, morpho-lexical, supra-lexical) over a lifetime.
- **Comprehension:** The active process of constructing meaning from text. It involves integrating the reader's background knowledge with information presented in the text.
- **Continuum (K-12 Literacy):** A seamless, developmentally appropriate progression of literacy skills and instruction that builds from foundational competencies in early grades through advanced reasoning skills in later grades, as opposed to fragmented, grade-level silos.

D

- **Decoding:** The process of translating written words into spoken language using knowledge of letter-sound relationships (phonics) and word patterns.
- **Deep Reading:** A sophisticated level of reading that involves critical analysis, inference, synthesis, and the ability to transfer understanding across contexts, often leading to new insights or perspectives.
- **Developmental Architecture (of Reading):** The conceptual framework of the book, illustrating a structured, continuous system for literacy development across all grades (K-12) and tiers of instruction.
- **Disciplinary Literacy:** The specialized ways of reading, writing, and thinking within specific academic disciplines (e.g., how a historian reads a primary source differs from how a scientist reads a research paper).

E

- **Elbow Room Model (Wolf's):** An instructional metaphor by Maryanne Wolf that visualizes the dynamic, shifting emphasis between "Expanded Foundational Skills" and "Comprehension Processes" throughout a reader's development, rather than a fixed or sequential approach.
- **Expanded Foundational Skills:** A broader conceptualization of foundational literacy skills that goes beyond just phonics to include phonological awareness, orthographic patterns, the alphabetic principle, *and crucially*, semantics, syntax, and morphology.
- **Explicit Instruction:** A structured, systematic, and effective methodology for teaching academic skills. It involves clear modeling, guided practice, independent practice, and immediate corrective feedback.

F

- **Fluency:** The ability to read text accurately, quickly, and with appropriate expression (prosody), allowing the reader's attention to be directed towards meaning.
- **Foundational Skills:** The basic building blocks of reading, which traditionally include phonological awareness, phonics, and fluency. This book advocates for an "Expanded" view to include morphology, syntax, and semantics.

L

- **Language Comprehension:** The ability to understand spoken language, encompassing vocabulary, background knowledge, syntax, semantics, and verbal reasoning. It is a critical component of reading comprehension.

M

- **Metacognition:** The awareness and understanding of one's own thought processes; in reading, it refers to a reader's ability to monitor their comprehension, identify difficulties, and employ strategies to fix them.
- **Morpho-lexical Phase (Share's):** The second developmental phase in Share's Combinatorial Model, where readers learn to "unitize" or recognize meaningful chunks within words (morphemes) and whole words, moving beyond letter-by-letter decoding.
- **Morpheme:** The smallest meaningful unit of language (e.g., prefixes, suffixes, root words). Understanding morphemes is crucial for vocabulary development and word recognition.
- **Morphology:** The study of word structure, including how words are formed from morphemes (roots, prefixes, suffixes) and how they change (e.g., pluralization, verb tenses).
- **Myth of Mastery:** The misconception that foundational reading skills (especially phonics) are "mastered" by a certain grade level (e.g., third grade) and no longer require explicit attention, leading to a neglect of advanced foundational skills.

O

- **Orthographic Mapping:** The process by which readers store written words in long-term memory for instant retrieval. It involves forming connections between the sounds, spellings, and meanings of words.
- **Orthographic Patterns:** The visual patterns and conventions of a writing system, including letter sequences, spelling rules, and common letter groups.

P

- **Pendulum Problem:** The cyclical nature of educational debates where instructional approaches swing between two extremes (e.g., phonics-first vs. whole language), often leading to fragmentation and incomplete solutions.
- **Phonemic Awareness:** A specific type of phonological awareness that involves the ability to identify, segment, blend, and manipulate individual sounds (phonemes) in spoken words.
- **Phonics:** A method of teaching reading that explicitly connects letters or groups of letters (graphemes) with the sounds they represent (phonemes). It is essential for decoding.

- **Phonological Awareness:** The broad awareness of the sound structure of spoken language, including the ability to recognize and manipulate syllables, rhymes, and individual sounds (phonemes).
- **POSSUM Acronym (Wolf's):** Maryanne Wolf's acronym representing "Expanded Foundational Skills": **P**honology, **O**rthographic patterns, **S**emantics, **S**yntax, **U**nderstanding the alphabetic principle, **M**orphology.
- **Prosody:** The rhythm, stress, and intonation of speech. In reading, it refers to reading with appropriate expression, reflecting an understanding of the text's meaning.

R

- **Reading Rope (Scarborough's):** A visual metaphor developed by Hollis Scarborough, illustrating skilled reading as the intertwining of two major strands: "Word Recognition" and "Language Comprehension," each composed of several sub-components.
- **Reasoning:** In the context of reading, the cognitive process of analyzing information, drawing conclusions, making inferences, and solving problems based on text.

S

- **Science of Reading (SoR):** A vast, interdisciplinary body of research from fields like cognitive psychology, neuroscience, and education that provides evidence-based understandings of how reading develops and how it can be most effectively taught.
- **Self-Teaching Hypothesis (Share's):** David Share's theory that children primarily learn new words for sight recognition by using their phonological decoding skills to "sound out" unfamiliar words encountered in print.
- **Semantics:** The study of meaning in language. In reading, it refers to understanding the meaning of individual words (vocabulary) and how words combine to create meaning in sentences and texts.
- **Simple View of Reading:** A formula (Decoding x Language Comprehension = Reading Comprehension) proposed by Gough and Tunmer, suggesting that reading comprehension is the product of a reader's decoding skills and their language comprehension abilities.
- **Sub-morphemic Phase (Share's):** The initial developmental phase in Share's Combinatorial Model, where novice readers primarily focus on decoding words by breaking them down into individual letters or small letter-sound units.
- **Supra-lexical Phase (Share's):** The highest developmental phase in Share's Combinatorial Model, where readers integrate sentence-level syntax, context, and sophisticated reasoning to construct deep meaning and resolve ambiguity.
- **Syntax:** The set of rules governing the structure of sentences and phrases in a language. Understanding syntax is critical for comprehending complex sentences.
- **Systematic Instruction:** A teaching approach where skills are taught in a logical, planned, and sequential order, moving from simple to complex concepts.

T

- **Third Grade Cliff:** A widely observed phenomenon where students who have struggled with foundational reading skills in early grades experience a significant drop in academic performance around third grade, as curriculum shifts from "learning to read" to "reading to learn."

U

- **Unitizability:** In Share's Combinatorial Model, the ability to recognize and process words or meaningful word parts (morphemes) as automatic, integrated units, rather than having to decode them letter by letter.

V

- **Vocabulary:** The bank of words a person knows and understands. A robust vocabulary is a strong predictor of reading comprehension.

About the Author

Anthony Fitzpatrick, Ed.D. serves as Assistant Superintendent for the Delsea Regional and Elk Township School Districts in New Jersey and is a professor at the University of Phoenix. A former Director of School Innovation at the New Jersey Department of Education, his work focuses on building coherent, K-12 systems grounded in the Science of Reading, educational leadership, and Visible Learning. He has partnered with multiple school communities, to develop and refine the practical, research-based models that form the foundation of *The Evolving Science of Reading*.

www.ingramcontent.com/pod-product-compliance
Lightning Source LLC
LaVergne TN
LVHW081527060526
838200LV00045B/2032